W9-BGP-911

WOODSTOCK

*The Summer of
Our Lives*

WOODSTOCK

The Summer of Our Lives

Jack Curry

WEIDENFELD & NICOLSON

New York

Copyright © 1989 by Jack Curry

All rights reserved. No reproduction of this book in whole
or in part in any form may be made without written
authorization of the copyright owner.

Published by Weidenfeld & Nicolson, New York
A Division of Wheatland Corporation
841 Broadway
New York, New York 10003-4793

Published in Canada by General Publishing Company, Ltd.

Grateful acknowledgment is made for the following:

Excerpt from "I-Feel-Like-I'm-Fixin'-to-Die Rag." Words and music by Joe
McDonald. Copyright © 1965 Alkatraz Corner Music (BMI).
Used by permission. All rights reserved.

Illustrations in the photo section have been supplied and are reproduced by
kind permission of the following: p. 1: (top, bottom) courtesy Penny Stallings;
p. 2: Burk Uzzle/Archive Pictures, Inc.; p. 3: (top) Charles Harbutt/Archive Pic-
tures Inc., (bottom) Burk Uzzle/Archive Pictures, Inc.; p. 4: Charles Harbutt/
Archive Pictures Inc.; p. 5: (top) B. Friedman, (bottom) Charles Harbutt/
Archive Pictures Inc.; p. 6: Dan McCoy/Rainbow; p. 7: B. Friedman; p. 8: Ken
Regan/Camera 5; p. 9: (top) Ken Regan/Camera 5, (bottom) Bill Eppridge/Time,
Life Pictures Agency; p. 10: Dan McCoy/Rainbow; p. 11: Dan McCoy/Rainbow;
p. 12: Dan McCoy/Rainbow; p. 13: (top) courtesy Tom Constanten, (bottom)
Burk Uzzle/Archive Pictures Inc.; p. 14: (top) John Dominis/Time, Life Pictures
Agency, (bottom) Dan McCoy/Rainbow; p. 15: Dan McCoy/Rainbow; p. 16: Bill
Eppridge/Time, Life Pictures Agency.

Library of Congress Cataloging-in-Publication Data
Curry, Jack, 1952–
Woodstock : the summer of our lives.
1. Woodstock Festival.   I. Title.
ML38.W66C87   1989   784.5'4'007974734   88-33757
ISBN 1-55584-040-X (alk. paper)

Manufactured in the United States of America

This book is printed on acid-free paper

Designed by Irving Perkins Associates

First Edition

1   3   5   7   9   10   8   6   4   2

THIS BOOK OF RECOLLECTIONS IS LOVINGLY DEDICATED TO EILEEN B. AND JOSEPH P. CURRY, MY MOTHER AND FATHER. I TREASURE THEIR MEMORY AS MY FINEST POSSESSION.

ACKNOWLEDGMENTS

CLEARLY I owe the greatest debt of gratitude in completing this book to the people who granted me the time and the candor it took to create the profiles that make up this chronicle. Each in his or her own way opened another path back to Yasgur's farm; each put up with my probing and my repeated requests for follow-up information; together they demonstrated an enthusiasm and commitment to preserving the Woodstock spirit that reaffirmed my belief in the value of a book repopulating the event.

Others, however, played key roles in the book's development and progress. I'd like to thank especially Dick Berg, who listened to my rough ideas for a Woodstock history and helped me rethink them into a viable publishing proposal. His continued support since then has been a major motivating force whenever obstacles arose. I'd also like to thank Rona Elliot, the NBC News reporter and Woodstock Ventures veteran, who helped me wend my way through the still active though arcane network of friends—and enemies—who brought the festival into being. She guided me to many of the candidates I eventually interviewed, and beyond the contacts she contributed an excitement about the project which gave it early momentum.

Thanks also to my editor, Mark Polizzotti; my agent, Richard Pine; my colleagues at *USA Today*; my family; and my dear friend Patti Harrington.

CONTENTS

Joy and relief make themselves felt. So, too, music has power to ease tensions within the heart and to loosen the grip of obscure emotions.

From the I Ching, as quoted
in the official program of the
Woodstock Music and Art Fair

FOREWORD

THE FIRST question nearly everyone asked me when I mentioned I was writing a book about the Woodstock Festival was "Wow, did you go?" There was almost universal surprise when I told them I had spent that weekend at my summer job at a pancake house on Long Island, and that since I was just sixteen at the time, I didn't even think to ask my parents if I could go, knowing they wouldn't even consider it. The unspoken critique behind the surprise reaction was "How are you qualified to write a book about Woodstock if you didn't even go?" But I soon found that not attending impeded my research very little. After all, the actual details of the weekend—who performed, when it rained, what the hippies were doing in the field—have all been documented in both film and print. These were to form the backdrop for the more personal tales I was interested in. *Woodstock* isn't really about the public events so much as about the people behind them. And by not bringing my own set of memories to the project, I was better able to draw out, respond to, interpret, and present the recollections of the subjects who make up the book.

Of the tasks associated with this project, locating people who had attended the festival was the easiest by far. A few ads elicited hundreds of responses from people now in their thirties and forties, all eager to be involved with a book about this key weekend in their past. The hard part was sifting through the candidates, looking for those who would be most suited for the particular approach of this work. I didn't want history, I wanted personal life stories; I needed to know not that it was hot and rainy, but how the heat and rain affected the individual. As it turned out, many of my potential informants couldn't understand this slant, and their comments about the festival were all about exterior occurrences. They saw themselves as eyewitnesses and wanted desperately to tell what they had seen. But when pressed to talk about what was happening in their own lives at the time, they balked. The subjects I finally selected were those willing to open themselves up and reveal personal truths that gave the happening its individual relevance.

Naturally, for a work of this kind, I have relied extensively on the subjects' testimonies, and when it is appropriate have quoted them directly. At the same time, this is not simply an oral history; in reshaping the reports into a single coherent story, I augmented the recollections with details gleaned from primary material—books, magazines, newspapers—from 1969. To the degree it was required for narrative purposes, I corrected the obvious mistakes and memory lapses. However, since the work is based on the recollections of individuals, I strove to stay true to the Woodstock they described, even if their descriptions sometimes created an implausible, albeit richly imagined, tableau.

INTRODUCTION

FOR ABOUT five years beginning in 1978 I shared an apartment with Howard, an old college roommate, in New York City. Our Seventy-third Street place was by no means a luxury bachelor pad, and since neither of us boasted any particular decorator flair, it remained pretty sparse, containing only the meager possessions of our immediate post-student days. It was a vault for the few valuables from our youth we had dragged in paper bags and cardboard boxes into our adulthood.

Early on in our tenancy, Howard went over to the milk-crate bookshelves and pulled out his green high school yearbook. He opened immediately to a page he had obviously gone to often before and pulled out two aged tickets. They were unused, ancient-looking. Handling them with the respect one lavishes on treasured souvenirs, he held them up for me to inspect. It was clear I was not to touch them: the invitation was for observation only.

"They're tickets from Woodstock," Howard announced proudly. "I never used them, be careful."

Tickets to Woodstock, untorn. Like me Howard had been sixteen at the time of the historic concert that took place on August 15,

16, and 17, 1969. We were both old enough to feel the magnetism of the event, yet too young to escape parental restrictions against attending. He had bought the tickets hoping against hope that his father would relent. When his father did not, he held on to them, listening avidly to the numerous television and radio accounts that chronicled the phenomenon as the single largest assembly of young people in history. Thruways closed. Thousands convened. Music played. Peace reigned. He took his tickets and stashed them away. And now years later he still cherished them, symbols of his unbroken connection with that event in which he—and everyone else in our generation—participated even if we never actually traveled to White Lake, New York. Unripped, intact, the yellowing, frail tickets represented the delicate but tangible bond that still existed between his adult world of responsibilities and the world of his youth, forever associated in his mind with the three-day festival.

Around 1980 we went through an experience most New Yorkers know pretty well: our apartment was robbed. Sprinkled about the tiny place were the few objects left to us. My high school ring—a hunk of bad gold with a big "1970" stamped on it—was my major loss. Howard had collected some Confederate Civil War coins, scoffed up by the misled felon, who must have thought he had made a numismatic killing. But as we tallied the damage, I heard a triumphant whoop from my roommate, who had begun to put the riffled books back into the milk crates.

"They didn't get the Woodstock tickets," he roared. And he placed them back in the yearbook, back into the crates, back into his future.

In a sense, many of us figuratively treasure our own unripped tickets to Woodstock—the powerful images we retain about that legendary weekend of music and peace. They still moved Howard, and he hadn't even attended. His own profound link with that weekend connected him with his past in a way that pierced through the clichés that have come to encrust mass culture's perception of those three days. The media, in their attempt to seize the larger significance of the concert, had created those clichés, with analyses that turned into platitudes, with celebration that turned from hype to jibes. But in Howard's individual connection with the event there resided something, if sentimental and nostalgic, nonetheless vital and real. Imagine how much stronger the feelings must be for each of those kids who actually attended, or each of those performers who took to that stage, or each one of those organizers who brought the thing into being, or each one of the townsfolk who found themselves one morning invaded by hippies. Multiply those individual feelings by thousands and the magnitude of Woodstock's legacy begins to come into focus.

It is most richly and profoundly a legacy of individual experience. Yet almost everything written about the festival immediately afterward, and certainly during the two decades since, has emphasized sociology, crowd psychology, the weekend's cultural relevance or, increasingly as years sped by, irrelevance. To think about Woodstock, more and more, meant to think about a herd. As with any mass movement, the personal stories in which the true significance of the event lies have become obscured by the collective blur of the media spotlight—not lost, merely not chronicled. This book, then, is an attempt to recapture the vibrancy of the Woodstock Festival by repopulating it in microcosm. A tapestry woven from the strands of memory from a handful of disparate souls in that crowd, it grows out of the belief that for at least 500,000 Americans walking around today, Woodstock still signifies something enduring and powerful. What follows is an attempt to give a handful of participants the chance to pull out their tickets to Woodstock and prove to that petty thief Time that he hasn't managed to run off with some of our best goods.

Memories collide when it comes to Woodstock. The Woodstock Music and Art Fair: An Aquarian Exposition, despite that imposing name, itself lacked clear definition and direction when it happened, so it seems natural enough that now, twenty years later, vagueness characterizes its participants' recollections about the three days. Those who were there talk of enjoying performances by groups who didn't play during the concert. Time sequences from concertgoer to concertgoer conflict. The usual tricks memory plays are multiplied by the extraordinariness of the weekend, by the drugs so many indulged in, and by the fact that so many of those who went were so young. Like an early, innocent Christmas, when lights seemed brighter and gifts more overwhelming, Woodstock resides in a corner of memory where fact has long ago succumbed to the irresistible tug of wish fulfillment.

My particular pathway to 1969—the memories of others—provides an access route with its own idiosyncratic precision. Sacrificed is the documentary's accuracy and gained is an appreciation of lived experience. And whether or not the festival took place as the sixties waned, as the spirit of cooperation and optimism that ruled that decade foundered, it exists now in the memories of those who populated it as a magical embodiment of their best hopes and dreams. Consistently, the recollections focus on the uniqueness of Woodstock and on its seminal role in the life of the recaller. Often enough the embellishment of details and the individual's exaggeration of his or her role clued me in to the probable inaccuracies embedded in the account. But the emotional content of the stories could never be doubted. Being at Woodstock had become a cherished distinction, a mark of honor, a personal landmark to last for life.

Culture no longer acknowledges the singular role of Woodstock: the type of event it represented and the images it conjures up are passé, bankrupt of potency, rejected as hopelessly naive and outmoded by the current generation of tastemakers. For the media that perception may be only natural: the festival took place two decades ago and witnessed an outpouring of sentiments that are no longer felt, much less understood. But mass culture aside, the festival's unerodable aftereffects are still working on the men and women who attended. For them Woodstock won't go away. For them what happened on Max Yasgur's farm created memories that still hold a primary place in their personal autobiographies.

Oddly enough, an event that at first gained its distinction for its sheer size has had its greatest impact in tiny ways. Interpretations of the festival have always focused on the macrocosmic meaning of it all, treating the individuals there as only so many particles in a mass social movement. The key to understanding the event, though, lies in the secrets and private stories of the weekend's cast of thousands. Yes, someone died there, and yes, someone was born there. But for the vast majority the weekend produced no such easily documented life change. Instead, for each in a personal way, the weekend touched inner conflicts, shifted emotional centers— changing the course of lives, perhaps, but sometimes in ways so subtle that the concertgoer himself can only now see the impact.

It is really no particular irony, considering how rapidly we Americans create, embrace, and discard our icons, that the very word "Woodstock" has become something of an accepted cultural joke. We've all grown up and the passions and fashions associated with that August weekend now make us blush the same way many excesses of youth do. It's like a summer fling we dove into with all our might two decades ago that causes mild embarrassment when recalled in maturity. Then, too, by most measures, the essentially ephemeral nature of the event further emphasizes its ridiculous- ness. It's always uncomfortable to hang onto the party spirit when the party is so obviously over. But if this particular party still has vitality—and it is my contention that it does—it is because it lives on in the memories of the faces in the crowd. Detailing the exact historic hour-by-hour occurrences of the festival, which is what several books have already done anyway, fails to capture the essence of Woodstock's potency today. Confront a subject with a fact—for instance, that Joni Mitchell *didn't* sing the song "Wood- stock" at the festival, a commonly held misconception—and you will be rebuffed with the certitude of an acolyte reciting his cate- chism. In the true believer's mind, the recollection is the event. Stitching some of those memories together does not produce a documentary of the weekend; rather, it delineates the outlines of the still-present, still-pulsating, still-relevant place in the heart where Woodstock still lives.

If that sounds mawkish, it's only because sentimentality is a key component of meaningful memory. True, hardship and adversity chart their own course in our reserve banks. But life's good times eventually take on a whimsical sweetness that has its own protec- tive properties. The stories people tell of their weekend on Max Yasgur's farm in White Lake, New York, are fuzzy around the edges, even sugar-coated. Youthful sex, neighborly cooperation, rain that cleansed, helicopters that dropped daisies—the dreamscape panorama created by selective memory is so perfect that it must be inaccurate. And yet, for the purposes of a memory play such as this, that subjective backdrop is exactly the setting desired. So, in retelling the Woodstock tales of the handful here, I've taken my tone in large part from their nostalgic, elliptical, genuinely loving attitudes. Journalists—and especially that particular variety who write about rock-and-roll events—often distrust the sentimental. It's just too good to be true, they protest. Perhaps, but this is a work dedicated to preserving memories, not destroying them.

Inevitably the big stories of that era and this one impose themselves onto the scene, even though the focus here is the intimate stories of several Woodstock lives. A friendship between two young women becomes a tiny battleground in the sexual revolution; a rock performer's trendy antiwar songs make him a Woodstock darling but stamp him with a damaging political label. By the book's end, AIDS, yuppie angst and the earmarks of a return to youthful activism in the 1990s all intersect the disparate paths individuals set out upon that Monday morning in August 1969, when 500,000 people left White Lake to filter out into America and into the rest of their lives. The unripped tickets they brought back with them, uncollected and intact, became their passports to a future that, for most, would be forever altered.

"We used to think of ourselves as little clumps of weirdos. But now we're a whole new minority group," Janis Joplin told the multitude from the rickety stage on Max Yasgur's farm. And now, twenty years later, the Woodstock Nation—spread out far and wide across the face of the country—is so much more than that. They are us.

Part I

THE
PEOPLE

WOODSTOCK VENTURES

*What we're doing here is celebrating, and at the same
time we're checking each other out, and what we see is
a bunch of fools rushing in where angels fear to tread.
And hooray for us; we've been fearful angels too long.*

> —From the official Woodstock Music and Art Fair
> program

WOODSTOCK VENTURES was formed in February 1969 in a quiet
office in Manhattan. John Roberts and Joel Rosenman, the money
partners, shook hands with Michael Lang and Artie Kornfield, the
creative partners. They would produce a festival like none there
had ever been. It would be a first, a perfect combination of counterculture entertainment and capitalism. Three days of peace and
music in the countryside, bigger than anything anyone had ever
seen. And they would get rich. The ultimate happening, the ultimate business proposition.

Four men cordially and enthusiastically shaking hands: their
pact would soon set off a series of chain reactions sweeping hundreds of their friends, colleagues and business associates into a
chaotic whirlwind of often comedic, sometimes traumatic activity.
With that handshake a gravitational center formed, jerking into its
orbit a wild cross-section of the young generation. Some of the best

3

professionals working the American concert scene at the time, and some of the most incompetent, got involved. The majority of the several hundred who eventually became part of the Woodstock Ventures team had never before participated in organizing a rock concert. It was a concert for babes in the woods, by babes in the woods. What united them all, however, was their destiny. Once in the Woodstock farrago, all of these staff members, organizers, employees, hippies and tag-alongs would feel that their lives were redirected.

How perfect, in retrospect, that the festival would go down in history bearing the name of a town miles away, connected to the weekend's paranoia and euphoria by the slimmest of sentimental quirks of the event's creators. Cofounder Michael Lang lived in the artists' community of Woodstock, New York, a hippie retreat north of New York City made cultishly cool by its proximity to the Big Pink home of the Band. It was there that Lang first envisioned the grandiose scheme that would evolve into the Aquarian Exposition, a dream constructed on even more elaborate dimensions than the mega-happening that finally resulted. In addition to the concert weekend, the plan called for the building of a permanent recording facility, the ultimate sixties rock retreat: state-of-the-art technology inside; creeks, birds and tranquillity outside. The concert in fact would serve in large part as the promotional launching pad for the ongoing facility. Very soon after naming the business Woodstock Ventures, it became clear that nowhere in the township was there available land that could support the size of the proposed concert. And as the various permutations of zoning, local hostility, bureaucratic incompetence and scheduling exigencies pushed Ventures farther and farther away from its hometown, the company and its dream retained the same name, ironically one of the few things that didn't mutate into something completely different by the time August rolled around.

Several weeks after the fateful handshake, Penny Stallings joined on as an office administrator; a week later Lee Blumer came to work on the security detail. By June Rufus Friedman had traded his office job in Manhattan for a laborer's job on the upstate site; and by the end of July, Henry Diltz was flying in from California to serve as the official photographer of the event. Each from his or her unique perspective observed the creation of the immense apparatus that propelled Woodstock into being, as well as the daily crises that nearly aborted it. And they would all learn from Woodstock that they had abilities they never imagined. On that winter morning Penny slept late, Lee made her business calls, Rufus ran a package of proofs to a client, and Henry spilled developing solution in his lab. Meanwhile, Roberts and Rosenman and Lang and Kornfield were making a pact, envisioning nothing less than the largest youth event in history. We can pull this off, they said to each other.

Penny certainly believed they could when she was invited to join the staff—but then she wanted to believe it. It meant she'd finally have a job. And more important, somewhere to fit in. Never in her life had she felt more alienated than during the months since graduating from Southern Methodist University in Dallas and moving up to New York. A position with Woodstock Ventures, whatever it entailed, would be better than the hanging-out existence she was currently leading.

Not surprisingly, it was Barry who got her the job. Not surprising, because it was Barry who also got her to leave Texas, Barry who got her to come to Manhattan, and Barry who taught her what little she knew about rock-and-roll management. They had met when they both were working in the fashion business in Dallas in the mid-1960s. He was a displaced New Yorker, the worldly older man to her southern belle. And he was Jewish, which was exotic to Penny's white-bread sorority sisters in Tri Delta. Her parents didn't approve of the relationship, and their stance further divided them from their already alienated daughter. When Barry moved back to Manhattan in 1968, he asked Penny to come along. Will we get married, she asked. No, he said matter-of-factly. Well, my mom doesn't want us to anyway, so why should it bother me? When do we leave?

The transition from Texas cheerleader to New York working woman proved more difficult than Penny had imagined. She was self-conscious about her drawl and tried to disguise it, which only aggravated the accent. She had always been an impeccable dresser, but here, among the hippies and sophisticates, her clothes were all wrong. She attempted to adapt with a vengeance, donning the Earth shoes and Indian fringes of the day, while clinging to the mascara and eye shadow of her sorority days. The ensemble made her feel a little like a cross between Ann-Margret and Buffy Sainte-Marie. And worst of all, there was her lifestyle—or rather, Barry's lifestyle. Hired on by old neighborhood buddies as a manager of the Electric Circus, one of the East Village's hottest clubs, Barry lived according to a crazy nocturnal schedule. He didn't get home until six in the morning, didn't get up until noon, and didn't go to work until eight or nine at night. Because she had no agenda of her own, Penny fell into Barry's pattern. Daunted by Manhattan chic to begin with, the southern belle nightly headed off to a far-out dance hall where she saw the city's beautiful people en masse. It was, to say the least, a blow to her Texas pride.

Penny had made some vain attempts at applying her college degree in social work, but she was quickly put off by the dehumanizing character of big-city welfare. On the other hand, she wasn't about to live off her boyfriend forever. She needed to find a job. And when Barry said, You want to work on this music festival some friends of mine are going to do upstate, she said, Yes, yes, yes.

For all the celebrity this particular festival was to gain, when Penny signed on there was nothing really exceptional about the endeavor. Its promoters may have privately envisioned an event of unprecedented magnitude, but in the early stages of development it sounded like just another of the many festivals coming together that summer. With the advent of new amplification techniques and the growing popularity of electric music, large outdoor multiday festivals were becoming an established part of the pop scene. They had evolved into more than mere concerts: they were huge gatherings of youth, complete with art shows and bazaars and natural-food kiosks. Two years earlier, in June 1967, the granddaddy of the sixties festivals, the Fantasy Fair and Magic Mountain Music Festival, had taken place outside of San Francisco. Its success—and the relative absence of violence or crime—inspired the explosion of festivals across the country. Even though it was an era when the prospect of large assemblies of young people caused the establishment alarm, cities and parks accommodated more and more of these events, for which as many as 100,000 long-haired kids would show. With the Monterey Pop Festival, earlier in 1967, came another breakthrough that lent further impetus to the festival boom: the organizers put their event on film. They could then repeat those good vibrations over and over again, first live and then in movie houses. By the time Penny entered her new career as a Woodstock Ventures administrative assistant, the field of festival management was nearly as mainstream as banking or plumbing.

What will I do there, she asked Barry when he told her she had the job.

Who knows, he said, running out to work. Everybody just does everything.

To Penny's conventional thinking that sounded chaotic, and it took very little time for her to realize her premonitions had been right. High finance and big business had never mixed easily with rock and roll. But the new demands for crack coordination and management that came with the organizing of large festivals clearly overwhelmed many of the hippie entrepreneurs getting into the act. Converting racetracks and mountainsides into Aquarian oases, complete with every counterculture creature comfort from head shops to Portosans, took experience, brains and talent. And Harvard wasn't giving out degrees in pop planning. Because of the inevitable screw-ups and outright fraud, several major concert weekends had turned into extended bad trips for kids, and prominent black eyes for the industry. By the time the Woodstock Ventures principals got together, a pall had already begun to descend over the benign memory of Monterey and Magic Mountain. Festivals were still hot, but they were suspect as well. Many of the charges levied in the alternative press against promoters were naive attacks against their making money off the counterculture. Legitimate concerns were voiced too about overcrowding due to uncontrolled ticket sales, about security and about talent no-shows. Still, the momentum behind the festival phenomenon was not to be derailed. And the huge success of the Miami Pop Festival just before New Year's Eve 1968—the first major music weekend on the East Coast—provided enough good vibrations to set the mega-concert movement in motion again. Many of the staffers responsible for Miami Pop were joining the Woodstock team, which encouraged Penny. Little else she was experiencing during her first weeks supported that optimism.

For one thing, the organization itself seemed schizophrenic. She shared office space in Greenwich Village with Lang and several of his operatives, while Roberts, Rosenman, Kornfield and their support staff worked uptown in the Fifties. Were there two production companies or one? All the money seemed to be spent downtown: primarily by Lang signing up groups, but also on elaborate initial expenditures for preparation of the site, in Wallkill, New York. Meanwhile, all the worries about running overbudget came from uptown. Even from Penny's mid-level desk job, she could discern a problem: one branch of Woodstock Ventures didn't know what the other was up to.

What do I know, though, she would say to Barry, content to let the big boys make the big decisions. She was happy just to be working, proving to Barry she was more than the country bumpkin. The growing independence was nice, but she didn't expect it to come in such big doses: after barely a month in the Greenwich Village office, she was told that operations were moving up to the site in Ulster County. She'd have to move up there until the August concert, meaning two months away from Barry—who had set this whole thing up in the first place. Two months in the Catskills with these hippies, who sometimes made fun of her makeup and her cute cropped blond hair. She agreed to go, but as she packed to leave her apartment, she thought, How did I get here from SMU?

At that point the concert was still booked on the original site in Wallkill, New York, about forty miles from the event's eponymous town and about fifty miles north of Penny's Manhattan home. It had been her job to call ahead and find lodgings for the preliminary work crews, easier said than done without notice at the beginning of summer. Following recommendations of several of the staffers who as kids had spent holidays there, she reserved bungalows in a small family-vacation resort near the site. When she finally arrived there herself, in early June, rather than feel like the hostess welcoming guests to the accommodations she'd arranged, she felt alone. The small handful of advance workers consisted mostly of older men (the bosses) and girls (the clerical staff). Penny felt apart from both groups, since she didn't have the official responsibilities of the former but clearly had more important work to do than the latter. Within weeks their numbers would grow out of control as workers of every hair length and stripe were added to the payroll. But at first there seemed to be no one for Penny to fit in with. No one except Lee Blumer, the only other young woman who wielded any degree of authority up there. The blonde Texas belle and the dark-haired Brooklyn Jew moved in together. And like two girls meeting at camp, they shared secrets all through the summer in voices just loud enough to bridge the gap between their narrow cots.

At first it was Lee who had the best secrets. Just twenty-four, by 1969 she had already been in rock-and-roll management for four years, and she brought to Woodstock a well-developed radar for the type of shenanigans perfected by music honchos. If Penny was Alice in Woodstock Wonderland, Lee was the Sadder but Wiser Girl of the Aquarian Exposition. She hadn't yet turned cynic; the decade's infectious optimism hadn't curdled into seventies disappointment. Lee's years in the business had simply accustomed her to the view one had upon entering the hall of distorting mirrors that was concert management. Everything's cool, everything will work out, these fun-house reflections suggested. Lee wasn't about to throw a brick through any of those mirrors, but she didn't take any of their surface illusions as truth either. Penny, you ain't seen nothing yet, she told her roommate while dressing in front of the vanity table they shared, one morning early in their stay at Wallkill. This thing is going to get hairier by the day.

She was right, but then she had witnessed rock-and-roll chaos firsthand ever since she took a job with Dick Clark's promotional group back in 1966. Her first assignment: the Monkees' summer tour. Working the phones, she'd arrange the group's accommodations from New York, occasionally accompanying them on the road. She watched with amazement as this foursome—actors cast as musicians in a TV sitcom—became a live-performance hit across the country. Their opening act was the new discovery Jimi Hendrix, whose innovative music was rejected by the kids shouting for the Pre-Fab Four's bubble-gum rock. She liked the Monkees personally, remembering them as four little guys suddenly at the center of an unprecedented phenomenon. For the first time TV had created a rock-and-roll act rather than simply exploit an existing one. Instead of someone earning the medium's recognition on the basis of demonstrated abilities on records or in concert, the medium fabricated those assets—image, songs, personalities—whole. Lee may not have been an old pro, but even this newcomer realized the Monkees' success had little to do with innate talent. If the Monkees can outshine Jimi Hendrix, she said to herself as she watched the guitarist playing another sizzling set to yet another unappreciative audience, we're obviously not operating in the real world here.

Practical and down-to-earth, Lee rejected an offer to move to California when Clark's enterprises relocated on the West Coast soon after the Monkees tour. Move 3,000 miles to work in rock and roll! She wasn't about to uproot herself for something as frivolous as that. So for the next few years, she drifted from one job to the next within the business, networking about her ever more impressive circle of contacts and connections. She secured glamour spots others her age would have killed for without ever thinking she was really building a career. Sure, she worked with Albert Grossman, legendary pop music manager and impresario, whose client list at various times included Bob Dylan, the Band, Janis Joplin, and Peter, Paul and Mary. She baby-sat for Mary's kids. She worked for Bill Graham, owner of the Fillmore East and Fillmore West, the era's most influential rock arenas. She'd bump into Jim Morrison at the back door. From both organizations, though, she was fired on the whim of autocratic bosses, and the dismissals reinforced her skepticism about this business. She had never taken the whole thing too seriously anyway, though, so when she got laid off was hardly the time to start.

Ambition didn't much affect Lee's thinking about a new job, nor did she realize how marketable her experience had made her. The veteran of pop music wars thought she'd just see what came along. So when she received a call from the Woodstock Ventures office, she thought, Why not? At least it would get her out of the city for the summer.

It's starting to get hairy, like you said, Penny whispered to Lee one night. It was moving toward July; the festival opening date, August 15, was fast approaching. The camplike atmosphere still pervaded the crew, now expanded to over seventy, mostly kids. As the ranks filled out under them, the women's own standing rose. The men still made the festival decisions, but Penny and Lee managed most of the on-site living arrangements. They were privy to the glitches the men were meeting.

Have you heard about the threatening phone calls? Townspeople are telephoning telling us we've got to get out of here, Penny said.

Have you heard about the talent? Lee responded. They're paying incredible amounts of money to the acts, like, more than $10,000 for the Who. And they're getting people you never heard of. Joe Cocker? Who's that?

They can't decide what sort of a stage they want.

They can't find policemen to staff the festival.

They can't possibly meet the zoning requirements Wallkill is suddenly issuing.

I miss Barry, Penny finally said.

It's beautiful up here. I never knew you could see so many stars, said Lee.

They can't find water, said Penny, drifting off to sleep.

They can't find food, whispered Lee.

No idle gossip, the women's nightly litany of snafus outlined perfectly the minefield Woodstock Ventures had partially created for itself and partially walked into. While zoning battles continued

in local courts, financial disarray mounted in Manhattan. Ticket
receipts had suddenly disappeared. Ulster County support for the
weekend, feeble to begin with, dwindled into a series of quibbles
over adequate parking, sufficient sanitation, noise levels. A few of
the rented cars had vanished. Tensions among the partners grew;
Roberts and Rosenman's bankroll shrank at an alarming rate and
Lang's activity progressed at a distressing one. Elaborate but ill-
conceived efforts were initiated to involve all possible elements of
the counterculture in the event. They're flying in people from that
Hog Farm commune, Lee said. They're renting an Indian tribe
from New Mexico, Penny said.

For all the mounting tensions, the two young women found
themselves enjoying the work and the play of their Woodstock
summer more than either expected. The daily tasks defied preparation, every day introducing new items on their must-do agenda.
Penny had to find out where goat-milk dairy products could be
bought in bulk in upstate New York, since that was all the Hog
Farm hippies would use. Lee, commissioned to solve Ventures'
tattered public-relations image in the neighboring towns, had to
set up dances for local kids and mini-concerts in local jails. Beyond
the ever-challenging work, though, there was the ever-growing
compound of coworkers. As roommates, Penny and Lee had each
other as solid anchors; their little bungalow was their shared base
of operations in that wild world. But as July sped on, both women
reached out into that loose and freaky band, each of them discover-
ing an unexpected soulmate and mentor there who held the
answers to questions they didn't even know they were asking.

For about three days Lee thought she loved Don Ganoung, a San
Francisco priest and social worker who was working with her on the
security and community relations crew. What she remembers now
more than the romance is respect. It was perhaps the first time she
had felt admiration for someone like Don. He represented a religious system, Christianity, that she disdained. He was much older
than she. And he had served in Korea; like many young women her
age, Lee felt that military service did not make a man particularly
appealing. But Don exploded her prejudices. He encouraged her

criticisms of Christianity and added a few of his own. He may have been older, but his maturity engendered a hip wisdom, not inflexible attitudinizing. And although he had served his country in one Far Eastern war, he was not blindly supporting the one in which it was currently engaged. Everything else she witnessed on the pre-festival landscape reminded Lee of the same chaotic hypocrisy she recognized from her music business days. But in Don she saw integrity and optimism. And faith. Don had faith that miraculous good would come out of the gathering they were working on. The festival might actually prove to be that breakthrough experience of peace and love youth was waiting for. For the first time, Lee believed that they could, indeed, make it happen.

Penny remembers that when she first saw Jean Ward she felt little affinity toward the woman. Among the groupies, free-lovers, and one-night-standers who made up the Woodstock encampment, Jean had a clear-cut distinction: she was married and her husband was with her. The Wards headed a small battalion of art students from the University of Miami who had been commissioned to oversee the design of the festival, maintaining the area's natural rusticity amid the psychedelia and high-tech equipment. At first Jean spent all her time outside and Penny spent all her time in the Wallkill Ventures office. Then a few things changed. Bill Ward left for home, and Jean decided to stay. Thirty-plus and refusing to take on a roommate, she was still an anomaly. But without a husband, Jean seemed more accessible than before. Meanwhile, Penny's increasing work load took her out to the fields more often, out to where Jean's group industriously worked the land. Penny watched as this strong, capable woman felled trees, drove a backhoe, took command. Ah, shove over, she'd bark at one of the daffy hippies stripping the gears on a tractor. Do it like this. It was the first time the girl from the Deep South saw someone of her own sex handle machinery and men so competently.

At the same time, Jean was the one other woman Penny recalls wearing makeup, and it made her own fastidiousness seem less ridiculous and strange. Jean demonstrated to Penny how a chain saw worked, but her nails were polished as she took the buzzing beast back from Penny's manicured hands. Penny's mother had taught her manners and expectations. Jean showed her that being a woman and being powerful were not mutually exclusive.

You will not believe this, not this one—after a summer of one-upping each other with snafu reports, Lee thought she finally had the topper.

I'm way ahead of you, said Penny, already packing her bag in the bungalow. Negotiations and renegotiations with the board of supervisors had finally and ultimately collapsed. The Wallkill site on which they had been working since June had been scrubbed. It was July 16, one month until the concert, and Penny and Lee and the rest of the motley Ventures crew was being kicked out of Wallkill. A month earlier they might have taken the reversal more easily: for Penny it would have meant an early return to Barry, for Lee just another letdown in a bad-luck year. At this point, though, the roommates had quite a deal more invested in the success of the festival.

Rufus Friedman waved over his shoulder at the other festival grunts, an assortment of cowpokes and overgrown kids gathered at the edge of the woods. And with an almost sexual excitement, he drove his tractor through the uncut alfalfa that covered the field Max Yasgur had rented to Woodstock Ventures. It was the first gash made into those hilly acres which within three weeks would host 500,000 grooving, moving freaks. Many more cuts left to be made, many more ditches dug, much more wire run, much more sweat sweated. Rufus shifted the thresher up a gear. Let the promoter-bosses and executive ladies wring their hands over the details back in White Lake; he and the other grunts were having a great time hustling to make up for time lost in Wallkill. The new festival site had been determined, and now with barely three weeks to go a farm had to be turned into an amphitheater. A dream, one not necessarily his own, had to be kept alive. Heading deeper and deeper into the sea of high grass, Rufus wondered, Can we do this?

Of course, as the lowest of the low in the Ventures pecking order, he had no detailed knowledge of the full magnitude of chaos now occurring. Nor did he crave any. He and the other Bastard Sons, as he had dubbed the crew of manual laborers, weren't let in on the particulars. Officially, all Rufus and company knew was that a rushed deal with Yasgur had been made to substitute his Sullivan County dairy farm for the Wallkill site. That was information enough for the Aquarian Exposition's beasts of burden. With three weeks to go until the first amp blast, he and the rest of his buddies just expected to take orders, follow them, and come back for more. But as is always true, the masters can never keep everything from the slaves. And with the intuition and cunning unique to the proletariat, Rufus was able to keep attuned to the day-to-day crises among the Ventures elite.

What an enormous fuck-up, he'd say to himself as Lang strode by the grunts on horseback, like the great white master surveying the darkies. Shirtless and drenched, Rufus and another field worker carried a stump they had just cut, occasionally dropping it or stumbling on the uneven terrain. Lang shook his head. We'll get this job done, Rufus thought to himself. What about your job? What about the cops? (New York City officers had just been prohibited from working the festival.) What about the buses? (Transportation to and from the site hadn't been worked out yet.) What about the stage? (The construction of the six-story complex hadn't even begun.) Even the grunts knew about those loose ends. And as Rufus glared at the big boss, Lang tumbled off his horse onto the field. Christ, Rufus thought as the grunts exploded into bold derisive laughter, this gets better every day.

If making the festival succeed assumed greater and greater personal significance for Lee and Penny as the event approached, site prep remained just a good-time summer fling for Rufus. But for him that good time was significant too. At eighteen the scrawny New York kid was still struggling with the psychic aftermath of a congenital heart disorder that had plagued his childhood. A series of operations had corrected the problem by the time he was in his teens, a ragged red scar across his front the only physical remnant. But memories of his coddled boyhood, when swimming and running and team sports were impossible, lingered. To be with other guys, doing physically challenging things, playing rough . . . Rufus had missed out on that. Once he was cured, he picked fights throughout high school as a way of compensating for the youthful weakness. And he developed a personality in which bravado, outspokenness and bluster covered up his sense of inferiority. But these more or less hostile responses could never restore what he had really lost: the good-natured, nonviolent rambunctiousness of boys together. He really didn't want to beat his classmates up, he wanted to climb trees with them. And play cowboys and Indians. And nail skate wheels on soap boxes. Being a Woodstock grunt let Rufus back into the playground he wasn't allowed into as a kid.

To join on, he had left a low-paying job with people he didn't like at an advertising agency where he was going nowhere. No big deal. In return, the lightweight late-teen was accepted as an equal by the other, bigger, cooler guys who had all been hired out of the SoHo rehearsal studio where Rufus loved to hang out. Together, all crammed into the back of a van like desperadoes crossing the border, they were transported up to the country. What a band of burn-outs, hippie poets, vets and Village street people they were. But to Rufus, they were right-on. He idolized the group so much that he didn't even care, once he got up there, that his respected comrades and he were cast at the very bottom of the Ventures echelon, the beggars at the love-in. He took pride in the abasement. We are the Bastard Sons, he told his new fraternity of losers with the swagger of the virile downtrodden. Let's show 'em.

The blood-and-guts adventure he embarked on hit highs and lows. It wasn't easy to sustain macho fantasies when so many of your buddies were flakes. Few of the other men shared his gusto for the hard life, and some were simply incapable of meeting its challenges. After all, how much youthful vitality can one feel when teamed on a tree-cutting crew with a tripped-out space case? Rufus remembers more than once narrowly escaping injury as a carelessly axed branch crashed down nearby. Paul Bunyan didn't have to put up with lumberjacks on 'ludes. And even the ultimate boyhood dream, operating construction equipment, ran into noncooperative hippie realities. Once he was nearly tossed

out of a cherry-picker bucket when the freak at the controls decided
to experiment with the levers.

But for all the setbacks, Rufus's fantasy stayed alive. The hours
were long and demanding, and meeting that challenge alone gave
the young man a sense of physical accomplishment he never had
before. Even though some of the grunts were flipped-out dudes,
more were solid, decent, robust men with whom Rufus relished
the male bond. They worked hard and they played hard, scouting
the hills for local girls on nights off. Their ethos was unique, a
subculture within the Woodstock subculture: the camaraderie of
middle-American beer-drinking overlapped with the laid-back
openness of pot smoking. They were hippies and they were hard
hats. Rufus recalls no ill will between him and two other grunts,
each of whom had slept at one point or another with the same Hog
Farm gal. That's cool, man. Enough to go around. Sexist, imma-
ture, insular, the Bastard Sons were everything Woodstock was not
supposed to be, and exactly what Rufus wanted it to be.

One night in the large dining hall of the Diamond Horseshoe,
the bungalow colony they took over in White Lake, the Woodstock
Ventures ensemble shared supper. Lee and Don sat together and
talked about nonthreatening crowd-control techniques. There
won't be any cop uniforms at the festival, you see, Don said. The
security force will be in T-shirts and jeans, distinct but not hostile.
Penny and Jean sat at another table, looking around at the collection of freaks and geeks who had been drawn to this mad enterprise. I enjoy it because it is so out of control, Jean told Penny. Well,
maybe, the younger woman replied. But I'm worried. There are
going to be half a million kids here. I don't think anyone realizes
that. Rufus arm-wrestled with a large bearded man, and lost.
There's a dance in one of these towns around here—let's go raise
hell, he yipped like a terrier as the older men drank beer and
tolerated him. It was the counterculture's ultimate cafeteria.

On a late July night, everyone finished dinner and moved into
the hotel lobby, where a TV, ignored for these last few weeks,
was the center of attention. They watched silently as on the gray
screen the astronaut placed the stiff American flag in the crater.
Men with tattoos and women with nose rings gazed blankly into

the set. Hippies and dopers and hustlers and sorority girls and vets and lovers and cheats focused on the small scratchy image. In this run-down retreat in the green hills of New York where boisterous sounds of chaos and enterprise vibrated through every night, you could hear only the static crackle of the picture tube. Do you think it's really happening, someone said.

Rufus was in the field on an August afternoon working on the concession stands. What are they going to sell here, natural hot dogs, he joked to one of the other grunts. The older man just continued to shovel. The plot they were working was sunny and hot, but because of the recent rains there was mud all over the place. Severe storms had hit the nearby Delaware River valley, flooding low-lying areas and turning the resort area into a soggy, boggy mess. Local authorities in Pennsylvania and New York tried to get their governors to declare the counties affected a disaster area. Here in the higher Catskills the rain had not caused the same degree of damage, but it hampered the already overworked crew substantially. The fence around the site had not even been put up yet, but Rufus had been yanked from that detail when the men who purchased the food franchise hollered that their facilities weren't constructed yet. Everyone was spread thin, and like most of his colleagues Rufus took small hits of acid to keep going, not enough to zonk him out, just enough to pick him up. Still, everything this August afternoon seemed hazy, diffuse, distant.

Rufus noticed Penny walking through the field, in a hurry but still graceful. A man, following her, took her picture. Rufus watched Lee get into her car, and the man took her picture. He was a short, gnomish fellow whose camera equipment, dangling in front of him, made him look like a bizarre tourist lost from his tour group. The photographer started over toward Rufus and the other grunts, and they shouted and hollered for him to take their picture. We may be only the Bastard Sons, but we deserve a shot, don't we? We're the ones really working to make this thing happen. Shoot us.

Of course, Henry Diltz did take their picture. Henry Diltz took everybody's picture. With an omnivorous passion for photography, the man roamed the fields those pre-festival days like a kid in an amusement park that never closed. "Official concert photographer" . . . he really didn't even know what that meant. The other times he had been so named, the contractors never even asked to see the contact sheets afterward. Rolls of film went unrequested by the bosses who hired him. Just come and shoot anything you want—that had always been his job description. It was like telling Fred Astaire, Just come and dance. Henry loved nonstudio work, simply recording images the way he found them. If no one wanted to publish them afterward or even review them, that didn't make a difference. Henry participated by isolating the given event into individual crisp images. And never before in his career had he been surrounded by so many strange and wonderful subjects. He shot Rufus and the Bastard Sons as they posed foolishly, like a wrestling team in a yearbook. But eventually, ego-stroked, they went back to work, and that's when Henry really began to click.

Unassumingly and inconspicuously he moved among the Ventures workers, separated from the phenomenon of Woodstock-in-the-making by a lens, but also connected to it through the same filter. Men with dark, oily ponytails that hung down their wiry backs hammering nails into the enormous stage. Teenage boys smoking pot, shirtless and fair, waiting for the next truckload of Portosans to unload. Commune women dipping naked babies into a green pond in the sunset light. Michael Lang, his brown curls bobbing up and down, motorbiking through a blue field toward the road. Townspeople in baggy clothes and funny hats, driving out to the site to laugh and stare. Penny laughing with Jean. Lee laughing with Don. Rufus, dwarfed between two burly bearded men, laughing by himself. What the bosses planned to do with these, Henry had no idea. But he knew he was glad he had decided to come all the way from California to capture those moments.

In a way it was right that Henry should be the photographer of the biggest musical event of the decade: he had been a professional musician himself before turning to photography. During the early sixties, when folk was king, he played banjo in a group called the Modern Folk Quartet. The foursome recorded several albums with Warner Bros. and toured extensively around the college campus coffeehouse circuit that was booming during the era. The moderate

success of the group was not enough to keep its members interested when the popularity of its music began to die out in the
middle part of the decade. Soon after it disbanded, Henry, who
had always dabbled with cameras and film, accepted his first
professional assignment, to photograph the Lovin' Spoonful for
their first album cover. Soon he established himself as part of that
group's Greenwich Village circle, which included the Mamas and
the Papas and the Hollies, all of whom he shot as well. He found
that his preference for natural portraits coincided with the rock-
and-rollers' disdain for posed, artificial shots. And his former
experiences as a musician gave him a natural affinity for their
temperaments and lifestyles. Soon, he earned a reputation as one
of the hottest rock-and-roll photographers in the business, which
was not all that much of a distinction since the business at that time
was very small: he recalls never seeing a paparazzo or even an
amateur photo buff during his year on the road with the Lovin'
Spoonful.

When the popularity of mega-concerts began to soar, Henry was
already connected with the talent and the promoters who were
making them happen. Planning these weekends with an "event"
mentality, their organizers—even as scattered and ad hoc as many
of them were—naturally felt documentation of their activities for
posterity was a must. They were making history, after all, and with
that in mind they hired Henry to make sure it was duly recorded.
He had been photographer for both Monterey and Miami, two of
the best music weekends so far. And when he was called to Woodstock, he had a feeling this would be the most extraordinary
festival of them all. And the most personally meaningful, perhaps.
Now a full-fledged long-hair sixties hippie, Henry a decade earlier
had passed through this part of New York on quite a different
mission: he was heading to West Point, where he spent a year
grappling with the restrictions imposed by the strictest military
school in the country. The two terms were enough to snuff out the
young man's service zeal and send him reeling away from the
academy and its rigidity, jingoism and machoism. I've left all that
behind, he said to himself. I'm a hippie now. And yet something
about being back in upstate New York was calling up forgotten

memories. Naked babies and commune ladies, freaks on tractors, a stage bigger than anyone had ever built . . . and yet why was he thinking about West Point? Why did he look at the stage and think of a battleship floating in a sea of alfalfa? Why did he look at the construction engineer, a blond, bearded young man, and think of Custer?

I told them this was going to be a disaster. I told them we should pack supplies to bring to the site, because we'll never get back here once the concert starts. I told them . . . Penny stopped herself. She looked at Lee, lying across her cot, listening but not responding. There were only days to go before the concert and the two women were frazzled, frustrated, exhilarated and exhausted. Penny wasn't telling Lee anything she didn't know. Together they had watched as food and water supply arrangements had collapsed, as construction had been slowed down by rainy weather, as feuding among the executives mounted. Festivalgoers had already begun to show up, setting up camp in and around the site that the incomplete fencing could not protect. Power lines run haphazardly through the compound left exposed wiring everywhere. The stage was barely finished and staffers who had dared to cross it reported they found it rickety and unstable. I'm worried, Lee said.

Love, peace and catastrophe, Penny joked, flipping a feeble peace sign to her roomie before nodding off to sleep.

The Thursday before the festival, Penny, Lee, Henry and Rufus would all witness an overture to the crisis-fraught weekend ahead of them. Late in the evening, a dark clear one for a change, a fire broke out in the first floor of the Diamond Horseshoe. A short in the circuitry sent sparks into one of the clothes-strewn bedrooms and from there the flames leaped quickly around the cluttered corridor. Rufus held a hose, Henry took pictures. As they would for the next three days, the members of the Ventures crew were forced to face a crisis by themselves, isolated by the crowds from county relief teams, reacting minute by minute to an uncontrollable situation of their own making. As they would for the next weekend, this collection of misfits and flower children and heads tried to keep cool in the midst of near chaos. Eventually, the self-appointed firemen of the crowd extinguished the blaze, but while it raged it generated an ominous light. Lee and Penny held hands on the cold lawn outside the Horseshoe, their feet wet with dew, and watched as their summer home burned. They weren't worried about their belongings, they were worried about Woodstock. Can we pull this off?

ELEN ORSON

SHE WAS an odd sight in her bell-bottoms and frizzed hair, queu-
ing up with the commuters at the Clifton, New Jersey, bus stop.
Once on board the bus to Manhattan, seated businessmen in suits
eyed Elen, wondering if they should act out the strained etiquette
and offer the young hippie girl a seat. Or if they did, would she
snap a charge of chauvinism at them? Watch out! You may meet a
real castrating female, was what some of them had read in pam-
phlets handed out in Battery Park recently. In the summer of 1969
even commuting had become charged with sexual politics.

Elen certainly never looked expectantly at the men, as did some
of the older working women, who hoped the glance would prompt
an instinctive offer for a place. In fact, she seemed content—even
when the morning heat and humidity were unbearable—to hang
from a strap, swaying to and fro with a casualness and ease that
made her stand out from the harried men even more than her

unconventional look. As the summer of 1969 ran on, the commuters grew accustomed to the teenage girl with the backpack and
embroidered jeans.

If being a high school hippie in 1969 meant impatience with
homeroom nonsense, macho jock bravado and inflexible rules and
regulations, Elen was a high school hippie. But if that also suggested a generalized apathy and lack of focus, she was far from the
stereotype. At seventeen she was already on the career path that
would meet an early hurdle successfully at the Woodstock Festival. Years later that same professional arc would eventually bring
her across the country to Hollywood and the movies. A determined, directed, self-motivated teenager, Elen had no idea that
bus ride led upstate and to California. She was simply taking
advantage of the era's go-for-it attitude. Welcoming the outward
expressions of the trendy hippie lifestyle, she moved well beyond
its immediate lure of free love and drugs to embrace the more
subtle message of self-actualization and meeting one's individual
potential. In Elen, the hippie and the feminist intersected.

Remembering that year now, she never once casts herself as a
protofeminist or, as she would have then been called, a women's
libber. She doesn't talk about reading any of the new-conscious-
ness best-sellers like *The Feminine Mystique*, which a few years
earlier had become a rallying cry for militant women. She recalls
simply feeling unrestricted to set out to accomplish what she
wanted, freed of preconceptions about "normal" behavior by the
counterculture's invitation to do your own thing.

Earlier in 1969 the sports world was buzzing about Barbara Jo
Rubin, a nineteen-year-old horse trainer who had begun to break
down the gender barriers preventing women from becoming thor-
oughbred jockeys. "I'm not doing anything special," she would
tell reporters bustling about her in the winner's circle. "I'm just
doing what I love." For the younger women of the era, raised on the
baby boom's sense of prerogative and the sixties call for equal
opportunity, pioneering came naturally and without ideology.
Leave it to groups like the National Organization for Women to
picket the White House. Leave it to their older sisters to strip to the
buff when a speaker addressed them on the *Playboy* philosophy, as

a group did at Grinnell College in Iowa that February. The attention-getting gesture and the big statement were not for them. Like Barbara Jo, firm atop her racehorse across the river at Aqueduct, Elen simply presumed she could accomplish anything she set out to.

Elen would leave the Clifton commuters behind at the bus terminal and head off for the midtown production studio where she had found a job as an editing apprentice. Unlike most workplaces, integration of male and female employees was nearly complete here: management at this documentary-production outfit was staffed predominantly by the New York liberal media types who hired women for nonclerical positions without thinking twice. The bosses were still men, but at least here women editors were not an anomaly. It was Elen's age that distinguished her. There were few high school sophomores with the chutzpah even to seek out a situation like this, much less the experience to fulfill its demands. But then, Elen had already accumulated nearly two years of film tech work. While most of her peers were still earning their Girl Scout badges, Elen had begun her involvement in film editing, more or less hurled into that adult world by a family crisis.

The fifth of six children, Elen watched as her older sister went through an early hippie phase in the mid-sixties. From her vantage point as her father's favorite, Elen was able to observe the effects Janice's growing independence had on her parents. They were upset by her clothes and new friends. They had begun to read about marijuana and its use by middle-class youngsters. Children no different from their own throwing themselves out of windows, high on psychedelics. They wondered if Janice's odd mannerisms meant she might be experimenting with drugs. Their concerns were well founded: she was running into Manhattan and swallowing acid-coated sugar cubes. One afternoon, while tripping in Central Park, Janice met an intriguing Frenchman who described himself as a Leninist-Maoist radical filmmaker. Janice fell in love and soon moved out of Clifton and into the charismatic documentarian's apartment.

Elen recalls now how this defection upset the Catholic sensibilities of her parents. Her dad, the son of Polish immigrants who was orphaned on New York City's Lower East Side during his teens, placed a priority on family solidarity. Still, he wouldn't compromise his values to accommodate Janice's lifestyle. He hated to lose his daughter, but he also disdained the way she was living. Janice came home occasionally, never looking very robust, and that made her parents even more worried. You're running yourself down, they'd warn. Move back home, they'd implore. As a result of Janice's wildness, Elen was cast as the sensible one, the trusted one. She prefers to think of herself simply as more diplomatic; she just didn't throw her teenage pranks in her parents' faces. She was also more moderate by nature. When she and her friends would do drugs, she did one hit to their five. They would do it six days in a row, she got high about once a season. She knew when to stop. And she knew when to tell her parents the truth and when a lie served everybody's best interests. So when Janice asked fourteen-year-old Elen to move into the city for a while, her parents approved. If they couldn't force Janice back to Clifton, at least Elen could be their surrogate in her world. Don't accept anything they offer you there, they warned Elen. Don't smoke any of their cigarettes.

Janice had agreed to help the Frenchman on a film and was overwhelmed by the work load. Elen joined the team, and for the next year and a half, as part of this shoestring operation, learned everything about low-budget moviemaking. The radical Frenchman found antiwar protests intoxicating and around New York there was plenty of action to keep his motors running. Together with Janice and Elen he charged into the melees to record the sights and sounds of revolution. At his side, Elen would tote the bulky equipment and canisters required by pre-video location technology. Later, with Janice, she would thread the footage, looking for the most exciting scenes. It was more fun than baby-sitting brats in Clifton.

It was inevitable that her activities in Greenwich Village distanced her from her schoolmates, or rather further distanced her. Her Catholic high school was not the sort of place where Elen could find many like-minded kids. As did many of the others who would find their way to the Woodstock Festival in August, she felt herself an outsider. Even before her editing jobs drew her away from school as a center of life, she had begun to look for friends outside that narrow world. A group of well-to-do kids in nearby Montclair used to gather at a park in the middle of town, and she soon found she was more in tune with this crowd. One of the kids' parents owned a record store and he always had the newest rock music. He was also allowed to smoke dope in his own bedroom. She learned to use Magic Markers to draw peace signs and write slogans on her blue jeans, innocuous enough fashion statements but bold at the time. She had her first teen romance in Montclair. Compared to her own strict household, Montclair seemed like the promised land.

In school Elen remained aloof. She maintained a good average, but boredom set in. She was also exhausted: sometimes she would run into the city after school to help the Frenchman and not get back home until after eleven at night. She earned a reputation as an outspoken liberal in history class discussions that inevitably turned to the American involvement in Vietnam. Witnessing anti-war protests firsthand as a film crew member and being exposed to the leftist rantings of her French mentor had turned the girl into a pacifist. She would rail against those students who spouted domino-theory banalities. What, did you learn that from your parents, she would accuse, figuring that was the most demeaning put-down she could inveigh. Teachers relied on her to generate controversy and enliven otherwise soporific classes. One class, though, kept her attention in its own right; it was taught, ironically, by one of the few nuns left in the classroom among the growing number of lay teachers. It was the parochial school's required religion course, usually the most dogmatic and rigid of any part of the curriculum. But the post–Vatican II changes had affected religious teaching; one of the sisters took advantage of the new liberality to redesign sophomore religion, turning it into a comparative theology class. After years of catechism, Elen's intelligence was stimulated by the challenging concepts about spirituality she encountered there for the first time. She probed the teacher about the soul, the afterlife, the significance of the self. She read the Koran, the writings of Chinese philosophers. She began to think on her own about existence. So significant was this experience that later, when the nun who taught the class left the convent, the two women stayed in touch. Years afterward, when Elen married a Vietnam veteran, the wedding was performed in the older woman's home.

When summer vacation rolled around, Elen wanted a full-time job. Realizing she had enough editing experience to find better-paying work than the Frenchman offered, she sought a position at mainstream film labs. A series of temporary jobs took her through August, when she was hired at a midtown studio to help cut a documentary on outdoor survival. It was her first legitimate job as a skilled craftswoman.

The position placed an even greater strain on the relationship she had going with a local Clifton boy whom she had met at school. His father, a conservative member of the town draft board, did not approve of his son's seeing Elen, characterizing her as an avant-garde thinker, a radical and a troublemaker. Her work experience in the city made her seem much older than Brian. She turned him on to pot and filled his head with notions about draft evasion. She shared with him all the eye-opening things she would encounter in Manhattan. And when the posters for the Woodstock Music and Art Fair began to appear around town, she convinced him it would be a once-in-a-lifetime experience. This is a must, we have to go to this. It's going to be full of freaks.

Had the two teenagers eventually gone to the festival together, the weekend might well have turned out as little more than an exciting date for Elen. Instead Brian's father grounded the boy, and Elen was left to get there on her own somehow. And in so doing, she transformed that rainy weekend in the country into a test of her growing independence.

At the studio her disappointment over the disrupted plans was intensified by the fact that, at the eleventh hour, her colleagues at Wadleigh-Maurice Productions Ltd. had been hired to work on a major motion picture to be made of the festival. While she continued to work on the survival-movie footage, everyone around her scurried to arrange supplies, transportation, housing and funding for the three-day shoot. Rising stars like assistant director Martin Scorsese were signed on, signaling the priority being given the project. Elen felt like the Cinderella of the cutting room, uninvited and forgotten—and after so much documentary and location experience!

But Elen was remembered. On the Wednesday before the festival, she got a phone call asking if she'd be available to work in White Lake that weekend.

COUNTRY JOE MCDONALD

ALL RIGHT, he did have that one overtly political tune. His catchiest number—yes, the crowd did love it—happened to be about the war, about soldiers kissing their asses good-bye in the jungle and coming home in a box to Mama. "Do the 'Rag'," the fans screamed, and he willingly satisfied their requests. But he had other songs, about the aftermath of love, about the devastation of drugs, about finding happiness. The political thing, the issue-oriented material, that wasn't the whole bag. The audience and the media didn't seem to care, though. This was 1969, and being anti-American got you hot. In the peculiar climate of the time, even playful radicalism went over big. What was making Joe McDonald popular and famous, notorious even, was that audience-participation ditty about dying in Vietnam. Like the war itself, there was no getting around it.

Joe achieved his most significant career exposure during the

Woodstock show, between the size of the crowd and the subsequent inclusion of his "I-Feel-Like-I'm-Fixin'-to-Die Rag" in the hit documentary made about the weekend. And with that single performance, the singer locked himself into an image that would frustrate and constrict him for more than a decade to come.

Few of the hundreds of thousands who sang along with McDonald on the farm recognized the songwriter for the complex personality he was. The public persona sufficed: he was the lead singer of the Fish, an erratic and eclectic group that was finally moving beyond West Coast cult status to real success. McDonald himself was the most charismatic member of the ensemble, the flower führer, as he has been called for his peace-and-love dress and radical cant. He was different from a lot of the other protest rockers, though: he was funny. His politico-hippie performance style combined absurdist stagecraft with message music. He wore face paint, he rolled around the floor while performing, he combined comedy with iconoclasm. With Joe the fans knew they'd get hip New Left attitudes without all the melodramatic angst of other message rockers. What the growing number of fans didn't know was that beneath the psychedelicized exterior there was a vet. Country Joe McDonald, the author of the most well-known anti-military song of the late 1960s, had proudly and ably devoted the first part of the decade to his nation's service as a soldier in the U.S. Navy.

An enlisted man straight out of El Monte High School in southern California, Joe had shown early signs of his dual musical and political interests: he wrote the campaign song for his buddy's student council election. Once signed up, he went through boot camp in San Diego and then went to Kansas City for training as an air traffic controller. He drew an assignment in the Far East and was stationed at the air facility in Atsugi, Japan. At that time Vietnam was just one of a half-dozen trouble spots in Southeast Asia, one of the sites for which pilots occasionally requested intelligence maps. There was nothing special about that. Here you go, sir, he said as yet another officer asked for Mekong Delta charts. The situation in Indochina occupied very little of the young sailor's thoughts. And as for the service itself, Joe was happy to receive his honorable discharge in 1962, but he came out no more critical of the military than he had entered.

It wasn't until Joe returned to civilian life and enrolled at Los Angeles City College that he began to express himself politically at all. School bored him and he drifted into the coffeehouses around campus, where he heard late–beatnik era poetry and songs. Within a year he decided it was the coffee that interested him more than the college, so he moved to Berkeley, where the mid-sixties avant-garde scene thrived. At first he turned to publishing as an outlet for his thoughts, but music eventually became his main focus. The crossover was almost inevitable. In high school Joe's most rewarding experiences involved playing with a dance band. And now here he was in the Bay Area, the new Liverpool, the capital of acid rock. It was 1965 and the San Francisco sound was happening.

Spurred on by a large university population and a prosperous club scene, musical talents were flocking to this rock mecca, turning the city into a breeding ground for new groups. In commercial terms the Bank of America estimated that in 1967 rock amounted to a $6 million industry in San Francisco. But at least on the face of it, the explosion had nothing to do with commercial terms. The makeover or takeover of Haight-Ashbury by the flower children provided the metropolis with a hippie nerve center unrivaled in any other American city. The countercultural beat emitting from that most with-it of ghettos soon set off a musical reaction. Quicksilver Messenger Service, the Grateful Dead, Jefferson Airplane, Big Brother and the Holding Company: these were foundation stones upon which the San Francisco sound established itself. Actually, there was no sound per se, since each one of the groups to emerge from the city's rock melting pot had a distinct approach to music. They did, however, share a sensibility. Freaked out, psychedelicized, cheerfully blitzed, the rock that was earning San Francisco its reputation had the enhancement of drug-induced good times as its primary raison d'être. The emphasis was on live music, rather than record contracts, which was a handy preference, as studios and executives were all in Los Angeles and New York. The performers' lifestyle was communal, their professionalism arbitrary, and their politics vague. Aside from the implied rhetoric of long hair and wild clothes, the San Francisco musician was more head than thinker.

Joe was listening to the new sound crystallizing across the bay and adapting it to his own style. He was living in the more politically aware Berkeley area and the first gigs he came by were the numerous sit-ins and demonstrations at the University of California. Having learned Woody Guthrie's songs from his parents—labor organizers who had named him Joe after Stalin—he worked out a set that incorporated down-and-out Depression-era classics and his own love songs and folk songs. While that background and setting gave his performances political overtones, the trippy delivery connected him with San Francisco. His music at this early stage had a distinctly down-home simplicity; his first band was called the Instant Action Jug Band. While making the Berkeley circuit, he met the other musicians who would form the Fish, and together they began to experiment with more and more elements of the San Francisco sound: electric guitars, light shows and drugs all crept into the act. By 1966 the group consolidated into the membership it would keep through Woodstock and began perfecting its presentation at rallies and be-ins around the Northwest. Pretty soon Country Joe and the Fish had hit upon the style that would distinguish them nationwide: psychedelic rock with humor. You got your costumes. You got your pratfalls. You got your counterculture monologues. And, oh yes, you got your F-U-C-K cheer. And your "Fixin'-to-Die Rag." They started out as fun.

Sort of a vaudevillian shuffle, the "Rag" worked magic in a crowd of kids. It was like a camp song, in which you all took a part and joined in. Only, it was irreverent, "Row, Row, Row Your Boat" for dissenters:

> *Come on all of you big strong men*
> *Uncle Sam needs your help again;*
> *He's got himself in a terrible jam*
> *Way down yonder in Vietnam*
> *So put down your books and pick up a gun*
> *We're gonna have a whole lot of fun!*

> *And it's one two three, what are we fighting for?*
> *Don't ask me, I don't give a damn,*
> *Next stop is Vietnam*
> *And it's five six seven, open up the Pearly Gates*
> *There ain't no time to wonder why—*
> *Whoopie, we're all gonna die!*

Like a joke "Where Have All the Flowers Gone," the lyrics lamented the waste of young American lives in a foreign war, and did it with pizzazz. Copping a cynical attitude to damn the establishment's callousness, the "Rag" revealed more of McDonald's own experience as a soldier than anyone ever realized. Here was that G.I. Joe bravura all enlisted men get shoved down their throat, twisted against itself. Blackly mocking the Green Beret mentality of valorous, unquestioned death, McDonald's theme song connected the grunt's impotence with the antiwar rage of America's youth. Who else but a swabbie turned hippie could have made that linkage? The song was an instant hit. But though the Fish featured it at every live performance, and the lyrics appeared in print even as early as 1965, the group's first album, the 1967 *Electric Music for the Mind and Body*, did not contain the cut.

Alone, perhaps, the scathing antipatriotism of the "Fixin'-to-Die Rag" would have brought Joe the attention he needed to compete with the big talents of the Bay Area. With the song and the cheer combined, McDonald was clearly a standout. It's difficult to imagine that less than twenty years ago the collective vocalization of the word "fuck" could arouse so much passion. Not "fuck somebody" or "fuck something." Just plain, unadorned "fuck." The command form of the verb as used by Joe had no object; the insult, if that's how it was being taken, had no target; the expletive merely floated into the air like a puff of smoke from a giant bong. Still, by the standards of the pre–Eddie Murphy and Richard Pryor 1960s, you could get yourself in trouble saying certain things on stage. In the spotlight, Joe would say, "Gimme an F," and the crowd would shout, "F." "Gimme a U," and the crowd would shout, "U."

"What's that spell?" he'd cry at the end, like a cheerleader.

Even high as peace doves, the fans could handle that.

An audience-participation release valve, that's all the ritual cheer signified. These American kids, raised on high school boosterism, loved the chance to shout the F-word nestled in the protective anonymity of the crowd. Political? Perhaps the outrageousness of the cheer represented a challenge to the status quo; the profane word repeated over and over lost all its punch, just as so many other societal hang-ups had for this new generation. We don't want your dirty words and we don't want your dirty war, may have been the subtext. More likely, the cheer was little more than adolescent experimentation with cussing on a collective level. Regardless of its cultural underpinning, the phenomenon started apolitically enough. Not getting the notice he thought his group deserved, Joe had initiated the cheer as a celebration of the Fish. "Gimme an F, gimme an I . . ." Exactly when the spelling changed, no one can remember for sure. The song appears in its original version on the group's second album in 1967, *I-Feel-Like-I'm-Fixin'-to-Die*. Joe now recollects that it was only months before Woodstock that he first went from F-I-S-H to foul. It seems likely it was at least a year before: *Rolling Stone* in its 1968 year-end wrap-up makes mention of the act's being bluelisted for its public obscenity.

What's easier to trace is the mentality behind the initiation of the rag and the cheer. The songs on the radio may have said, "Paranoia strikes deep, into your mind it will creep." But for the most part, fear of reprisal—a legitimate concern of true radicals and subversives—didn't infect many performers in these heady days. The rock star operated as opinion maker and mass leader in a public forum, with thousands of supporters nightly spurring him on. The adulation skewed reality. It's not surprising that a false sense of invulnerability developed. Jim Morrison of the Doors flouted venue restrictions and began exposing his genitals onstage. Janis Joplin started to use her natural gutter dialect during performances. What can the pigs do to me? And Joe McDonald, the former Navy air traffic controller, found himself famous for singing a song about dead soldiers and inciting teenagers to scream "Fuck."

It wasn't until 1968 that the group began to catch heat for its material. A lucrative spot on Ed Sullivan's variety show was canceled because of reports about the cheer. The organizers of the Schaefer Brewing Company concert series in New York's Central Park said the group would never play there again after the Fish's first appearance. Looking back now, however, Joe says he was already uncomfortable about the way the rag and the cheer were dominating the act even before the crackdown came. If that's true, he certainly never said so in any of his interviews at the time. What can't be disputed, however, was that the group experienced unusual tensions during the late sixties. Something gnawed at Joe, some deep internal rift continued to rankle him. Between 1967 and 1969, the group broke up and reunited no fewer than five times.

Their much-publicized organization hassles earned them a reputation as a together-again/apart-again band. Several months after their successful appearance at the Monterey Pop Festival, and just weeks before their second album was released near the end of 1967, manager Ed Denson announced Joe's departure and the renaming of the remaining musicians as the Incredible Fish. By December the reunited ensemble traveled to England for a much-heralded gig as the first San Francisco band to appear in London. To quash rumors of their breakup—which they had started themselves—the Fish leaked to *Rolling Stone* in February 1968 a detailed song list from the group's just-completed album, the title of which was changed from *Hello* to *The First Golden Era* to the more appropriate *Together.* That LP hit the record stores at the same time as a new wave of breakup rumors. And while the group managed to stay intact through the end of the decade, everyone assumed it was just a matter of time before Joe's solo career took off. And when it did, his followers wondered, what new directions would the singer take?

Even as the group struggled with its internal rifts, they were ascending to national prominence. They were added to *Who's Who in America* in the 1968 edition, one of only eight rock acts so honored. They managed to continue producing albums to meet their contractual responsibilities with the Vanguard label. The negative critical reaction to the work, however, certainly didn't improve the situation among the members. Both 1967's *Fixin' to Die* and 1969's *Here We Are Again* were panned in *Rolling Stone,* the bible of the generation. Still, the material documents McDonald's maturing style and his attempts to broaden his appeal beyond protest music. The albums contained Eastern-influenced orchestrations, cabaret ballads and a modicum of pop rhetoric. The 1969 LP featured jams with members of Count Basie's band and backup from the Oakland Symphony. Typically, however, the media wanted to keep the performers pegged: the group's decision not to release the arch "Bomb Song" track as the first single off the *Fixin' to Die* album was criticized by the press. Instead the single chosen was "Janis," a love song to Janis Joplin. On again and off again, Janis and Joe were lovers in the mid-sixties. The relationship eventually broke off, Joe recalls, because her deepening addiction to hard drugs made her incapable of love. ("Janis" was one of the many songs of the period written about private romances between public figures. At Woodstock, where Joe and Janis ran into each other again, Crosby, Stills and Nash introduced "Suite: Judy Blue Eyes," a composition about Stephen Stills's onetime girlfriend Judy Collins.) Eager to escape stereotyping, Joe was encountering the frustrations of an inflexible image, even as he continued to play to it. His sell-out live performances gave his freaky fans exactly the mix of cutting up and cant they had come to expect.

After one of these performances the soldier turned protest singer had an experience that epitomized the career schizophrenia he was feeling. It was in August 1968 in Chicago. The riot-torn Democratic National Convention was in session: the city filled up with antiwar demonstrators agitating for a peace candidate on the ticket, storming the convention hall and battling with Mayor Richard Daley's police force. Throughout Chicago, the decade's ongoing tensions between "hippies" and "rednecks" flared into confrontations. Joe McDonald had traveled to the city at the invitation of Yippie leaders to entertain at a demonstration. Once in town, however, he sized up the situation and decided the hostility in the air could only lead to violence. He backed out of the appearance, instead playing a quiet gig at one of Chicago's rock palaces. As he returned to his hotel room that night, Joe and two members of the Fish crossed paths with three Vietnam vets, who saw nothing but long hair. In Chicago in 1968, a pigtail alone was taken as a political statement. Don't you like America, one of the vets taunted. Do you think you're better than fighting men? The musicians knew this conversation would only provoke violence and started to back away. Before he saw it coming, Joe felt the crack of a fist across his nose and tasted the stream of blood pouring down his face. One of his buddies was knocked into the elevator; another bounced off the wall. The three vets darted through the lobby toward the door and escaped.

Nothing will make you adhere to your beliefs as will getting beaten up for them. Joe was ready to take the licks his lifestyle might invite, but there was something just not right about fellow vets slugging him. Angry as hell, the young man picked himself up off the floor and wandered back to his room. He looked in the mirror and wondered who it was he was looking at. Joe McDonald, USN, protest singer.

A year later nearly to the day, Country Joe McDonald stood offstage at the Woodstock Music and Art Fair. If anything, his conflicts and frustrations had only increased during the interim between the Chicago melee and now. It had been another year, and the rigidity of his image was even more out of synch with who he really was. He had arrived early, before the rest of the group, to cool out a little, to groove on the peaceful vibrations of the Aquarian outing. Perhaps he would have some time with Janis. Out there, among the kids, it was all love and pot and happiness. Backstage was in chaos. The next group can't get through the traffic. We need someone to play. Now. Joe, can you help us out?

This would be his first major solo gig in years, a once-in-a-lifetime opportunity to redefine himself as an entertainment force and rock artist. This might be a chance to convince people once and for all there was more to Country Joe McDonald than F-U-C-K.

Can you help us out, Joe? Now.

RON STONE

Talk to enough of the 500,000 participants—no more than five or six will be necessary—and you're sure to pick up a theme central to the way people remember Woodstock. Maybe the first three will all tell you they thought it was going to be just a great party. Two more will say the music made them go. But pretty soon someone will say, I wanted to be there because I knew it was going to be a piece of history. As they rummage through their memories now, many of the 500,000 will describe their experiences, and what you keep hearing is this desire to witness, the need to take part, the conviction that they were living through momentous times.

While reading *The Washington Post* in his apartment, Ron Stone heard a DJ on the radio talking about Woodstock and knew it was history in the making. For this young man the generation's historical consciousness had been given a unique opportunity to develop early. A George Washington University senior, Ron boasted a sixties sense of being there which had been heightened to the point that he viewed himself as more than merely an observer of major events. He saw himself, perhaps legitimately, as one of their architects. For most of his high school and college years, Ron had worked as a congressional aide, first as a senatorial page in 1964 and then as a Democratic cloakroom clerk through 1967. Still a boy, he had had a close-up view of the Capitol Hill power plays and personalities shaping the decade. And as he recalls it now, his position provided more than good sight lines. By mastering the idiosyncracies of the nation's most exclusive club, Ron exerted influence, shifted votes, made things happen. He felt at the core of his nation's destiny, part of its posterity. It was the sensibility his generation shared. By the time Woodstock came along, his appointment had elapsed as political fortunes shifted in the Senate, sweeping out his sponsors. Ron's congressional access route to history had closed, yet his appetite for being a witness to history still remained strong. So when he heard the advertisement for the festival, old instincts quickened.

There is an almost fairy-tale beginning to Ron's congressional career: one night several years after his father had died, he and his mother were watching TV in their Chicago suburb home. He was a little old at fourteen for the Disney show but there wasn't much else on, so he sat back. The program that night was a dramatization of life among the pages, the young men selected to assist on the floors of Congress through a rigorous process of back-patting, favor-collecting and nepotism. Of course the Disney hour showed none of that, it simply emphasized the classy glamour of the lucky few who finally did get the post. Here was prestige that clearly didn't negate fun! The boy decided this was a job for him.

By the following June, the now fifteen-year-old Ron found himself in Washington, looking for a bed in one of the designated page rooming houses and hustling over to the Senate side for his first day of work. Somewhere along the way Chicago mayor Richard Daley signed a form. Illinois senator Paul Douglas got ahold of it. And young Ron, who had no influential relatives or connections, got a letter saying he had been accepted. What a fluke, he screamed to his mother. And not only was he appointed, but he had been assigned to the Senate floor, clearly among the more elite group of pages, since there were then only six of them. The career, serendipitously inspired by a Disney drama and even more fortuitously launched by a political fluke, had begun. As he remembers it now, his next three years in Congress—1964 through 1967, perhaps the most pivotal of the decade—would never prove any less thrilling.

Within the first week, the high school junior got his initial exposure to the intoxicating power of being present at key events. It was mid-June. Ron was still trying to master the intricacies of a page's duties: when a southern senator gets up to speak, Ron was told, he must receive a glass of Mountain Valley water from Arkansas; when a northern senator gets up to speak, he must receive a glass of Poland Spring water from Maine. The boy hardly knew who came from the North and who from the South, and didn't have an idea where the various region-specific bottles were kept. What he did know was that his basic training was taking place as one of the most bitter filibusters in modern times was occurring on the floor. The great Civil Rights Bill was still pending before the Senate, introduced before John Kennedy's assassination the previous November and still under attack that June by southern delegates. Its proponents, led by Hubert Humphrey and Everett Dirksen, wanted a vote soon, hoping that passage of the bill would quell race riots in the long hot summer ahead. But before a final vote could be taken, the filibuster, now in its seventy-fifth day, needed to be closed. And as Humphrey and Dirksen and even this green page knew, a vote to silence the filibuster was tantamount to a vote for passage. And suddenly, three days after Ron's arrival, the cloture roll was called.

Through various pressure deals, the act's advocates believed they had nailed together a block of dependable ayes large enough to carry. But their prospective majority was far from solid. Besides the inevitable swing vote, certain senators who would definitely favor cloture were in absentia. One of them was California Democrat Clair Engle, on indeterminate sick leave. Two months earlier, he had attempted to introduce a bill but couldn't form the words. Information about that poignant scene didn't take much longer to reach Ron than did the directions about the spring water. The senator's recuperation from two brain operations, the veteran pages told the newcomer, was taking longer than expected and hadn't progressed very far by June. Feelers had been extended to his wife about making him available for this key piece of legislation, and she had rebuffed them. So when Ron spotted the wheelchair at the chamber door midway through the roll call, he knew exactly who the unexpected gentleman was.

Mr. Engle, the clerk called, realizing the paralyzed senator was in fact on hand for the historic vote. Mr. Engle, he called again.

In the corner of the great hall, the crippled man shook. Everyone in the room knew he had made the trip to Capitol Hill to throw his support in favor of the act, but according to the delicate dictates of procedure, he had to make his own position known. Ron, who had moved near him to help with the chair if he needed it, watched the mute language Engle improvised. Struggling, Engle pointed his hand to his eye, to his eye. Ron remembers comprehending the gesture, suddenly feeling the responsibilities of an interpreter. Aye! the new page shouted. The senator is saying "Aye."

More than a few senators started when they heard the youthful tenor carrying across the floor; and later many chided the boy for his temerity—imagine a page voicing a vote. It was, though, just one more unprecedented aspect of what would turn out to be a precedent-setting day. Cloture passed, seventy-one to twenty-nine, and within a week the bill itself was passed. With it, it was hoped, a bright new era of equality in the United States was to begin. Back in his little rented room, Ron already felt himself something of a folk hero in the Senate. He said to himself, I've been here barely two weeks. This is history, and I want to be a part of it.

Even without becoming the first page to vote, it is likely Ron would soon enough have developed a sense of participating in destiny. This was the Senate before imperial presidencies and Washington scandals, when elected statesmen still wore legendary mantles. So important was the legislature that even those who worked in its remote and invisible recesses shared at least part of the limelight. *The Saturday Evening Post* focused on a few of the most influential low-profile employees, calling them the "unseen powermen." The piece, written in 1963, had the prescience to single out Bobby Baker, then secretary to the majority, as someone "who could find any number of ways to misuse [his] power." (He was convicted on a number of counts, including income tax evasion, in 1967.) But Baker had begun his career on the Hill as a page and certainly his ascent to senatorial power stood as an example for Ron's ambition.

It didn't take long, once the excitement of the Civil Rights Bill vote had passed, for another entirely different sort of drama to begin. This time it was war. And once again Ron remembers himself at the center of the action.

It was early August and the Senate was alive with a special buzz; something unusual was in the air. All through that Tuesday, gray-haired men whispered to each other in muffled concern that no mere bill or committee resolution could ever prompt. By evening a handful of the most influential members were called to the White House for a briefing with the president. Secretary of State Dean Rusk would be there, and so would Secretary of Defense Robert McNamara and CIA director John McCone. Something's happened in Vietnam, I bet you a million bucks, said one senior page to young Ron. Kid, there's gonna be a war.

Within hours all the nation knew what Ron had gotten an early inkling of: a series of bombings had been directed against American destroyers stationed in the Gulf of Tonkin as part of the U.S. intelligence operation against North Vietnam. "We seek no wider war," a tired Lyndon Johnson told TV audiences that evening, but by the next day he was asking the Senate to approve just such a move. Already he had discharged bomber jets to retaliate, destroying twenty-five PT boats and four major bases in North Vietnam. Short of a declaration of war, the president now wanted the legislature's broad-based consent to "promote the maintenance of international peace and security in Southeast Asia." At a meeting to discuss the proposed resolution, Ron poured coffee as Rusk and McNamara briefed Montana senator Mike Mansfield and Georgia senator Richard Russell. He offered the men cream as they talked about troop strength and missiles.

On Friday, debate was scheduled on what would come to be

known as the Gulf of Tonkin Resolution. This will be quick, everyone is in favor of this, Ron had heard. Not quite everyone. Using whatever tactics he could, Senator Wayne Morse of Oregon stalled the vote, hoping to persuade some of his colleagues that the motion amounted to a declaration of war. Like a fly on the wall, for pages were considered nearly as invisible, Ron stood nearby as Morse was bullied by resolution supporter Arkansas senator William Fulbright.

Nearing draft age himself, Ron feared the coming of war and couldn't see how the Gulf of Tonkin Resolution could fail to escalate the conflict. Years later, as the intensified hostilities continued to sap the nation's spirit, Fulbright himself would realize the error of granting so much authority to the president, thereby virtually relinquishing the Senate's constitutional right to declare war. By the time Woodstock took place, the devastation wrought in the aftermath of the resolution had come home, the nation was pummeled with surging antiwar passions. But on that muggy August morning, it seemed Morse's warning could gain only one supporter, a green page from Illinois, the youngest American in the Senate.

Because of his spiritual kinship with the Oregon senator, Ron felt he had personally failed later that day when, through a ruse, Morse's delaying tactics were undermined. As Ron remembers it, a staffer tapped Morse on the shoulder to inform him that a *New York Times* reporter had requested he come outside and talk about objections to the resolution. Morse is a hopeless media hound, the other pages had told Ron. He can't turn down an invitation from the press. And indeed, Morse left. As soon as he was gone, Fulbright ended his speech at the podium and called for a vote. The clerk yelled out, Any objections? Suddenly, Ron realized what had happened; the timing of the interview request had been too neat. If no objections were voiced, the vote would be called. Should I run out and get Morse? Where are his staff people? What's my responsibility? Frozen by his dilemma, he sat and watched as the debate was rung to a close and the roll call initiated. When, moments later, Morse charged onto the floor, duped and angry, Ron cast himself as the senator's silent partner as state by state the representatives voted aye. They looked on impotently as the Gulf of Tonkin Resolution materialized into fact, already casting, in their eyes at least, the terrible shadow of fruitless war.

Ron remained a page through his senior year in high school, eventually becoming head page. Upon graduation, he accepted an invitation to return as a Democratic cloakroom attendant, a full-paying position as a party staffer within the Senate. It was one of those linchpins every organization includes, instrumental and influential and virtually invisible. Knowing where to find senators twenty-four hours a day, and where not to find them, was his strong suit. He developed a keen awareness of the members' voting behavior and, through a call to a restaurant or a hotel, could make sure the right senator was on hand when needed. The point man in the Senate's communication center, Ron again was privy to history firsthand. During the Arab-Israeli Six Day War in 1967, Ron received a call from the White House for Senator Russell. While the statesman conferred on the phone, Ron again heard the ominous buzz of pending calamity. When Russell came out of the phone booth, looking ashen, he walked over to the clerk's desk. Would you be willing to fight a war in the Middle East, he asked the soldier-age young man. No, Ron said without reservation. Within minutes the news wire was carrying scattered reports of a bombing raid on the U.S. Navy communications ship *Liberty* off the Sinai Peninsula, initially believed to be a Russian attack. It turned out to have been an accidental attack by Israel. But while the world tensed for the aftershocks of the incident, at least one senator already felt he knew how America's young people would react to more U.S. intervention abroad.

Under different circumstances the young men who held the cloakroom jobs attended college part-time, if at all. But since Ron needed his college deferment from the draft, he was required to enroll as a matriculated student at George Washington University. His first priority remained the Hill, but attending school outside government precincts added interesting wrinkles to his personality. He already had a reputation as something of a liberal in the Senate: he wore a green suit and a contrasting yellow shirt, considered flamboyant and an outward sign of free thinking. On campus he witnessed strident antiwar demonstrations that made Senator Morse's most fervent speeches seem like lullabies. His own sympathies grew more pacifist, although because of his government job he was unsure about actually demonstrating. He attended rallies as an observer, but never felt it possible to join in. At the same time, his job on the Hill made him something of an outsider in the classroom as well. The firsthand knowledge he possessed about politics made it difficult for him to tolerate the often misguided academic theories he heard in class. That's just not the way it is, he would say to himself as a professor with no experience in the real world of Congress explained the true motivations of senators Ron knew personally. Rarely did he contradict the teachers by citing his own experience, but the disparagement he felt for them affected his grades. Ron was not a very good student.

The war and his belief it should be ended are the reasons Ron now cites for leaving the Senate in early 1967. It was a decision peculiar to these times. Only during a period when young men like Ron feel they can in fact alter history do they grow frustrated when they cannot. Such despair requires optimism. Recalling his departure, Ron doesn't mention the fact that his own support base within the Senate had eroded. Paul Douglas, who first secured his page position, lost his Illinois seat in 1966, and incoming Texas senator John Tower took a dislike to him. But more important to Ron were his efforts to stop the war and his inability to make them effective.

As part of his job, Ron had assessed the members' war positions, and predicted that there would be enough votes for a Vietnam measure if it were presented correctly. Robert Kennedy had been elected and with him came strong end-the-war muscle. Senator Eugene McCarthy was pushing for just such a vote, establishing the platform he would use to run for president in 1968. On campuses dissent was erupting and it was likely the spring would bring more violence to the universities. Senator Mansfield refused to support a vote. Too divisive to the party and to the nation, he said. But you can get the majority, Ron insisted. I've figured it out. His tallies were ignored. No end-the-war measure moved out to the floor. Disgusted and defeated, Ron decided to look for other work.

Eventually he chose a job as a lobbyist with American Airlines, mainly because he loved the chance to fly anywhere in the nation it gave him. And with reduced passage to the skies, Ron became addicted to weekend jaunts, hops out of Washington to wherever it seemed likely significant events were happening. If a riot broke out in Boston, he'd fly there after work on Friday for a look-see. When the Apollo missions took off, he'd use his old White House ins to firm up entree to the launch and fly there on the cheap. But for all the travel and improved pay that came with the new job, it couldn't match the headiness of working on the Hill.

By the spring of 1968, Ron was again looking for change. At first he thought he'd go to Hawaii for the summer, to a university program there in Asian-American studies. The airline had agreed to giving him a leave. But this diversion held no real weight; it was just the alternative of the moment. His real plans involved working with the Robert Kennedy organization once the senator won the party's presidential nomination in the fall. He had already held conversations with campaign representatives he knew from the Hill days. And once the campaign successfully placed Kennedy in the White House, Ron expected a new government appointment, a job that would once again offer him a vantage point to history.

But in early June, Kennedy was dead, shot in Los Angeles just as his campaign had reached its apex. Distraught over the assassination and not a little dejected about his own dashed dreams, Ron walked through Washington, past the Senate office buildings, around Capitol Hill, and felt hopelessly detached and unconnected. A page from a newspaper blew by him on the street, its headlines drifting aimlessly into the air.

At twenty, a year amounts to a good chunk of one's life. The time dragged for Ron. Each day seemed another eternity away from those golden years in Congress. He continued to travel around the country, trying to stay plugged into the beat of the times. He was free now to participate in antiwar activities and frequently went to New York City for sit-ins and protests. His final year at George

Washington began. Nineteen sixty-eight merged into 1969, the spring into the summer. Around him, others swelled with that sense of destiny he had felt earlier in the decade. We can change the world, they said. We will make a difference. Then Ron heard about Woodstock, the biggest counterculture event of all time. This sounds like history, he thought. I have to be there.

JOCKO MARCELLINO

REGISTRATION DAY, Columbia University, September 1968. You could observe in a glance the old order and the new restlessly rubbing against each other, like giant underground plates just before or after an earthquake. The setting was the backdrop for one of the many small epiphanies that occurred during the latter part of the decade with great frequency.

On folding tables in the quad in front of Low Library's pillared façade, orientation committee volunteers arranged their printed materials, folders emblazoned with the official university insignia in crisp blue and white. They had banners and mascots and other reminders of the Ivy League school's two-century-old legacy of superior higher education. Here, information on extracurricular activities. Here, hints on getting around the city. They wore buttons welcoming the freshmen and their parents to Morningside Heights. With the atmosphere on campus this fall, their service to the university tradition could be considered only as heroism or folly.

Nearby, at another folding table, a second group of students proffered their printed material and paraphernalia. Blotchy black-and-white fliers from the Students for a Democratic Society informed the newcomers of the progress achieved since the previous spring's takeover of the university, or liberation, as it was referred to. What's SDS? said a frosh. The Columbia Student Coordinating Committee had printed up a position paper arguing in favor of group amnesty for all leaders of the April strike, not a case-by-case review as the administration proposed. That's a plot to separate the leaders from the rest of the strikers, a tired fascist maneuver, explained the smudged handout. Available free of charge: Yippie buttons, armbands and strike posters. Welcome to Columbia, a girl said to John Marcellino, who was shy about asking if anyone knew where the glee club sign-up was. The leftist sophomore tried to cram a little red book into his loose-leaf binder.

Look, there's Mark Rudd. The girl began to straighten up the material she had allowed to fall into disarray on the table.

John turned and got his first up-close glimpse of Rudd. He looked like Rodney Harrington, Mia Farrow's boyfriend on "Peyton Place." Or like the kid who played "Dennis the Menace" on the sitcom, only grown-up. Even though he was just a freshman, John recognized Rudd: how many other Columbia kids had their picture in *Time* and *Newsweek*? All of May, John saw this unexceptional face, usually with a microphone stuck in front of it, alongside the startling and inflammatory news reports about the SDS strike that closed the school. The university is shut down, Rudd told the newsmen, and they printed what he said. Even *The Boston Globe* back home covered the uprising at Columbia, despite similar activity at Massachusetts schools. But things went a lot further at Columbia than elsewhere. Final exams never took place. Entire sections of the university were held by student groups. They had even kidnapped the dean! Yes, John knew that face, the preppie clothes and beach-boy hair, parted neatly, which seemed inconsistent with the rhetoric. That was the face his parents saw on the TV back in Quincy when they began to ask themselves, Should we be sending John down there? It's so wild. Their worries echoed the concerns of hundreds of parents.

Rudd crossed the quad, stopping often to exchange words—secret orders from strike central?—with his comrades. Even if he hadn't seen the upperclassman's face a thousand times before, John would have picked him out as someone special. He walked with the self-consciousness John recognized as the mark of big men on campus. In other times that distinction was earned by point-scoring jocks and student council presidents, just the way John had earned it back in high school. At Columbia things would be different, though. At big universities brainy revolutionaries were the top dogs. Rudd was prohibited from registering because of the suspension still in effect against him. But the punishment only added to his stature here on this day. Having battled against the enemy for student rights and university reform, he was at registration to underscore the personal repercussions of his fight. With the pride of a wounded general he passed among the new recruits, as *The Village Voice* recorded it, "like a god."

Mark Rudd, Columbia University's most famous delegate to America's radical elite, drifted by John Marcellino, the newest lineman on the school's doormat football squad. Young men's lives, intersecting for the first and last time. Within a year, Rudd's revolution would be disintegrating, fractured by the political fickleness of youth, while John would be performing at the largest event the sixties counterculture produced, spearheading a new craze that swept the nation and continued to ripple throughout the next decade, and establishing his group as one of the entertainment industry's most versatile novelty acts. But as Mark Rudd walked by, John was not thinking about nostalgia rock and roll, or the group Sha Na Na, or sharing the stage with Jimi Hendrix and Janis Joplin in Sullivan County. The lineman from Quincy was thinking about football practice and joining the glee club. And how small Rudd looked.

Although it might be supposed that at least a portion of John's fellow freshmen had selected Columbia specifically because of its new notoriety as an outpost of radicalism, certainly that had nothing to do with his choice. Sympathy for the cause? Except for the fact that the spring's rebellion frightened his parents, John had nothing against the SDS. He just had very little in common with them. There were "pukes," or radicals, and there were "jocks," or straight kids, according to James Kunen, who wrote about the 1968 Columbia revolt in his best-selling diary, *The Strawberry Statement.* Kunen himself was something of a split personality, rowing crew while stoking the fires of insurrection. In between practice sessions he chalked up the administration building with the grafitto, "I'm sorry about defacing the wall, but babies are being burned and men are dying and this University is at fault quite directly." He shared the wall with a woman who had chalked: "Up against the wall motherfucker." John suffered no such identity crisis: he was "jock" all the way, and loving it. He arrived at Columbia a one hundred percent old-fashioned golden boy. He was that simplest— and rarest—of campus figures, the standout regular guy.

Like most regular guys, in high school he was one of those kids who seem to have the world at their command. On nearly every teen front, he scored a victory. All-state football, student council president, honor roll. But essential to the regular-guy mystique are rough edges, intimations of humanity that assure peers that down deep you're, well, regular. And John had his share of wrinkles. He was active in the student council, but he wasn't a nerd. Outside of school, he was a healthy cut-up. He'd even join in on the forays into Boston Common, where a counterculture oasis had sprung up. You could buy pot and hang out. They bought pot and hung out. And even though he was a hard-ass jock, with half a dozen broken noses to his credit, he wasn't a macho dink. He was in a garage band, the one sure-fire route to cool. And beyond just being in a band, he was the drummer for the band. Inspired casting. Say he had been lead singer, the kids might have been turned off by the spotlighted ego display. But high on the platform, behind the singers, drummer was perfect: ever since Ringo, the drummer was the oddball, the goofy one, the everyday schmo. With the A's, the varsity letters and the stix, John perfected the nearly unattainable persona: golden boy as regular guy.

There was one more key characteristic to John's personality: leading man. Ever since he was a kid, working with the Boston

Children's Theater, the athlete and scholar secretly craved the musical stage more than the football field or classroom. He remembers catching the bug early while watching local stock productions of *Finian's Rainbow* and *The King and I.* Throughout grammar school, whether it was a Christmas pageant or a St. Patrick's Day review, John had the lead role. At his Catholic high school he ran into his first conflict of interest when his football training interfered with participation in the fall musical. Of course, the gridiron took precedence; his older brother, who went on to play professionally with the Patriots, had established a Marcellino football dynasty, which John promised to continue. Besides, you didn't get scholarships for singing "Edelweiss." Football meant college money. So every November, the all-state guard, the student council officer, the honor roll student would go to the high school auditorium and quietly die as someone else played the one role he most wanted.

God works in mysterious ways, the boy had heard over and over again in religion classes. Maybe it was true. Nixed from the fall musical, John looked forward to the spring variety show with all the more excitement. While he gladly took the backseat, literally, as drummer with the band, the leading man in him seized the opportunity to perform on the stage each April. One year, he decided to present a series of rock-and-roll impersonations, gyrating around the stage with some buddies, lip-synching a couple of Temptations hits. It wasn't just imitations; John produced the numbers, complete with lighting and costumes. He remembers asking one of the nuns if he could borrow her black cloak for his friend's James Brown routine. Who's James Brown, she wanted to know. It was John's first success with rock-and-roll revivalism.

Not surprisingly, considering his accomplishments, six schools offered John football scholarships. Only one of the colleges he applied to offered him an academic one, however, and that was the scholarship he accepted. But picking Columbia over the others had more to do with his secret ambitions than with endowment allotments. Columbia meant New York City and New York meant theater. And by the time John was in his final year in high school he had decided the stage, not the locker room, was his future. He'd

still be playing ball at college, but in the puny Ivy League confer-
ence. His tightly contested high school league was probably more
competitive. Opting for Columbia in 1968 meant turning his back
on a football career in favor of what he really wanted to do.
Throughout the spring, as the reports of campus strife and
upheaval at Columbia filtered into Quincy, John just kept thinking
about Broadway.

As little as the student rebellion interested the freshman, the
revolution in theater intrigued him. Sixties culture shock
recharged the performing arts, and John hit town at the height of a
rebirth. Improvisational techniques, new candor and a vital off-
Broadway explosion blew off the dust that had settled during the
early part of the decade. Outrageously avant-garde dramatic
works, calculated to draw gasps, competed with each other. They
even prospered commercially. *Futz* opened in June and was still
playing when John arrived in Manhattan that fall. In it a farmer, in
love with his pig, tries to convince townsfolk of his right to self-
expression. But even John's favorite genre, the veritable old musical, was undergoing a renaissance. *Cabaret*—a song-and-dance
show about Nazi Germany—was running. There was a hippie
interpretation of Shakespeare in *Your Own Thing*. And the gaudy
excess of musical overproduction had been successfully jettisoned
in the minimalistic if syrupy adaptation of *Peanuts* called *You're a
Good Man, Charlie Brown*. It was a good time to be open-minded
and a musical buff in New York.

Soon after registration, John discovered the Columbia Kingsmen, an apple-pie and crew-cut choral group that was attached to
the university glee club. A tight-harmony, a cappella octet, the
Kingsmen wore matching jackets, performed at nursing home
Christmas parties, and sang the Columbia University fight song.
They were barbershop in an era of long-hair rock; they drew more
inspiration from the Lennon Sisters than from John Lennon. But
they had chutzpah. And they were good. On weekend nights, if a
few of them found themselves in one of the coffeehouses around
the campus, they'd show off their harmonies on old doo-wop
songs. These were half-forgotten numbers that tapped into the
kids' collective memories and conjured up images of transistor

radios stuffed under pillows and turned to countdowns on AM stations. John heard them one night and his impresario instincts awoke. Hey, how about adding some instruments to the act, he suggested, and really getting into the fifties thing? The kids will hate that, a tenor scoffed. A greaser act, now? At Columbia? If we do it all out, they'll love it. Trust me, John said. They did.

John had already joined the university's theater group and secured a part in a production of a Bertolt Brecht play that fall. Knowing the rehearsal schedule, he managed to reserve the theater on a night when no event was slated. In addition to himself and the original coffeehouse doo-woppers, he found a few more Columbians who grooved on the idea of a fifties group, bringing the performing ensemble to twelve. Relying on the old workhorse of the movement, the mimeograph machine, he printed up fliers inviting Columbia and nearby Barnard students to "take a night off from the Revolution for a Greaser's Ball." What's a greaser, asked a Barnard freshwoman. John was determined to raise her consciousness. Whipping out a tube of Vitalis, he showed the other collegiates how to slick up their hair and comb it back. In three months on campus, his own crew cut had grown out and he needed half a tube to get the whole crop glopped. Who's next? No way, the Kingsmen screamed. It's so square. This from guys who know all the verses of the fight song, thought John. Convincing his colleagues that grease was an essential ingredient for the act was just the first hurdle. After rehearsing—barely—for two weeks, he was informed the night before the Greaser's Ball that the group couldn't use the stage because the Brecht set couldn't be struck. Not to worry, John improvised. We'll use the stage as is. Typical of student productions of the day, the set was a somber gray void meant to suggest urban alienation. It's a street corner, John decided. Like one in Philly or Brooklyn where doo-woppers used to sing. We'll just hang some clothes from a string over here and it will look great. Sha Na Na was born.

John remembers that night vividly. Any minute he expected the SDS to barge in, take over the event, and stage a liberation exercise. Just to make sure the revolution didn't interrupt—and since the crowd had turned up so early—the show started forty-five minutes before schedule. And didn't end until three hours and twenty-five songs later. Crude, unsophisticated and problem-ridden, the performance was a smash. Relying on gym class routines for choreography, the entertainers did jumping jacks during instrumentals; the Kingsmen, freed of their blazers, proved to be hunky dudes in dungarees and T-shirts. It was the Columbia revolution's silliest be-in. And no one was more surprised and delighted than John, who that night became Jocko forever.

It's easy to see now why the novelty act clicked so well, although at the time its popularity defied the reigning zeitgeist. By playing authentic good-time rock and roll under the disguise of camp, Sha Na Na seduced its rhetoric-dazed audience into letting go and having fun. Without the grease and the shtick—which told listeners this was a joke—the group would have been dismissed as hokey, corny, retrograde. But the show biz trappings called attention to the group's distance from the material, to their awareness that in 1968 this music had become hokey. That music, though, still had pizzazz. Compared to the head-trippy and bluesy compositions of the day, these primal rock sounds had catchy melodies and foot-stomping beats. Sha Na Na didn't condescend to doo-wop, nor did they consecrate it. They exploited the tunefulness of songs like "At the Hop," "Blue Moon" and "Get a Job." They presented them as the generation's curios, each enjoyable in its own right, and as reflections of old values thought to be dying. They reminded their relentlessly forward-looking audiences that they shared a blitheringly daffy past.

If a meteoric rise to fame can include dismal treks downtown on the IRT, then the group's ascent was indeed that. More Columbia gigs—their revue, Grease Under the Stars, drew fans from several Ivy League campuses—led to a string of appearances at the Fillmore East, Manhattan's premier rock spot. At first they were signed on for a quick twenty-minute set, between Three Dog Night and Canned Heat. John had his own ideas about that.

You've got to forget about that light show for our act, Jocko told club managers the day before their first gig there. No bubbles for Sha Na Na. We want to show the back wall, the brick wall, and hang our clotheslines up. That's the look we want. It's Brechtian. And you should let us go on before Three Dog Night. We get the audience charged.

No, they told him. Just do as you're told.

The next night, after the crowd went wild for Sha Na Na, the bubbles went out, the clothesline went up, and they opened the show. Here they are, greased and ready to kick ass . . . Sha Na Na.

For all the unexpected success John was encountering, he never at this point thought of the group as anything but an extracurricular activity. With a dozen members sharing whatever pay they received for the gigs, no one was getting rich enough to consider the act a career. Equipment, stored in lockers around campus, was expensive too. Money was tight, and requests for appearances grew. But John and most of the other Columbians refused to put the act before their education. Honoring the demands of his academic scholarship, John set down scheduling guidelines that continued throughout his school years: no Monday, Tuesday or Wednesday shows, no commitments two weeks before exam period. Still, there was enough money coming in to make it feasible for the group to remain in New York over the summer after John's freshman year. We can share apartments, they told each other. We'll get gigs.

Gigs as they never imagined possible. With the Fillmore success as an imprimatur, Sha Na Na began to receive offers from some of the city's hottest rock clubs, dingy basements that teamed with funk. One of these, the Steve Paul Scene, was particularly significant for John. Located on Forty-sixth Street, the club sat across Eighth Avenue from the theater district that had first attracted him to the city. Now in a costume and with a troupe he could have never foreseen, he was pioneering a whole new sort of rock-and-roll theater. Throughout the summer, some of the biggest stars of popular music dropped by the Steve Paul Scene, and the incandescence they generated brought John and the other performers back down to earth. They were after all little more than a novelty act with a local cult following compared to the likes of Jimi Hendrix and Janis Joplin. They were just a bunch of college kids interrupting the revolution with doo-wop. Then one night two young men showed up after their show asking about their availability in August.

I've heard about this Woodstock thing, John told his friends. I think we should do it.

SYLVIA GREENE

Rᴇʙᴇᴄᴄᴀ ᴅɪᴅ and Sylvia didn't. More precisely, as Sylvia remembers it now, her best friend, Rebecca, did it a lot, and Sylvia didn't do it at all. And for all their homeroom laughter and sleep-over confidences and teenage chatter, inevitably it would be their sexual experience that divided them. In the late 1960s adolescent girls like Sylvia and Rebecca were feeling the dark and confusing tug of that primal competitive pressure traditionally shared by high school and college boys: losing one's virginity. Going all the way, once a mark of shame, became a female status symbol: the ritual significance of being pinned replaced by the real thing. Or at least that's what a free-love counterculture contended. But different girls responded differently to the glib hippie urgings to gather rosebuds. By the time Sylvia and Rebecca would go to Woodstock, sexual friction—all the more complex because for girls it was so new—had pretty much sabotaged the innocent camaraderie that had sweetened their youth. One did, the other didn't, and at Woodstock that made all the difference.

Not surprisingly, this friendship had its roots in competition, in the simple and universal jockeying for attention that's always been part of high school relationships. Initially, however, Rebecca was a prize rather than a rival, as Sylvia attempted to establish herself in her new high school by securing the popular girl as a friend. As a result of her mother's divorce and subsequent remarriage, Sylvia had moved around several times during her middle and high school years. The circuit covered classrooms as far afield as Long Island and Texas. As is frequently true with such rootless kids, Sylvia relied on her siblings, especially her older sister, for companionship. Unlike relocated teens, however, Sylvia hadn't lost her ability to socialize well outside the home. In fact, she had developed an almost pragmatic approach to friendship: she would determine a likely candidate and go out and introduce herself. With no cushion of time to let things evolve naturally, she pinpointed her buddies. With Rebecca, Sylvia's calculations hit the bull's-eye, but the resulting relationship was far more intense than the cool reserve of her pragmatic technique would have suggested.

In the spring of 1966 the family relocated again, this time a short hop from Hackensack to Fort Lee, New Jersey. This uprooting was less traumatic than earlier transitions. In fact, Sylvia commuted through the spring to finish out her term at her old high school. But once summer came she found herself in a strange town full of kids she didn't know. Plus, she was acutely aware that her sister would be heading off to college soon, leaving her without the home-front support she depended on. She made one friend, a fellow incoming junior who lived in the same apartment complex, and together they filled July and August planning Sylvia's debut that September. If the summer was a dry one for the girls, they were going to make a big splash in the fall.

But the school was full of cliques, and in early September Sylvia encountered a degree of factioning she had never experienced before, in which members of one group absolutely shunned those of another. What dismayed her most were the ethnic lines of demarcation: cliques divided into Italian clans and Jewish ones, and verbal hostility between them filled the corridors. The "Wops" and the "Kikes" were like the Blue and the Gold teams of Fort Lee High. Even before she associated herself with any group, Sylvia was subjected to anti-Semitic incidents that left her more shocked than intimidated.

In such an environment Sylvia gravitated toward the other Jewish kids, but that presented problems too. The cool group was hopelessly greaser, and for all her desire to be in, there was no way she was going to don the heavy mascara and tight skirts of the girls in that clique. One girl in that crowd stood out, though. Behind Rebecca's gobs of makeup and tough-girl attitude, Sylvia sensed the presence of a soul sister. She was popular with boys who repelled Sylvia, those slicked-back hoods in T-shirts and pointy shoes. And Sylvia assumed the girl's involvement with them meant she was willing to "put out." Certainly that was the reputation of the other girls in the clique, especially Rebecca's best friend, Esther. With the same determination that she had mustered to date the best-looking boy—a campaign progressing nicely—Sylvia set out to win Rebecca away from the captive greaser gang.

Rebecca responded warmly to Sylvia's overtures. She had an artistic temperament, as did the newcomer: Rebecca painted, while Sylvia acted. But their similarities ran deeper than that. Both girls had watched as their parents' marriages unraveled. Rebecca's experience was more recent and therefore more painful: her mother, she claimed, was having an affair with her uncle. Her favorite uncle. Sylvia offered her empathy, but she showed vulnerability too: she was suffering from the ongoing animosity between her mother and father, which prevented her from seeing her dad as much as she would like. Linked by their family problems, the two girls began spending more and more time together, much to Esther's dismay. Sylvia suspected that part of what really may have rankled Esther was the defection of a fellow sex initiate. Rebecca and Esther had been bonded in the group by their willingness to hook into new, casual attitudes about fooling around with boys. It was cool, but the experimentation demanded the reinforcement of several girls' doing it. And now Rebecca was stepping back, befriending a girl known to go slow, leaving Esther on the sexual frontier, exposed and unsure how she got there.

My cousin is a musician, Sylvia told Rebecca. We can go listen to him and his group at a club. It was her second cousin actually. Leslie West, a fast-rising hard-rocker, was then making a name for himself as a member of a bar band called the Vagrants. Later, under the aegis of top producer and bass guitarist Felix Pappalardi, he would form a larger, more ambitious combo called Mountain, which would make one of its earliest appearances at the Wood-stock Festival. One of the reasons Sylvia and Rebecca would go to the weekend concert was to see the new-star relative. But even back in high school he was an enticing draw for the girls. He can get us in the back door, Sylvia assured her friend, even though we are underage.

With this invitation, Sylvia played her trump card and won her new friend over for good. For all her experience with boys, Rebecca was far less worldly in other matters than Sylvia, whom she ideal-ized as a sophisticate. She had already begun to copy her dress, substituting the clique outfit for the sort of modish fashion to which Sylvia introduced her. Together they had gone out and bought the first pair of bell-bottoms Fort Lee High had ever seen, then a radical departure from the skirts girls were wearing. Choos-ing to premiere them at a wrestling match had been another Sylvia-inspired flourish: where better to flaunt one's avant-garde style than at an interscholastic sweat-and-grunt meet. Their entrance together guaranteed that everyone would from then on identify the two girls as inseparable buddies. Well convinced that Sylvia held the key to breaking out and truly becoming hip, Rebecca flipped over the prospect of backstage passes to a rock performance. The next time Leslie West played in Manhattan the two girls went to see him.

This was to be just the first of many trips they made into the city together. Few actually involved seeing Sylvia's cousin, or attending anything special at all. They simply became addicted to the excite-ment of downtown, where the streets teemed with older kids and wilder kids and kids who seemed more experienced than their high school peers. No, not kids. Boys who seemed older and wilder and more experienced. And even men. The pair was too young for bars, and they weren't interested in the drug scene. The trips amounted primarily to adventures in flirting. The girls went to try out their attractiveness, to exercise their allure, to cock-tease.

Sylvia would drive into the city in her parents' car and park in Greenwich Village. She had been taking acting classes in Manhattan for several years and knew it well. It was hers to present to Rebecca. They would join the scene on Bleecker Street. They loved the fact that the streets were full of Europeans, handsome young men who had flocked to the hippie mecca eager to meet American girls. American girls enjoyed sex, the Europeans were reading in their home newspapers. A cultural revolution had liberated them from puritanical restraints, they told each other on the plane over. They may even pick you up, the European men hoped. It was easy to get laid in Greenwich Village.

Sylvia and Rebecca toyed with these boys. In coffee shops and on park benches, they would cross their bell-bottomed legs in a come-on that the foreigners lunged after. It was Friday night, and the hippie's version of cruising was in full tilt. In tie-dyed T's instead of Jockey muscle shirts, in bare feet instead of black boots, the horny young men would eye the girls. Local boys would go after them too. But the girls liked the visitors more. Their accents were cute, their English broken. The girls were more in control with boys like that. The game seemed less dangerous that way. We're such brats, Sylvia would say to Rebecca.

The two had a number of long and open conversations about sex. Sylvia assumed that Rebecca had far more experience with boys than she did. Rebecca felt it was healthy to be involved with boys, to respond to her body's urges. Sylvia agreed, but said she just didn't feel comfortable about intimacy yet. What she really wanted to know, though, was what it felt like to go all the way. What was that like? Well, I don't know. I never have, said Rebecca. I want to but I haven't yet. Sylvia was astounded. She had just assumed Rebecca had had sex. She suddenly realized that when it came right down to it, they were sexual equals.

We'll, I'll be a virgin when I get married, said Sylvia.

And Rebecca looked up from the magazine she was paging

through, smiled in a way Sylvia had never seen before. Well, I won't, she said.

Such was the sexual climate in the years leading up to Woodstock: a sixteen-year-old girl could pledge herself to premarital intercourse and expect approval from her best friend. For Sylvia to express objection would have been to reveal herself as hopelessly square, since censure contradicted so many contemporary cultural messages. The popular media of the day virtually urged young people to consider sexual experimentation. As Dr. William Masters was quoted as saying at the time, "the sixties will be called the decade of orgasmic preoccupation." The rallying cry of the era, "Make Love, Not War," lifted nooky to a political plane. *Time* magazine labeled the trends in pop culture by saying, "Clothes-lessness is next to Godliness," and continued: "Hippies, nudists, protesters and naked-theater advocates have somehow managed to equate the altogether with the unattainable: total honesty, inno-cence, understanding, peace and in the same breath revolution." Articles in every popular magazine probed the impact and signifi-cance of the new freedom, tracing its effect on theater (coital simulation came to Broadway in *Oh! Calcutta!*) and screen (by 1969 the Swedish sex documentary *I Am Curious (Yellow)* was a succès de scandale). High school kids watching the Franco Zeffirelli film adaptation of *Romeo and Juliet* as part of their homework saw a nude bedroom scene. They danced to the Rolling Stones' "Let's Spend the Night Together." Meanwhile, in the schools themselves, kids listened as parents and teachers wrangled over the pros and cons of sex education. As the debate raged on, more such courses were offered each year throughout the nation.

But for all the information and explicit encouragement, girls like Sylvia and Rebecca still received don't-do-it warnings. It's not unlikely both girls had read an editorial in a 1968 issue of *Mademoi-selle*, titled "On Virginity," in which the author intimated virginity was a prerequisite to real romance. He—it was a man who wrote the piece—frequently used the pejorative term "promiscuity" when referring to sex. In an issue of the magazine they could have read just before going to the festival, another male editorialist criticized sex as a new status symbol. "It is more disreputable to be a virgin than a bore," he complained of contemporary mores. Then he went on to deplore the era for "confusing sexual freedom with political freedom."

In his massive 1968 tome *The Sexual Wilderness,* social-trend spotter Vance Packard attempted to chart the new terrain young people were exploring. Read now, of course, some of his analyses seem somewhat stodgy: one hallmark of the "new environment for sexual awakening" he cites is "the promotion of the dissolute look." And as proof he adduces this irrefutable sign of wantonness: "In 1964 a *Seventeen* magazine survey indicated that whereas in 1948 only 2 out of 10 girls were regular users of mascara, by 1964 9 out of 10 [were]." Yet for all its stuffiness, the book is a clear record of the pressures girls of Sylvia and Rebecca's generation were facing, which their counterparts a decade earlier, and certainly their mothers, never had. "The social changes of the past quarter century have had their greatest and most obvious impact on the lives of women," he wrote, and most specifically their sexual options. He quotes another survey conducted by *Seventeen* of 1,166 teenage girls that showed 25 percent had had sex before they were nineteen. And his own survey of 1,393 student-age Americans conducted in the mid-sixties showed that by age twenty-one, 43 percent were "coitally experienced." Still, his findings also indicate that 47 percent felt a girl should wait until she was married before she had her first sexual experience.

Sylvia and Rebecca fell along this great female sexual divide of the sixties. Sylvia held back, keeping the sexual stance that had the weight of history behind it and, in fact, seemed to be the prevailing attitude. Rebecca wasn't going to wait. And because culture now legitimized her sexual appetite, Rebecca's decision to do it, far from labeling her a slut, made her a formidable rival. For if Rebecca offered sex to boys, how would Sylvia ever compete?

Their adventures into Manhattan continued through the school year. They went through a series of boyfriends, both of them dating older men. Sylvia's interest in theater and her cousin's entertainment connections led her into liaisons with several performers. She dated a member of the *Hair* company. She remembers now how she loved to walk through Central Park with this incredibly cool guy with his cast jacket on. She also began seeing a rock musician and singer whom a year later, as one of a crowd of 500,000, she would watch perform at Woodstock. With neither, however, did she have sex, although she realized they began to lose interest in her when she refused.

Is it really so bizarre that Rebecca called Sylvia in the middle of the night within minutes of her having intercourse the first time? The college man she was dating must have wondered what this girl was doing when she dashed for the dial. For Rebecca the need to share this moment with Sylvia was paramount, the experience wasn't real until Sylvia knew. Her chevrons had been won and she wanted her best friend in boot camp to know. Are you mad at me, she wanted to know. No, of course not. I'm not mad.

And throughout senior year Sylvia watched as Rebecca grew more and more experienced with sex. She developed a theory she still holds to this day: that her friend was more receptive to the sexual license of the era because she lacked confidence, and she used sex to feel popular. And in particular, more popular than Sylvia. Sylvia remembers several occasions when Rebecca took men away from her. The suitors knew Rebecca would sleep with them and Sylvia would not.

It was natural for the two girls to go to Woodstock together. By the summer of 1969, each had been away at college for a year, and the distance allowed them to conduct their own love lives separately without collision. They enjoyed seeing each other again during vacation and were excited about the plans to spend the weekend upstate. It was not to be a fulfilling time as friends, however. Their different attitudes about sex would again come into play at the festival, and it would become the girls' last adventure together.

BILL PELLIGRINI

NINETEEN AND a bum. No one was more surprised at this turn of events than Bill Pelligrini himself. As he grubbed a cigarette from a fellow derelict he asked himself how he had sunk so low. He had gotten a 98 on his chemistry Regents and was on the state-champion crew team, and now he was panhandling for change around Manhattan, crashing in unoccupied apartments around Alphabet City.

By August 1969 street life would be over for the good-looking, affable young man. Chance encounters he'd have at the Woodstock Music and Art Fair would derail his skid-row existence in a way he never could have anticipated. But that spring, when his derelict drift seemed unalterable, he could foresee only season after season of hand-to-mouth scrounging. Where did it all go wrong?

Dropping out had a cachet in the late sixties that corresponded little to Bill's day-to-day life in the Bowery. There was supposed to be poetry in the free and easy ways of a bohemian. On Broadway, just blocks away from Bill's bleaker part of town, theatergoers were lining up to see *Hair*, the musical that tunefully celebrated rebellion against cultural norms and the flouting of convention. It depicted ad hoc communal living as a supportive, nourishing environment without bothering to explain exactly how its flower-children characters managed to feed or clothe themselves. Similar dropout fantasies cluttered the pop culture landscape, few dramatizing the difficulties of making do without in an urban setting. Dropping out was part of letting the sun shine in, a romantic escape from convention.

That fantasy was the extension of a more serious questioning of values; radicals of the day criticized society's institutions, acclaiming as heroes those who rejected the establishment. Student protesters focused on the schools and their failure to meet contemporary needs. High schools and colleges were irrelevant, and young people who turned away from them—some 400,000 a year by certain estimates—were legitimate seekers of alternative truths. In response, educational authorities mounted campaigns urging kids to stay in school, hoping to stem the rising level of dropoutism. Without at least a high school degree, the campaign argued, youngsters could never expect to find work, support themselves, live. Failure to graduate was equated with a future of abject poverty.

Hair's prettified presentation of life on the periphery, unfortunately, had little to do with the realities that Bill faced. Nor was there any well-thought-out political commitment or ideological decision behind his leaving Woodbridge High before finishing his junior year.

Bill's problems began simply enough and in a quintessentially sixties way: he didn't want to get his hair cut. He was living at that point in Hicksville, Long Island, with his mother and her new husband, a man who was struggling with the demands of relating to a teenage boy who wasn't his own son. Bill was usually not a problem. Bright and well mannered, the kid distinguished himself as a backstroke swimmer and rower, accomplished in upscale sports the middle-class family had never taken much interest in before. In fact, early tensions mounted when his stepfather refused to make concessions to the boy, who was overstressed by his accelerated academic program and sports commitments. I want you back here by six on the dot, his stepfather would say. Even though he didn't finish practice until five-thirty, he was required to be home promptly for supper or face punishment. He'd run the three miles home to make the deadline, hauling the books he'd need for homework. He remembers that because of the stress he occasionally suffered from stomach convulsions.

Still, Bill was happy at school, more popular by far than Billy Joel, who happened to be in his class and whom he vaguely resembles. With-it and cool, he began to let his hair creep over his ears into a Beatles cut, as many of his classmates were doing. The look, then perceived as wild and uncontrolled, enraged his stepfather. He insisted Bill have it trimmed back to the crew cut he had always worn before. When Bill refused, the animosity between the two that had been roiling under the surface broke out into violence. The next day Bill left home.

He headed off for Woodbridge, New Jersey, a town he knew nothing about, except that his natural father lived there. Ever since his mother divorced, she had maneuvered to keep Bill and his younger brother away from their father. She restricted visits and tried to thwart those that were court approved. Bill had seen his father twice a year at most since he was about seven years old. Battered by his stepfather, he seized on this little-known relative as his best hope of starting over.

Bill got off the bus in Woodbridge, a factory and warehouse town in middle New Jersey, and wasn't even sure where he was going to go. Luckily, the first person he asked knew his father—who, ironically, had set up a haircutting business in the town—and where he lived. Bill sat on the stoop of his father's house for hours, waiting until he came home. When he did, the man listened to the boy's story, thought a minute about the possible ramifications, and said, You don't have to go back there again.

With a new living arrangement, Bill thought he'd be able to reestablish the happy high school existence he knew on Long

Island. He would soon realize Hicksville had been a breeze compared to the hassles awaiting him in Woodbridge. His hair would again be a problem even before enrollment: during his placement exam that fall, an administrator warned him, You better have that hair cut by the time you start classes. Bill spent the afternoon in the library tracking court cases on a student's right to wear hair of any length in a public school. He was prepared with those citings when he was again confronted by the belligerent administrator on the first day of classes. He pushed Bill up against a locker, and said, I don't care what the law says. You'll just feel a whole lot more comfortable if you get it cut off.

Bill had started Woodbridge High expecting the same degree of sophistication from his peers and acceptance from his teachers. He met neither. Greaser behavior still dominated; black pointy shoes, white T-shirts and cruising were the hallmarks of the in crowd. Bill wanted to fit in so he tried to adapt. He'd pile in a car with a bunch of guys and head out to Perth Amboy, where in ritual progression the cars would circle the designated block as the sixteen-year-olds drank beer and looked for girls. Bill went along for a while, but it wasn't going to work. For one thing, he was too old to go backward. Born in December, he had been held back from first grade a year. And because of the many moves after his parents' divorce he lost another year. Then a bout of mononucleosis nixed the athletics he might have used to make a place for himself in the new school.

Two years older than his classmates, Bill began to chafe at the narrow constraints of Woodbridge life. He buddied up with a few closet intellectuals in the student body whose Leonard Cohen albums and copies of Kerouac served as common grounds for friendship. Still his hair—he never did cut it—stood out enough to mark him as a hippie and to draw the attention of local boys. Despite the love affair the media were having with hippie fashion, its small-town proponents often drew flak for following its dictates. Typically, cars returning from the Saturday-night cruising Bill now avoided would slow down as they passed him on the street. Toughs would get out, call him "hippie faggot" and threaten him. They'd throw their malteds on him. He had been reading some of Gandhi's writings lately and had become interested in nonviolent resistance. So during one skirmish when fists were about to fly, he simply stood there. Get back up, you pansy, they taunted him. And he got back up, not realizing that Gandhi himself would have stayed down. Each time he got back up, he was unwittingly challenging the greasers to throttle him again. And they met the challenge. To their minds, this passivity meant Bill was the effeminate weakling his clothes and hair suggested. After that incident, he couldn't eat solid foods for a month. He also learned a key principal of passive resistance: stay down once knocked down.

Along with his dwindling popularity, his classwork deteriorated. His English teacher was the wrestling coach, his art teacher was in the Army reserves. They looked at Bill with his longish hair and saw a freak. Without setting out to become a high school radical, he found himself cast in the role. Small gestures of defiance began creeping into his behavior. Insignificant in their own right, they reinforced his negative reputation. Once he refused to stand at a rally when the football team made its entrance. He was scolded, or rather humiliated, in front of the entire student body. By midterm Hicksville High's golden boy was failing most of his courses, even gym. A year before, he had rowed to a state championship, and now he was failing gym!

Counselors harped on his hair length, telling him his problems with his teachers and peers would disappear if he would just get it cut. When his father realized how poorly his son was performing in school, he too insisted it was all because of the hair. He gave him a five-dollar bill and told him to stop wasting everyone's time and just get it cut. He then added an ultimatum: Don't come home until it is.

Confused, Bill crashed at a friend's house for three days, missing school without an excuse. When he finally went back, they presented him with this catch-22: New Jersey law barred him from going to school if he didn't live with a guardian; and if he did live with his father then his father could be fined $1,000 a day for Bill's unexcused truancy. Fearing they really would slap a penalty on his father, Bill left school and never went back.

The expulsion, far from filling the boy with carefree jubilation, terrified him. Although he had acted stubbornly, he never thought he'd be cast out like this. He felt guilty and lost. The prospect of failure at such an early age filled him with dread and morose thoughts. Not knowing what he would do with his life, he drifted away from Woodbridge and into the streets of New York City. It was early 1969.

If the tides of change had not washed through Woodbridge High School, they were certainly flooding every corner of Manhattan. Along with San Francisco's Haight-Ashbury, Greenwich Village was the center of new consciousness and hippie lifestyle. Like a magnet, it attracted young people who had been disenfranchised from their hometowns. One result of this migration was the growing number of young people joining the city's homeless population. Some were burn-outs from the drug culture, and in that they weren't so different from the addicts and alcoholics who had always taken to the streets. But there was also a new subset of itinerant youths huddling in alleyways and showing up at soup kitchens. Scraggly and skinny, they weren't incoherent from dope or booze; they were simply dropouts. And Bill was one of them.

His education in street smarts took place quickly. He hooked up with a mysterious fellow named Joey, who introduced Bill to Alphabet City, the ghetto section of Manhattan divided by Avenues A, B, C and D, near the coffeehouses of St. Mark's Place. In the neighborhood's run-down and seemingly deserted buildings, young people were setting up funky homes with little more than a month's rent and a mattress. Bill hung around Alphabet City; soon enough he had mastered slum survival skills, which amounted to little more than waiting for opportunities to happen. With the casual courtesy of the era, two girls who were abandoning their tiny pad told Bill he could just move in. They said, You never have to pay rent. Just keep two six-packs of beer around and when the landlord comes to collect, just get him drunk. Tell him a sob story when he's loaded and he'll go away. He did, but the burglars who came by twice to see if Bill had anything worth robbing were less cooperative. They held a gun to his head, picked over his meager belongings, then left.

Becoming increasingly dissatisfied with street life, Bill began hanging around the New York University campus. It was a short way from his neighborhood and represented all he was missing in his current existence: comfort and affluence and well-heeled free-thinking. The fact that he was an unemployed, long-haired dropout didn't necessarily make him a pariah among the liberal collegiates there. To their minds, his life was exotic. They invited him for pot parties where his familiarity with Kerouac and Oriental philosophies provided him with suitable material for the raps. The encounters only made Bill more frustrated about his situation, because eventually the party would be over and he would once again take to the streets. There he would run into the winos and degenerates whose lives he feared he was emulating. But what he still had that they did not have was good looks and sex appeal.

It was May and nearly time for school to let out when one afternoon a girl from NYU more or less picked him up. In all his trips into the dormitories before this, conversation and pot were all Bill had been offered. But this was exam time, and Carol seemed to know what she wanted as a study break. Although this was his first real experience with sex, Carol's eagerness and the comfort of the dorm surroundings eased Bill's nerves. He didn't leave the dorm until Carol went home for summer vacation in Poughkeepsie, taking Bill with her.

Her plan had been simple, although it obviously grew out of the false sense of independence a year at NYU had engendered. Together, they would go upstate and on her savings set up an apartment somewhere in her hometown. To Bill this sounded very grown-up, since to this point he had never had to deal with such adult realities as rent and deposits. He had no idea what sort of work he was supposed to do once he got up there to help support the household. Still, he liked the idea of getting away from the bums and derelicts with the first classy person to pay him any mind in quite some time.

The question of earning his keep came up more quickly than he had thought. No sooner had he and Carol moved into the small room than her father and brother stormed the place, bundled up her possessions, and corralled her out the door. Suddenly Bill found himself in Poughkeepsie without a job, without a partner, without any money. His career as a gigolo had been short-lived.

Aimlessly wandering around the neighborhood, Bill noticed a small crafts shop. It was the type of love-beads-and-jewelry joint cropping up around the suburbs, those storefronts where locals once bought Christmas cards or garden equipment, now converted for hippie consumers. You could buy posters there and black-light lamps and occasionally even drug paraphernalia like bongs and papers. Most of the craftwork was made on the site. Above the retail section, in a cramped room, the owner, a friendly Santa Claus of a hippie, had set up a series of tables which were surrounded by boxes of string and beads. It was a self-contained factory, a small-time capitalist's way of making legitimate cash off the counterculture. Got any work, Bill asked. The storeowner sized up the gangly, hairy young man and pointed upstairs. Bill had his first crafts job.

As it turned out, Bill was good at his menial task. The more elaborate necklaces, which required complicated two-handed maneuvers, called upon the dexterity he had developed in shop classes. He recalled the problems he used to have with his counselors in high school because he was interested in shop rather than straight academic classes. But you have a 160 IQ, why do you want to take shop? Those hours familiarizing himself with tools certainly were paying off more now than his algebra and history courses. He was good at using his hands and he enjoyed it. Besides, he really liked Greg, his boss. Soon after Bill began to work with him, the employee-employer relationship blossomed into a warm friendship.

The months in the Poughkeepsie love-bead business began a process of realization that would reach its full epiphany at the Woodstock Festival that August. Bill accompanied Greg to a weekend concert in Atlantic City, New Jersey, in early August. One hundred thousand turned out for this overture to Woodstock, listening to many of the groups who would soon travel to Max Yasgur's farm, including Santana, Jefferson Airplane, Creedence Clearwater Revival and Joe Cocker. In Atlantic City, Bill observed his friend's full retail operation in microcosm: just how one bought and sold and kept honest. Then, with a clearer idea of low-budget crafts marketing, he returned to upstate New York less than two weeks before Woodstock. The bungling of Bill's education was over. The dropout was getting a crash course in real-life success, 1960s style. He would prove to be a very quick study.

JOHN SEBASTIAN

HAD WOODSTOCK taken place a mere twenty-four months earlier, there would have been no doubt about the necessity of having the Lovin' Spoonful on the bill. To have excluded them or failed to sign them on would have been to announce to the potential ticket-buyer that in fact this was just a B-list, second-rate concert weekend. To have scheduled the event without first checking the Spoonful's itinerary would have been an enormous blunder. Universally liked, enormously effective in concert, crowd-friendly, and beyond all else top-notch musicians, the four men who comprised the Lovin' Spoonful were both respected by in-crowd arbiters of hip and adulated by teenybopper singles buyers. In the mid-sixties few other American bands enjoyed the popularity and esteem the Spoonful did, and few American bandleaders and composers so distinguished themselves as real artists the way John Sebastian did. And few groups disintegrated and disappeared so rapidly and silently as did this one.

By the summer of 1969, as the Woodstock Ventures talent drag-net was being thrown wide over the landscape, the Spoonful was but a top-of-the-charts memory, and John Sebastian but a faded star with deluded ambitions about a solo career. But if anyone deserved to have a second chance it was John Sebastian. And if any event could deliver that instant reconsideration it was Woodstock. Down on his luck and, worse, in a state of mind totally inconducive to a comeback gig, the twenty-five-year-old singer nevertheless, almost in spite of himself, benefitted from his time on that stage more than any other performer. Flying into the site on a helicopter full of musicians scheduled to play, Sebastian came to Woodstock a hanger-on, a has-been, a groupie. Within hours he would be a star again.

Stardom had often seemed elusive in a career that by 1969 had already gone full circle from down-and-out bar-band leader to nationwide media darling to blast from the past. In fact, fame had seemed so distant in the beginning that Sebastian almost decided not even to pursue it. The son of the country's foremost classical harmonica player, John had grown up on the periphery of fame, albeit the marginal fame that a noted harmonica player could attract. Woody Guthrie and Burl Ives had been dinner guests at his family's Bank Street home in Greenwich Village. He himself star-ted playing harmonica at age five. But despite the musical richness of this household, the boy's inspiration to learn guitar came from TV: he saw Elvis, and like millions of other American kids he wanted to strum. All of these early leanings were redirected, though, when the eight-year-old moved to Italy for a sojourn there with his parents that lasted more than five years. The rock beat that was tearing across the States was but a distant echo in the Italy of the mid-fifties, and young John soaked up the romantic lan-guage and the folk syncopations indigenous to that country. The seeds of the unique sounds he would bring to the American pop mainstream a decade later were already being planted.

When the family returned to their Greenwich Village base, they found themselves in the middle of a bubbling downtown stew that was whipping the beatnik's jazzy cool into what would become the hippie's freaky high. As liberal as Mom and Pop Sebastian were, they thought it best to send John off to boarding school, just to let him grow up a little more before allowing him full exposure to the wildness that surrounded the boy back home. So four years were spent in the posh environs of Blair Academy in New Jersey, where the intense academic pressure again largely distracted John from any serious thought about a career in music. Although he had grown up with living proof that such alternatives existed, he opted for an academic curriculum when he registered at New York University after graduating from Blair. Not unlike most freshmen, he really didn't have any idea where the combination of language and liberal arts courses was going to take him, but it seemed the most natural extension of what had preceded in high school. Plus, NYU was located smack in the middle of Greenwich Village, right near to Washington Square Park and a shout away from the clubs and bars where early-sixties music was being born. Clearly, John was drawn to NYU for more than just its language labs.

The Village at the time was America's hothouse for a musical movement that defines the entire era, though this jaded urban landscape seemed a most unlikely center for its flourishing. To this most frenetic part of one of the world's most sophisticated cities, thousands of young people flocked, ironically, seeking the simple, direct, almost reactionary sound that was becoming hip: folk music. While the explosiveness of fifties rock and roll momentarily settled down, the country-inspired acoustic harmonies of farm worker songs, spirituals and hootenanny nonsense ditties began to fill coffeehouses and cellar dives. Here was an authentically American sound, presented with heartfelt emotionalism that proved compatible with the dawning of a new antimaterialism. Here was a purity of expression and artistry that rock's big beat couldn't touch. True, the plaintive bleats of the Village's early folk avant-garde seemed at odds with the subway rumble and taxi blare that filled the New York night. But perhaps it was just that external cacophony that made the soft strummings in cafés throughout the

Village all the more sweet and welcome. For a brief period during the Camelot era, big tough New York gave itself over to the folkies. And it was not long before John was drawn out of the groves of academe and into the grooves of the new folk consciousness.

Though the movement subscribed to a simple esthetic, its popularity inevitably created stars with giant followings and big contracts. With performers like Peter, Paul and Mary, Phil Ochs and Tom Rush, folk became an industry that challenged the then-flourishing soul and rock, and even offered American ballast to the British invasion. And when Bob Dylan burst onto the scene, first as a mumbling guitar poet at the Bitter End and the Gaslight and then as a nationally embraced demigod of existential pop on vinyl, folk ascended to near-mythic status.

At this point, during the early acoustic period of folk, this music sounded much like the unadorned mandolin tunes John had first heard in Italy. And the pedigree of folk, tracing back to the delta and the cotton field, the country church and the square-dance hall, shared lineage with the harmonica blues numbers his father played around the house as diversion from the restraints of his more restricted performance repertoire. Beyond the ear, though, the folk music also struck his heart. For all the pessimism of a "Tom Dooley" or the biblical references of a "Michael, Row Your Boat Ashore," folk's most overriding character was its optimism, its upbeat sense of the curative, benevolent power of music itself. It was the music's message that most affected John, who very soon would begin to graft this sense of magic onto the even more popular folk-rock songs that would lead him and his group to the top of the charts.

Within a year and a half, John was out of NYU, content to accept the fact that college life was just not for him. After wandering around the East Coast, in 1963 he drifted back to the Village and to the other young people who, like him, had responded to the charm of the folk sound and fallen under its sing-along spell. But unlike many of the Village folkies, John Sebastian had talent, and the good fortune to meet others with more of the same. One of them was Cass Elliot.

In hindsight, it is easy to isolate the qualities that would eventu-

ally catapult both John and Cass to stardom. Good-looking, literate, gifted with a tune, bearing a noteworthy musical pedigree,
Sebastian would seem a natural for celebrity. Charming, effusive,
vocally unique, Elliot would seem destined to mature into the pop
diva she finally became in the latter part of the decade. But as the
two of them shared harmonies in their grungy Village apartments
that winter, neither of the future stars felt the inevitability of
success. Cass had left her home in Washington, D.C., to join in the
nonstop Village hootenanny at which she quickly established herself as a colorful regular. Her gargantuan size and overgrown
personality got her plenty of attention, but she was dismissed as a
folkie kook, just another of the hundreds of eccentrics who added
spice to the scene. The outrageous clothes and behavior, however,
were just the exterior trappings of a will and an ambition that set
her apart from the other flakes. Hey, look me over, she demanded.
Lend me an ear. Together with fellow Village hang-alongs Zal
Yanovsky, Denny Doherty and Sebastian, she willed the Mugwumps (a group named after a faction of political independents
from the 1880s) into being. The musical career Sebastian had never
really considered seriously took off, given birth by one of the most
domineering and forceful women he had ever met. And for the
next year, he played, sang and traveled with the Mugwumps along
the club axis that stretched from Elliot's hometown through Bal-
timore, up into Philly, all around New York and on to Boston.

If the strains of traveling and living hand-to-mouth broke the
group up by 1964, each member departed a more assured, confident and determined musician than ever. Through mutual connections Cass and Denny would meet up with John and Michelle
Phillips, whose East Village pad became the breeding ground of
the Mamas and the Papas. Sebastian often traveled across town to
play for John and Michelle some of the tunes he was working on,
and Papa John still recalls the first time he heard his friend sing
"Do You Believe in Magic" at their home on Avenue D and Seventh
Street. He predicted it would be a hit, but his enthusiasm for
Sebastian's early compositions was not shared by the downtown
club owners who refused to give the singer-composer a shot on a
bill. Along with Zal, who was also renting rooms at the dingy

Albert Hall, John practiced in the hotel basement, perfecting the folk-plus sound he believed in. Borrowing generously from ragtime, Nashville jug band and standard pop, John and Zal developed a melodious, feel-good sound that bridged a gap between sometimes dour folk music and the rowdier rhythms of rock and roll and R&B. Although the mix now seems obvious, at the time it was considered radically innovative: folk-music purists believed in an unalloyed roots sound, no electric guitars or organs, please. The rocking of folk really took off only in 1965, when Dylan himself went electric on *Highway 61 Revisited*. But until the great god Bob sanctioned the marriage, Sebastian's toying with the two musical traditions was considered freakish, unnatural and certainly not commercial. Still, he and Zal pushed on. Realizing that to be considered a "band," and not just a novelty act, the duo needed a percussionist and a bass, they actively sought out two more like-minded members through their substantial circle of friends: Steve Boone and Joe Butler, formerly of a Long Island band called the Kingsmen.

What should we call ourselves, the four young men asked one day, hoping against hope they would someday need to sign a contract as a group.

I love my baby by the lovin' spoonful . . . John idly mumbled through one of his favorite blues tunes, a little-known John Hurt song called "Coffee Blues." And from that afternoon on, that's what they called themselves—and not long after that, that's what every club owner in town was talking about. Breaking in finally at the Night Owl, the Spoonful quickly became the word-of-mouth sensation of the Village. Burning out on pure folk, the in crowd embraced the group's good-time music, presented with good-time verve by four good-looking guys, perhaps the long-awaited American answer to the Beatles. Uninterested in political statements and unable to feign the pseudo-angst of the other folkies, the Spoonful sang happy—and the crowd responded. Kama Sutra records signed them on and mounted for the Spoonful the sort of hysterical promotional campaign the sixties were famous for. This time around, the hype was merited. With John's solid musical talent and highly individual sensibility as its creative engine, the group pumped out hit after top-ten hit throughout 1965 and 1966, rarely disappointing its growing number of fans.

"Do You Believe in Magic," their first single, went to number nine; "Didn't Have to Be So Nice" hit number ten. In 1966, both "Did You Ever Have to Make Up Your Mind," and "(What a Day for a) Daydream," soared to number two, and "Summer in the City," complete with jackhammers and traffic noise, hit number one. "Rain on the Roof," "Younger Girl" . . . in all of these songs, John's deep-down affability shone through. "Our music isn't what you respond to by screaming," he told an interviewer, suggesting the difference between a Spoonful concert and a Fab Four confab. "You smile, maybe," he added. And smile millions did. "It's the sweet-est, most lilting and joyous American sound of the pop music sixties," *Look* magazine said in a November 1966 article celebrating the group's four weeks at the number-one position with "Summer in the City."

At the height of their success, the Spoonful represented the sweetness and innocence that even the upper echelon of rock could still retain in the mid-sixties. Wearing their signature horizontally striped shirts, and with their just-long-enough hair, the Spoonful boys came across as hip but happy, cool but collected. As the first whiffs of drug rock and psychedelia began to waft in from San Francisco, the Spoonful's hits sailed gracefully to the top of the charts, temporarily warding off the advance of the acid riffs. And music this authentically gleeful could be produced only by men enjoying the fame without getting caught up in the attendant junk. Sebastian says he experimented with marijuana occasionally back then, but that he soon found it incompatible with performing and dropped it. Though they were making money, they spent it admi-rably: they bought houses and cars for their parents, for instance.

"You and me and rain on the roof . . . maybe we'll be here for hours." All around them rock stars were beginning to stumble on the pitfalls of skyrocketing fame and the peculiar madness of celebrity in the sixties: Sebastian's good friend John Phillips would become a heroin addict. But within the group, the youthful enthu-siasm and joie de vivre of the era stayed alive for longer than might have been expected. On March 19, 1967, two days after his twenty-third birthday, John Sebastian sang two Spoonful hits on "The Ed Sullivan Show". They were at the height of their popularity: within months the group would begin to fall apart.

With such a clean-cut image, the band's undoing in a drug bust seems most ironic. But later that year, according to *Rolling Stone* accounts, Yanovsky and Boone were picked up for possession of a small amount of pot. Worse, when pressed by investigators the two musicians informed on their source, fingering him in exchange for dismissal of their charges. The deal was common enough—feds often let the small-time user off if he pointed to someone higher up the distribution chain who in turn could point even higher up. But the press got ahold of the story and smeared the group members as stoolies and turncoats. *Rolling Stone* referred to the incident as the Spoonful's "dope fink scandal." The music was still the same, of course, but the glow was off the golden boys.

Internal tensions began to build within the group. Perhaps the four men would never have survived the crushing demands of touring, recording, personal appearances and ego battles even without the damage incurred during the drug incident. But that extra weight bore down on them irresistibly: by February 1968 cofounder Zal had left the group, replaced by Jerry Yester. A generous review of the band's Philharmonic Hall appearance in the February 22 *New York Times* points out that the newly reconstructed group wowed the crowd, but that the crowd was much smaller than the reviewer remembered from his last Spoonful concert. Sebastian himself had already begun thinking about the viability of the band and had started taking on personal projects as a way of testing his prospects as a solo act. He wrote the scores for the films *You're a Big Boy Now* and Woody Allen's *What's Up, Tiger Lily?* He took on composition chores for *Jimmy Shine,* a straight play Dustin Hoffman was going to appear in, which required several songs although it was not a musical. The disenchantment with the group grew as the outside enterprises escalated. In October 1968 Sebastian left the Lovin' Spoonful; his departure for all intents and purposes dismantled the group.

Talented, in demand, Sebastian was not prepared for the difficult year that lay ahead. His record company encouraged him to complete an album he had been working on, but then informed him it would be released as a Lovin' Spoonful LP. While he was anxious for this latest music to reach his audience, he did not want it issued under the group's name—none of the other members had participated in its creation. Despondent over the record delays, he was also finding it hard to establish himself in performance as John Sebastian, singer. Not lead singer, just singer. Then, too, times were changing, and the soft, ingratiating tunes he had written for the mid-sixties seemed quaint and a bit passé as harder rock with a more cutting political edge gained in popularity. With his granny glasses and genteel manner, Sebastian failed to connect with the current taste for raunch, explicitness, anger. He may not have been feeling particularly happy, but his music still made him sound like a chirpy canary. Uncertain about his future, John decided to do what many lost people do: he moved to California.

With little more than an overnight bag and his instruments, the musician headed out to Burbank to a farm owned by a former member of the Modern Folk Quartet. The plot of land had a single house, already overpopulated by a commune of rock retirees, rejects from the pop charts living out their fall from fame together. John wanted little to do with the extended family indoors, and he set himself up in a tent at the far reaches of the farm, alone and primitively content. Occasionally he'd hitch a ride over the crest to a phone and check in with his agent to see how plans for a tour he hoped to make were coming along. But most of the time was spent in reflection; he participated in the commune's life when he felt like it. He remembers he particularly enjoyed the tie-dying sessions several of the women there held to create the shirts and jackets they would sell at festivals. His hands, strong from years of picking, were perfect for the squeezing and wringing the process required.

He grabbed a handful of those shirts and stuck them in his overnight bag the night he went back east early in the summer of 1969. And he wore them in front of the medium-sized crowds he was attracting in New England and upstate New York that July: they were distinct from the striped T-shirts that had become his signature during the Spoonful days. The tie-dyed T's, he hoped, would communicate his independence, his hipness. He hoped.

At the Albany airport he ran into some old friends, members of the Incredible String Band. Laden with the dozens of instruments they played during concerts, they greeted the lone singer enthusiastically. You *are* going to Woodstock, aren't you, they asked, assuming Sebastian was heading off to the massive gathering. John looked at them and realized he hadn't been invited to the decade's biggest party.

SUSIE KAUFMAN

IT WAS, she says, the shock therapy that caused her memories from the sixties to jumble and crunch into the gnarled pattern of inconsistencies they are now. The rape, the pregnancy, the abortion, the breakdown—Susie Kaufman recollects these events from 1968 imperfectly, as if projected onto the screen of her life like photographs from someone else's album. Her past from that era exists only as a blur, but a compelling one. And it is a blur that covers much of her daily existence through 1969 right up until August, when with a dazzling clarity the haze of memory lifts to reveal the pivotal weekend of her young life. She went to Woodstock.

She drove away from the Morristown, New Jersey, neighborhood that had been the sight of much of her youth—and pain. Here in this affluent suburb, she had attended high school, feeling herself the ugly duckling of her class, and labeled the resident cootie by girls and boys alike. Certainly others had gone through the braces-glasses-scrawny phase she did, but Susie's gawky stage continued right through junior and senior years. The geek designation began early, when into the fashion-conscious corridors of the school she strode wearing the skirt and top her mother had made for her. Naive about trends, she had no idea of the social faux pas she was committing, but the outright mockery her dowdy clothes elicited soon raised her consciousness, until it became acutely self-depre-catory. The new sensibility and sensitivity couldn't make store-bought gear any more affordable, nor could they improve her father's meager schoolteacher's salary. Besides wearing creepy clothes, Susie played the violin—a hopelessly square avocation. Though she had been a star pupil in her Elizabeth, New Jersey, grammar school, Susie allowed her unpopularity—more, her overly developed sense of it—to affect her studies, and she began collecting the F's she would amass in spades through her high school career.

If the clothes and the violin weren't bad enough, Susie was flat-chested. As the other girls in her class began to fill out, the girlish bust Susie carried under her plain dress emphasized her self-imposed inferiority. She remembers the discomfort of disrobing for gym class, trying to hide her unmatured nakedness within the steely emptiness of an open locker. She would overhear conversations around her. Bobby is dying for me to let him feel me up. I've got to move up a cup size, this bra is too small for me now. Tommy and I did it. Twice. But these snippets of boy and bra talk flitted around her head like phrases from a foreign language. Because she simply didn't have the opportunity even to contemplate innocent adolescent sex play, she held onto the schoolgirl aversion to the healthy lust to which her peers seemed gleefully subjugated.

In one way only was the Susie of high school connected to the female yearnings she heard bandied about in the locker room: Susie, even at sixteen, knew she very much wanted to have a baby. She did not understand completely that the twittering secret activities Bobby and Tommy wanted to pursue with Angela and Ann were part of the same life cycle. And really, as far as the teen sexual imagination goes, they're not. Susie's unformed but clearly felt maternal instinct did not encompass a parallel desire for family, husband, security.

The drabness of these years was alleviated by music. Her classical training had honed her ear to recognize quality, even when it expressed itself in new and unorthodox forms. More than many young women of the period, Susie developed an avid if amateur expertise for rock and roll. Where most other female record buyers bought singles on the basis of how attractive the band members were, Susie viewed her tastes as more critical, informed. She looked down at other teenage girls' fan worship of the popular stars and ridiculed their swooning excesses. Music, didn't they understand, had nothing to do with boy-craziness. It was art. Still, her cool discerning demeanor met its match in the Beatles. She had heard of them early: before the official invasion, a young British man had whispered the group's name to her when she asked him about his strange haircut. And when the first albums came out, she already knew all about their sound, while all the other girls were talking simply about which of the four was the cutest. She complimented herself with a cognoscente's appreciation of the group's talents, yet she still was not totally aloof from the girlish thrills of Beatlemania. The night they appeared on "The Ed Sullivan Show," she found herself crying and in a cold sweat in front of the television.

She remembers feeling the same cold sweat the night of her first kiss. Because no one had asked her, and because none of her own classmates would have responded positively, Susie asked a junior to go to her senior prom with her. The football player who reaches down to the lower classes to pluck the most sensational cheerleader in the school can proudly march his young conquest into a dance. Susie's showing up with a younger boy meant only one thing: he was just as much of a nerd as she, and a class lower to boot. Still, Susie remembers enjoying the night thoroughly and thinks the moon was full and the stars ablaze as the boy walked her slowly home afterward; they stopped in a park, shared a swing. And then, because even dweeb boys try to score, he started to rub her shoulder, touch her dress, and began to kiss her.

A panic like nothing Susie had ever experienced rattled through her body. Not revulsion, just fear. This is what all the other girls had talked and talked about for years, and now she was in the middle of a kiss and didn't have the slightest idea what to do. Confused, she let the kiss continue for what seemed like minutes—and then finally pulled back, propelled more by terror than thought. Let's go, she managed to whimper to the unimpressed suitor. I think I should be home.

As aborted and fumbled as this first kiss was—whose isn't?—it nudged Susie into a new consciousness about herself and her sexuality. It left her shaken, but the reverberations would reshape her self-image. Soon after the kiss in the park, she had an opportunity to move even further out of her shell. It had already been planned that although she hadn't a chance in the world of going to a musical conservatory because of her grades, she would attend a summer camp for musically gifted children at Glassboro State College. On the way to the camp, sitting in the backseat of her dad's car, she decided something. Nobody knows me here, nobody knows I've never really had a boyfriend. I'm going to hit this place running. I will reinvent myself.

In order to underline the break with her past, she renamed herself. The Sue she had always been called became Susie. And as soon as she got out of the car, in a performance that could have won an Oscar for nerve alone, she raced up to the first two girls she met and enthusiastically introduced herself. Hi, I'm Susie. Hi, what's your name? Thus began six weeks that marked a metamorphosis as the depressed, introverted, insecure Sue blossomed into the winning, popular, confident Susie. She snagged the handsomest boy in the camp, a poetic, moony teen named Murray who composed heavy existential love songs à la Dylan. They kissed, and even though his open mouth frightened her, she felt herself tingle in the way the other girls had described back in the locker room in high school. More important, perhaps, she was accepted by the other girls in her dorm, participated in their pillow fights, and for the first time in her life felt as if she were their equal. Her total stay at Glassboro amounted to little more than a month and a half, but by the time she came back to Morristown, Susie had learned something new and unexpected: to like herself.

The new self-esteem met its first test during Susie's first year out of high school. Having decided to postpone any college plans, she took a job as a mail clerk at the enormous Prudential Insurance offices in Newark. Perhaps for most of the other seniors at Morristown High, youth seemed its most golden during their last year of school, but for Susie, being eighteen and at Prudential was being the most alive she had ever felt. In this bureaucratic environment, she bloomed. In the eyes of the older gray-haired men who populated those offices, this young thing was fresh air, vivacity, something to flirt with. Susie found herself playfully enacting all the girlish vamps and come-ons she had unconsciously studied in the corridors of high school, innocently practicing the wiles she never knew she possessed on men who never knew she was a nerd. With the spending money she began to earn, she no longer relied on mom's sewing machine and turned to Greenwich Village boutiques for fashions. She let her blond hair grow out and let her hemline ride up to Carnaby Street levels. The girl who couldn't get a date to the prom was working at Prudential Insurance as a much-admired American Twiggy a year after graduation.

Inevitably, Susie's growing up took its toll on domestic tranquillity. Though her parents were professed liberals, their daughter's burgeoning independence, especially after so many years of docility, unnerved them. She'd shriek when Mom came into her room without knocking, or when Dad would yell about her coming home late from a concert. Tensions arose over the smallest of irritations. And soon the cry heard round the country—What's becoming of our kids?—rose up in the Kaufmans' throats. With almost comic predictability they soon came up with the same uninspired antidote to their child's new behavior: Let's send her off to college.

I'm never even going to get in—remember my report cards, she protested. She had graduated 136 out of 136.

We can pull some strings, said Pop, connected as he was to various educational institutions. And indeed by the fall of 1966, Susie's bags were packed and she was shipped off to Kansas City, Missouri, to a school—Park College—she had never heard of before. By January she was back.

Her college semester was a dismal failure, officially at least. Classes were enrolled in to be skipped, homework assignments were given to be ignored. But like the summer music camp, the four months at Park served a more important role in Susie's personal development than in her academic history. Liberated from Morristown and all its negative associations, she also experienced for the first time life outside of her home, life away from her folks. What a seductive feeling: curfews were cut, rules abused. In order to put the memories of high school drudgery far behind her, she flaunted her free will by being a bad girl. The campus wild thing, she shocked the prim girls in her dorm but became the darling of the hayseed hippies who filled the rooms across the quad in the boy's dorm. They found her exciting and worldly. They sought her out. Romance wasn't necessarily the goal: she was just the most up-to-date thing in Kansas City, not just to date but simply to hang around with. The platonic admiration suited her just fine. Clearly the boys courted her, but since Susie still felt uncomfortable with sex, their middle-American politesse flattered without challenging. For the first time, she could enjoy the companionship of young men, these unsophisticated and laid-back boys of Park College with whom she could talk rock and roll and break the rules.

Finally she broke one too many. She was never expelled, but administration disciplinarians made it clear she need not return for the winter semester. It's a barometer of just how far along Susie's self-esteem had come that when she was informed of her dismissal, she accepted it as Park College's loss, kissed each of her boyfriends good-bye, and took a bus back home, enjoying the scenery in her perfectly matched fringe top and appliquéd dungarees. Older travelers who chanced to sit by her would comment on how polite and pleasant this hippie child was, how different from the dirty, foul-mouthed things they saw demonstrating and rioting on the TV. If the flower children had mounted a PR campaign, Susie could have easily gotten a job as its up-front personality. She decided during that trip that whatever lay ahead for her, she knew she could no longer live at home, where the phantom of her former self still lingered. And when she got off the bus, she never really unpacked her bags.

I'll be moving out, she announced.

You'll get in trouble, her mother warned.

That was the furthest thing in Susie's mind: she was still a virgin and hadn't really even had a boyfriend yet.

Looking back, she assumes her mother's warning about "getting in trouble" meant becoming sexually compromised. Perhaps not. Given the paranoid climate of the times, Mrs. Kaufman may have been expressing merely the fear shared by many Americans that random violence, escalating at an uncontrollable pace, would eventually strike home. Highlighted by the spectacular assassinations of the decade, the citizenry's awareness of its own vulnerability soared as the media riveted attention on the country's intensifying wave of vicious crime. Race riots added to the feeling of things reeling ever more perilously out of control. A sniper in an Austin tower kills thirteen, a demented loner murders eight nurses in Chicago. Where could one feel truly secure, safe?

All the while, peaceniks with two fingers extended tripped through the sixties, many sailing along on a false sense of security. The draft hovered as a distant threat, narcs a constant nuisance at home. But here among like-minded friends, the supportive, touchy-feely glow of love-ins and rap sessions deluded yellow submarine optimists into believing the demons that prowled the decade sought other prey. Susie moved away from home, buoyed out the door by the new sense of self that flower power had instilled.

It is around this time, mid-1967, that the cloud of forgetfulness drops over Susie's memories. She moved into an apartment house in Parsippany, New Jersey. She was attending classes part time at Fairleigh Dickinson University, and helping out at the student-union concert series. She was seeing a shrink at her mother's request. She was happy. And then one night she was raped.

What she remembers most is the immediate aftermath of the incident. Devastated, in her own living room, the biker who committed the violence gone, she slowly picked herself off the floor and flung herself up against the nearest wall. It would be the hard surface of that wall that created the strongest, most enduring image in her mind when she thinks about that night. Terrified that there might be someone else in the room about to pounce, she pressed her body tightly to the wall, hoping to find in its firmness reassurance, protection. Revolted by the smell of this man on her, she inched around the room, hugging the wall, toward the bathroom.

The cops weren't called, her parents weren't told. In a single evening, Susie reverted into the gangly, inarticulate child she had been in high school. Her anger and shame were turned inward, twisting her confidence and contentment into adolescent shyness. On the night she lost her virginity, she again became a little girl. She carried on normally enough, hoping time would allow her to cope with the rape. But time only made things worse: she realized she was pregnant. And while motherhood had always been one of her fondest aspirations, this wasn't the way she had thought it would be delivered to her.

You've never heard this before, I know you haven't. Perhaps it isn't surprising that the first person she told about her predicament was a minister from her childhood church. She hadn't attended Presbyterian services there in years, but she needed to feel the warmth and security and dependence she associated with an earlier time in her life. So she poured out her soul to a young clergyman whose reaction indicated she had been right, he never had heard anything like this before. But by simply saying the words— rape, pregnant, me—Susie set into motion a series of events over which she had no control. Her parents and psychiatrist were informed. They all expressed their disbelief. A doctor was found, papers were authorized, a hospital room was scheduled, anesthesia was injected, a gurney wheeled her into an operating room, an abortion was performed. Heavy psychological counseling began.

Susie spent two years struggling to make sense of the random act of evil that had fallen upon her in her own living room. And by the summer of 1969, with painful shock therapy behind her, she was almost whole again. She would make it, she knew, but would she ever thrive? Would she ever again feel the self-confidence and the inner worth, would she ever again enjoy her own womanhood, the way she had when she walked into her Parsippany apartment that terrible night? Would she ever really trust men, would she ever again feel equal to other women?

My son is going to the Woodstock Festival, her shrink said, one hot July during their regular session. Have you heard about it?

Um. Yeah. Sure. Everybody's heard about it.

Maybe you should go. You like rock-and-roll music. There will be lots of people, but I think you'll feel safe. It might be good for you.

JIMMY JORDAN

THE SEX was great in 1969, if availability was your primary criterion for greatness. Getting laid was easier than it ever had been. Getting involved, getting committed, getting serious—that was another matter. But there was no denying that the permissiveness that created the open-air orgy at Woodstock really did affect a large portion of the generation, the first to mature in a society in which birth control methods and medical advances reduced the usual obstacles to promiscuity. It was only natural, really, given the rebelliousness of the day, for youngsters to appropriate scientific advances the establishment had made possible and use them to erode and overcome taboos. The great sexual revolution of the late sixties, however, wasn't really all that great for many. Jimmy Jordan was one of them.

First of all, Jimmy was a romantic. Critics have described the entire era as romantic: everything from its noble belief in changing the world to its pastoral fashions was idealized and unrealistic. Jimmy was romantic in the more old-fashioned meaning of the word: he was in love with love. Sensitive, caring, passionate, he envisioned a relationship based on equal partnership, long-term goals, mutually fulfilling sexual sharing. During hedonism's finest hour, he was an inveterate Cyrano, determined to pursue a finer, more emotional satisfaction than the one the Rolling Stones sang about.

But something else separated him from most of the young people he would join at Woodstock: Jimmy was gay. And while Woodstock was the sixties' coming-out party for free love, it was more specifically the coming-out party for free straight love. Permissiveness was king that weekend upstate. But in 1969, as Jimmy was to find out painfully, permissiveness did not include two men hugging.

Jimmy himself had begun to accept the fact that he was gay really only within the last two years or so. He had grown up in Chicago in a home he remembers as loveless, barren and deadening. His mother and absentee father raised him with none of the nurturing that TV families throughout the fifties unthinkingly wallowed in. The difference between his lot and what he nightly witnessed on the tube couldn't have been more pronounced. The slightest infraction resulted in draconian punishments and humiliations that included isolation in the basement boiler room and extended stints standing in a corner. One entire summer he was restricted to his room for mistakenly ripping a slip of paper that belonged to his dad. The sterility of his home environment produced an insatiable need for friends and companions—not just as buddies but also as surrogates for the support system he couldn't count on in his family. No one could possibly meet the demands his needs engendered, and as a result he experienced alienation in school as well.

At seventeen, disgusted with the life he knew, he joined the Navy simply to get away, to escape. In the Navy, Jimmy began to sense growing homosexual urges within himself, but he assumed these were just legitimate feelings of friendship. And in fact, for the first time in his life, he developed male bonds that were fulfilling

and rewarding. The barracks, he discovered, were the most sexually charged surroundings he had ever encountered: men openly
discussed their female relationships, which Jimmy found crude;
others, more secretly, actually engaged in homosexual acts, which
Jimmy found repulsive. His own asexual proclivities became the
butt of gentle ribbing by friends who assumed he was straight, but
just uptight, shy and overly sensitive.

Still a virgin when he was discharged in 1962, Jimmy moved to
Philadelphia, where he found work with a shipping line and, more
important, found a nightlife. He had always been a jazz fan, but it
wasn't until he settled there that his exposure to live music stimulated his own interest in performing. He fell in with the community of bohemian types who populated the city's early-sixties
pre-hippie scene.

It was also in Philadelphia that he had his first homosexual
experience, undertaken, with a sense of exploration, with a friend.
It turned out to be an utterly hopeless exercise: aside from nervousness, Jimmy couldn't perform because of his romantic ideals
concerning physical intimacy. Despite the lapsing moralism of the
day, he held onto the increasingly unfashionable notion that sex
and love went together. The more experienced friend told Jimmy it
might mean only that he wasn't his type, but Jimmy read the
incident as proof positive that his attraction to men was purely
platonic and that the high expectations he placed on his male
companions did not necessarily mean he was gay.

If Jimmy was actively denying his sexuality, others beyond his
little world were busily campaigning to force society at large to
cease such denials. It had been some two decades since Kinsey
announced that, according to his findings, 10 percent of all American men were homosexuals, but America still didn't want to
believe it. In the mid-sixties arrest and harassment were still real
threats to adult men merely congregating together, if police suspected forbidden activity was going on. But the growing number
of homosexuals living in major U.S. cities—and the growing sense
of civil-libertarian entitlement—created centers of revolt and self-
assertion. In 1968 a riot broke out in the streets of Greenwich
Village when a squad of policemen raided a gay bar, alleging

liquor-license violations. Gay rights groups were popping up across the country, picketing the White House, the Pentagon, local statehouses. Never before had the words "gay" and "pride" been considered candidates for placement in the same sentence.

Society's reaction to this new self-esteem among gay urbanites was subdued panic. Hollywood began to crank out a series of films that hoped to commercialize on the new sensibility, though even the best of them—say, *Midnight Cowboy*—depicted the orientation as a weird sickness. Even the liberal national press treated the movement with a smirk. And in a 1968 article about a book on the gay society that grew up in Cambridge and Oxford between the wars, *Time* magazine reported without blinking that the author "is moderately encouraged by the fact that the form the current youth revolt is taking is not homosexuality but drug addiction." In Kew Gardens, Queens, in the summer of 1969, a grove of trees in a park was mysteriously cut down one night after community gossip erupted that the stand had a reputation as a gay meeting place. A poll the same year reported that 67 percent of Americans viewed homosexuals as "dangerous."

And Jimmy, as Jefferson Airplane would coax him to do, just wanted to find somebody to love.

He moved to New York City in 1966. At a late-night session at one of the clubs he frequented in Philadelphia, he had improvised with a visiting pianist on a version of "Round Midnight." After one chorus, the musician turned around stunned. You can really sing. You need training in a couple of areas, but you can really sing. With the thought of finding the best teachers and possibly making a career out of singing, Jimmy arrived in a New York whose homosexual community was among the most outspoken in the world. He quickly enrolled in voice classes, found a meaningless day job as an insurance investigator, moved into the East Side studio he still lives in today, and made a discovery: some of the best piano bars in town were gay.

Within months, Jimmy was sitting in on open-mike nights at an East Side bar where he remembers Barry Manilow being the house piano man. More and more of the clubs around town were converting to folk or rock music, and for a while Jimmy even considered switching to a more contemporary kind of singing. He liked the popular music of the era, especially Joni Mitchell and other balladeers. Their socially aware lyrics attracted him, as he was picking up on the era's activism. But crooning the standards, though it seemed a dying art, still corresponded better to his personality. Being around gay men at the clubs reduced his anxiety about that lifestyle, although he was still sensitive to suggestions he himself was gay.

Then Jimmy met Michael in Central Park. With the same sense of casual experimentation that he had brought to his unfulfilling Philadelphia fling, he had tried one-night stands with other pickups. These had failed too. But with Michael, older and more stable, he actually had a courtship. It was only after several dates and the establishment of an emotional intimacy that the two slept together, and for the first time Jimmy's hopes for a physical and sexual unity were met.

The honeymoon was a short one, and insurmountable differences between the two men soon emerged. But even for all its brevity, the affair had moved the young man out of the closet and onto a path of sexual self-discovery that would take him a year and a half later to Woodstock.

The liberating effects of living in New York during those years and of weathering his first affair influenced Jimmy's entire outlook. As he remembers it, his transition into homosexual self-acceptance came easily, though his search for suitable mates remained difficult. Riding high on the era's feel-good attitudes, the city's gay community was enjoying a feast of carefree frolicking, albeit covert. Commitment was perhaps even harder to find than in more closeted times, but even romantic Jimmy took advantage of the unfettered sexual sampling. Eventually he quit the insurance job and took a more flexible position as an assistant manager at a record store. The new job allowed him to expand his musical tastes beyond the crusty catalogue of hits from the forties and fifties. He began to go to more and more contemporary concerts, added spots like the Fillmore to his list of hangouts, and started smoking a little pot. During one high in the spring of 1969, Jimmy met Evan.

The bar on East Seventieth Street that Jimmy liked to go to was one of the few places in the city that dared allow its homosexual clientele to dance; Jimmy's athletic dance routines made him a notorious figure on the floor. He walked in, buzzing nicely from the tokes he had had back in his apartment, and saw a newcomer standing across the room, young but exuding a self-confidence unusual for his age. Jimmy asked Evan to dance.

Evan turned out to be a student at a college on Long Island, who still lived at home with his parents, drove their car, and generally accepted all the indulgence their affluence allowed them to bestow on him. It was a youth about as opposite to Jimmy's as can be imagined, and Jimmy found himself fascinated by this creature of bourgeois complacency. Perhaps he was even slightly envious of the fact that Evan had come to terms with his sexuality at such an early age, coddled into that acceptance by a home life in which his whim was law. If Jimmy's coming out had been stymied by his parents' failure to love, Evan, it seemed, came out with the sense of prerogative his parents' doting had inculcated. Jimmy and Evan danced, then dated, and for much of May and June and into July, Jimmy thought: This is it.

For the first time the older of the two, Jimmy nevertheless soon found himself in the submissive role in their relationship. It was Evan who decided when they could see each other, and Evan who decided what they would do. All the while feeling uneasy about his lover's adamancy, Jimmy found in the college kid a sensitivity that seemed to mirror his own. He wanted to make the relationship work, and so he focused on that sensitivity and tried to ignore the self-centeredness and coolness that went with it.

For the most part, they could see each other only on weekends, rendezvousing at the same dance bar where they had first met. This dating pattern was hardly the open celebration of love Jimmy had hoped for; in fact it quickly began to get old. He desperately wanted to find some other activity for them to share, some way of making their time together special, some way of creating with his new friend the enduring, lasting and mutually nurturing bond he had been denied all his life. Then he heard about Woodstock, the Aquarian Exposition, a festival of peace and love.

TOM CONSTANTEN

Many say that rather than signify the beginning of something, the Woodstock Festival actually served as the giant last gasp of—what?—a feeling, an ethos, a frenzy. Defining what was passing those three days has been frustrating observers and chroniclers of the event since it happened, but with the perspective of twenty years, now it seems clear to most that the weekend witnessed a glorious enactment of some incoherent last rites. It's unlikely the festivalgoers, high on the concert's delirium, sensed any of the finality that permeated the air; they spoke and dreamed of the new beginning of the Woodstock Nation's long life. But among the 500,000, at least some felt acutely the inevitable end augured on that hot and crazy weekend. No doubt one of them was Tom Constanten.

Standing backstage, waiting for what seemed hours to go on with the rest of the Grateful Dead, Tom silently watched as all around him the incredible whirl of activity pumped life into this voracious beast of a gathering. Rock stars and roadies, photographers and groupies dashed here and there in great eddies of motion and energy, at the center of which Tom perceived only a vast, inert emptiness. His sense of history forced upon him the realization that there was absolutely no permanence to this high, no foundation to this moment. Behind that realistic philosophic posture, there stood a more personal sense of closure that, more than likely, informed his reading of the day's events. It was August, midway through his first real year as keyboardist for the legendary San Francisco group, and on that muggy evening he stood shoulder to shoulder with Pigpen, Jerry Garcia, Bob Weir, Phil Lesh, Bill Kreutzmann and Mickey Hart, and knew his place in the band would disappear nearly as quickly as this magical and wild festival.

It would be hard to label T.C. (as he was called by the band) the odd man out, since the Grateful Dead has to be considered one of the most eclectic assortments of performers in rock history. If Tom didn't meld, it wasn't because he was any more different from the original six members than they were from each other. It was because, coming in as Tom did in 1968, he joined a Grateful Dead that had evolved into a nearly mystical fraternity whose cultish character clearly resisted a new face. Quite simply, Tom had missed the shared history the others had in common—and what a history it was.

Although the band's all-for-one image suggests equality among its members, Jerry Garcia is clearly its acknowledged leader. A self-taught guitarist, Garcia returned to his native Bay Area after an aborted military service in the early sixties. A jug band enthusiast but unambitious about his career, he worked at a record store and began hanging around the coffee shops in Berkeley. There music was taken seriously and the young man began to perform, becoming something of a magnet for a ragtag diversity of other sit-in musicians. Kreutzmann worked at the record store with Garcia and he joined in. Lesh, a classically trained trumpeter, found himself jamming on bass with the charismatic Garcia and a slovenly, heavy-drinking harmonica player who called himself Pigpen.

Others drifted in and out of the loose association of musicians, but a core group began to coalesce around Garcia. The idea to make their impromptu sessions official by giving themselves a name emerged casually, and by 1964 the Warlocks were playing covers of top-forty songs in pizza joints and topless bars all around the Bay Area.

Had the Warlocks come together anywhere else besides San Francisco at any other time than in the mid-sixties, they might have never achieved anything more than local recognition as a better-than-average bar band. But around the young men exploded the lifestyle that would make this city synonymous with the sex-drugs-and-rock-and-roll counterculture the Woodstock Festival would years later celebrate. And the Warlocks, who changed their name to the Grateful Dead around 1966, not only dived into this new pop mainstream but created part of the current as well. Living communally, heavily into the drug scene, the Dead expanded beyond their modest roots to incorporate the era's new values into a unique performance style. At first their concerts were truckbed improvisations in Golden Gate Park, outdoor jamborees for free. But eventually they moved into the city's premier rock showcases, where a quasi-spiritual aura enveloped them and the audience in a shared guitar-scored gestalt. The city was bursting with talent eager to exploit San Francisco's new notoriety as a platform for national recognition. But of all the new groups emerging against the backdrop of Haight-Ashbury psychedelia, the Dead generated the most intense hometown loyalty.

It was a loyalty that extended well beyond the Avalon ticket buyers and Golden Gate Park regulars. Even before they changed their name, the Dead had attracted the attention of the now infamous coterie of drug experimenters led by Ken Kesey that flourished around this time in Marin County and out to Big Sur. Regularly the far-out set threw Acid Tests, enormous parties where about four hundred people would collect somewhere, drop some drugs, and see what happened. Though the Dead's style was still in the developmental stages, the band's personality meshed wonderfully with the spontaneity essential to the Acid Tests, and its members became regulars at the parties. And if the band was the chosen entertainment because its music coincided with the feel of the Test, the blitzed-out tripping that they witnessed—experienced?—there wove the men even more closely together. It was as if the druggy milieu united the different musicians into a single multiheaded entity whose shared knowledge of the music amounted to a surreal intimacy. It was at the Tests that the group's now legendary fusion was born; without their exchanging a word or a glance the Dead's music flowed with an internal consistency and purity that astounded the audience.

Nothing could be further from this electric San Francisco scene than the Las Vegas Strip, but that is where Tom spent much of his pre-Dead life. Actually, if he had had anything to do with the tacky, neon-lit world we call Vegas his eventual hooking up with the Dead party boys might make more sense: you might look at the all-night hyperreality of casinos and nightclubs as the straight world's Haight-Ashbury. Oddly enough, Tom's Las Vegas was a world of piano lessons and recitals, scales and performances. To the country at large Las Vegas means little more than craps, but Tom spent his youth there well plugged into the city's classical music community—a tight little group, but a thriving one.

Tom moved to Las Vegas from New Jersey in 1954, when his stepfather, a Greek immigrant, received a job offer from the Sands Hotel. Just ten, Tom envisioned his new home as a Wild West outpost, and was surprised to find the glitter gulch the town had already become at that early stage of its history. Bright and bookish, he skipped a grade in high school and was already taking courses at the University of Nevada, Las Vegas, when he was a senior. Although the baton swingers at the growing number of hotels were mostly foppish hacks, among the musicians playing up and down the strip was a sizable population of classically trained pros, who almost secretly practiced their Beethoven sonatas on the side. Tom submitted a piece he had written at this point for a pops concert organized by these frustrated philharmonics, and it was accepted—his first publicly performed composition. The youngster was off to a promising start in classical music—Vegas style.

Like many bright young men of the era, Tom looked ahead to this future, and the most rewarding road led to outer space. These were the Sputnik years, and although he was receiving enormous support in his music, that alternative never seemed realistic. He was brilliant and brilliant people went into astrophysics. He applied to the University of California, Berkeley, and in September 1960 he headed off to the Bay Area. It was not to be a particularly rewarding semester—in fact it was his first and last. But at UC one afternoon he shook hands with a fellow student and it was a handshake that changed his life. Tom overheard a corridor conversation about avant-garde music during registration, and jumped in and quite knowledgeably declared his opinion about the exciting work being done on the very fringes of the classical community these days. A gawky blond boy turned to him and stuck out his hand as a greeting. Hi, my name is Phil Lesh. Tom took the extended hand and opened a door into rock-and-roll history.

While most adolescents at this time were screaming over Elvis, Tom and Phil shared passion for avant-garde music—conceptual, synthesized, atonal exercises only a student could love. Had the word been coined at the time, this odd pair would have easily qualified as nerds. But for all Phil's squareness, he had another side. At night he'd put away his arcane musical notations, head off to the coffeehouses of Berkeley, and jam with a group of beatniks who had come to accept him despite his straightness. Soon, as their friendship developed, Phil asked Tom along, introduced him to a folksinger named Jerry Garcia, and invited him to sit in on a session. Tom was playing with the band.

Eventually, Tom moved in with Phil—his apartment was closer to campus. But that didn't bring Tom any closer to academic success. His freshman classes bored him silly and he could find little concentration as his head was filled with the music he wanted to be writing, making. Tom dropped out after the first semester and convinced Phil to take some classes at more liberal Mills College, where avant-gardists were faculty members, and composition and concertizing were homework. Luciano Berio will be teaching there, he told Phil, naming a composer whose work they both admired. By day the two studied advanced music theories; by night they got down and funky with the bar band now called the Warlocks.

Well, not that funky. While Phil was able to find a connection between his academic musical pursuits and the barroom riffs, Tom could never really let loose and swing. His was a more considered piano, compared to Phil's wailing, free-soaring horn. Truth be known, the Las Vegas kid was accepted more as Phil's friend than as himself. As a result, Tom never considered the group anything but a youthful diversion, alien in a way, since its improvisational style was so different from his calculated, systematic approach to music. Jerry and the rest "felt" the music, Tom thought it.

It surprised no one, then, when in 1962 Tom decided to leave the group—it wasn't even really an official band yet—once he was accepted as a scholarship student abroad. Studying in Germany and Italy broadened his knowledge of the international avant-garde, and he wrote enthusiastic letters back to Phil about the exciting, ground-breaking work being done on the continent. But no amount of training would ever turn Tom's passion into a profession and he returned to San Francisco a more skilled musician— but not a more employable one. He followed Phil's lead and got a job at the post office, which is where he was working when he got his draft notice one rainy November morning.

Though he had been an associate of the group that would become nearly synonymous with the hippie lifestyle, in 1965 Tom accepted the notion of military service as something of an inevitability. The number of young men being drafted was increasing as the Vietnam conflict escalated. And though he continued to study at Mills, he was not matriculated and enjoyed no deferment. Still, the idea of military service was not anathema to him; he felt enough patriotism to preclude any thought of evasion. Resigned to his duty, Tom also knew there were much better ways to spend his three years than as a grunt in the Army, so he enlisted in the Air Force and by pulling some strings had himself assigned to a base near his parents' home in Las Vegas.

Hair cut off, in fatigues, Tom daydreamed about music, about the Warlocks and about the day so long in the future when he'd again be a civilian. More intelligent than most of his fellow fliers, Tom was assigned to the computer-programming division and quickly mastered the complexities of the then infant science. He also soon mastered the secrets of the military workplace: rule one being, If you look busy they'll leave you alone. So Tom filled up his days devising a program for musical composition by computer. At night, the erstwhile astrophysicist wandered off to a secluded portion of the base, set up his small but powerful telescope, and watched the age-old movements of the stars and planets. There was solace in their steady, unalterable sweep across the blackness above the desert. For a man with rock and roll in his future, these Air Force years were surprisingly enjoyable.

Back in San Francisco, the stars could have fallen right out of the sky and created less of an uproar than the changes in lifestyle sweeping through the streets of the city. Tom earned frequent passes for excellence on the job, and he spent his leave time with Phil and watched as both he and the rest of the band began to evolve their psychedelicized selves. They were all living communally now in the Haight, and were becoming famous—or notorious—for their talents as well as their habits. A drug bust at the house in 1967 put them on the front pages of the local papers. Gigs at the hottest clubs like the Carousel Ballroom and the Avalon were selling out. The Warlocks had become the Grateful Dead, their following had become cultlike in their devotion, their music had become even tighter and more enigmatic. Throughout 1966 and 1967 and into 1968 Tom watched as his old band became superstars and he pounded a computer for Uncle Sam.

By the time he was discharged, the shifting personnel of the band had settled down and membership in the Grateful Dead had crystallized. Jerry and Bob handled most of the vocals; Phil, Jerry and Bob handled guitars; Bill and Mickey handled percussion. Pigpen served as keyboard maestro on the sets that more and more consisted of original music composed by Phil and Jerry with words by unofficial Dead member Robert Hunter. Clearly, there was no need for another piano player—there was barely enough room on the stage for the members as it was. Tom moved back to San Francisco, but not with thoughts of joining the Dead.

Now famous for their legendary live performances, the Dead had earlier attempted to capture on record the uniqueness of their concert sound. The 1967 *Grateful Dead* largely failed to achieve the mystical something that characterized the group's seamless harmony, and the members realized they needed to reconsider their approach for their next studio effort, scheduled for mid-1968. As part of these reconsiderations Tom was asked to make suggestions, and he drew upon his background in avant-garde music to devise several production techniques involving innovative piano playing and electronic dubbing. The rehearsals turned into recording sessions, and when *Anthem of the Sun* came out, Tom Constanten was listed with the other group members. He was Dead again.

Straight out of the service and more classically inclined than rock oriented, Tom defied preconceived notions about pop musicians of the day. His personal style—low-key, pensive, intellectual—didn't exactly clash with the band's personality, but it was distinct from it. His friendship with Phil endured and prospered, and ironically he grew close to Pigpen, a logical competitor since both played piano. On the road, they roomed together and enjoyed the same pastime: chess. But Tom remained apart from the group, a newcomer and an odd duck at that. This separateness was never clearer than during performances: the very precision that made him invaluable during studio sessions—he would also appear on 1969's *Aoxomoxoa* album—impeded him from going with the flow during live concerts. Taking its lead from Jerry, the band had become extremely demanding in technical areas like amplification and equipment. Perhaps believing their own critics, they regarded themselves as artists and their music as art. This growing perfectionism improved their style, but it also made more glaring than ever any variance from the group's singular sound. And Tom varied.

When the acoustics of a hall were good, when the vibes among the men were solid, Tom knew the sweet intoxication of clicking with the band. There were times at the Fillmore in New York, one of the group's best houses, when his piano playing melted into the fluid stream of music coming from the other six. And after those special gigs, Tom reveled in the glow of oneness that made working with the Dead so special. But other evenings brought no such transcendence. If the crowd emitted bad karma, or if the acoustics on the stage prevented coherence among the band members, the entire evening would be a strain. Without technique to fall back on, relying instead on intuitive skills, the Dead were fragile maestros—and Tom the most vulnerable of all. He could fall out of sync far more easily than the others, unravel the slender thread of improvised harmony, get lost. Frustrated and isolated, he'd struggle with the line of music waiting to slide back into the elusive path Jerry was creating, and the way would never make itself clear. It wasn't that he'd overtly flub—no one in the audience would realize his predicament. But onstage they all knew. For years now, at Acid Tests, in Golden Gate Park, in their basement on Haight Street, the Dead had been growing together into a complex, interdependent entity. Tom had been in the Air Force in Las Vegas. During many performances this difference was clear. Woodstock was to be one of the last.

SCOTT LANE

BOTTOM LINE: Woodstock was fun. Heck, the whole lifestyle it embodied was fun.

Oh, you can find the kids who trekked there toting a knapsack full of woes, who sat in the rain and concentrated on—the rain. Lost boys and girls dragged themselves through a confusing decade seeking not just distraction but also salvation in the lyrics and ramblings of their heroes. That was a part of Woodstock too. And these despondent ones formed the segment of youth too often caught in the bleak spotlight of the news media, fascinated by the downside of sixties counterculture. Surely, the particular lures held out by the times created more frightening temptations to American teens than ever before. You could get addicted, pregnant, beat up or worse. And for some teenagers, sucked into the maelstrom of evil which was just a part of sixties life, what a drag it was being young.

But you could also just play, romp indulgently through the most intoxicating sandbox of an era into which the country had ever shoved its youth. The baby boom exploded into puberty, and adolescent pursuit of good times emerged as the national sport. For some kids, participation in the sex-drugs-and-rock-and-roll revolution signified active revolt, a political statement, a visceral response to the hypocrisy of their parents' generation. For others, plucking at the decade's erotic and psychedelic offerings amounted to sifting through an overstuffed stocking with their name on it, presented during a Christmas morning that began with their first toke of dope and lasted right through Woodstock. There was no better time to be young and on the make than the mid-1960s. Scott Lane was young and on the make.

These were good times for the senior at Spring Valley High School in a suburb some thirty miles north of New York City, who woke up each morning, looked at the new day, and wondered, What's in it for me? He had felt hungry for experience ever since he arrived in Spring Valley in 1966, late in his sophomore year, after moving that same school year from New Jersey, to Fairfield, Connecticut, to this suburban New York community beyond the Tappan Zee Bridge. A school psychologist reviewing his dismal attendance record and class performance might attribute his academic failings to these upsetting relocations. Anyone who knew him better would have observed that Scott's extracurricular zest for life had asserted itself long before he arrived in Spring Valley.

Take his short stay at Fairfield, for example, where he had spent about half his sophomore year. In this preppie capital of America, where students willingly wore button-down shirts and corduroys to class, Scott arrived in 1965, dressed in slinky black pegged jeans and Beatles-inspired hairdo. Too cool to be ignored, Scott soon attracted around him a band of buddies, garage musicians and hippie wannabes eager like their leader to sample some of the counterculture bounty they'd been hearing about.

As enthusiastically as the kids wanted to partake in sixties kicks, their curiosity found more conventional outlets for their boundless energies: juvenile delinquency. But Scott wasn't in the rule-breaking line for gain, he was in it for style. Like the time they hot-wired a yellow Volkswagen, not for the joyride but as a practical joke. Scott drove it to a neighboring town and left it where he found another yellow Volks of the same year. He then drove the second Volks back to Fairfield and parked it where he had found the first. Neat stuff. On another evening, following a similarly inane prank—he and his buddies gently tipped a Saab onto its side—a policeman showed up at his home to interrogate him about his involvement. Luckily, just before he had gone out for the prank, he had watched a TV show the detective had seen too. By bluffing out the plot of the episode Scott established himself an alibi. No one ever said Scott wasn't good at improvising.

Scott remembers one dream he had recurrently through his months in Fairfield. It was morning and he would be walking to school, passing friends and passing kids he hated. He'd get all the way through the parking lot and be heading for his locker, when suddenly he realized he had no clothes on. The dream faded as soon as he understood he was walking around Fairfield naked.

And he remembers one song. He was swimming in a harbor along the Connecticut coast where the rich people of Fairfield County moored their yachts. Suddenly he heard something differ- ent coming out of a transistor radio on a nearby dock: "Hey, Mr. Tambourine Man, play a song for me. . . ." He had never heard it before, and like a siren's song it beckoned him over. What's that song, man, he asked the guy playing the radio. It's the Byrds. It's "Mr. Tambourine Man." It's a Dylan song. I think it's about drugs, he told an intrigued and shivering Scott. It's about knowing things you could never know unless you did drugs.

This was a message Scott would find repeated over and over again, by songs, by pop literature, by the media. Drugs, drugs, drugs. In the mid-sixties America became obsessed with phar- macology, either through firsthand use of banned substances or through the endless stories and reports that news magazines devoted to such use. The greatest impact of the popularization of pot: getting stoned became an accepted form of socializing. The Food and Drug Administration issued reports stating that as many as 20 million had tried marijuana, while 400,000 used it regularly. It was no longer the vile habit of a plastered few. To party cool meant to party with drugs. Toking up became as accepted and widespread as drinking beer at teen parties. And while Scott never became addicted, the relatively gentle marijuana highs pushed open the psychological doors separating him from the greater unknowns: frightening as chemical drugs like LSD and speed seemed from a distance, kids like Scott wanted to try them. They were spooky, but kids like to be scared.

Scott moved to Spring Valley, but brought with him from that Fairfield harbor a fascination with Mr. Tambourine Man's promise of mind-expansion and delirium that acid held. It was, people said, more exotic and enticing than the marijuana he was regularly using now. It was also foreign: nobody he knew was doing it here. In Spring Valley he had secured the pot connection he couldn't make in Fairfield and had settled in nicely with a crowd of dopers with whom he felt comfortable. Some had already dropped out of school, and the ones still at Spring Valley High were just as uninterested in classes as he was. By mid-semester in the fall of '66, he decided he'd had enough and he scraped some money together for a trip to San Francisco, the mecca, home of the Haight-Ashbury freak scene, with which he had by now become obsessed. The day before Halloween he and a buddy headed for the airport, round-trip tickets bought, parents' permission granted, and with about a hundred dollars between them.

Fiasco from the start, adventure all the way, Scott's San Francisco journey typifies the goofy skin-of-his-teeth luck that seemed to characterize his youth. After making a throwaway crack at the check-in counter about a bomb he had in his carry-on bag, Scott and his buddy, Paul, were handcuffed and dumped into a police car. Released as unthreatening pains in the ass six hours later—they had stuffed all their dope down the backseat of the black-and-white—they waited for the next plane and met an older hippie type heading for the Haight. The scruffy dude offered them a place to stay when they arrived. He's got needle tracks up and down his arms, Scott whispered to Paul, which freaked the two kids out yet cranked the level of adventure up a notch. They went along, no turning back now.

Once they landed, they were picked up by two hookers and a

transvestite, who told them how cute they were. Just go with it, just go with it, Scott urged his friend. Halloween in the Haight, and Scott and Paul wanted badly to try some acid. They made their way through the macabre streets to a concert hall where the Grateful Dead were playing and where, as was the fashion at such Acid Tests, free tabs were handed out. At last: LSD. Within an hour after they dropped their first hit, both teenagers were back at the crash pad. Paul was stroking a cat, convinced it was dead. Scott became transfixed with a Stones song he played over and over. Hookers walked in and out, transvestites eyed them. Two weeks later they both decided to return home and see if they could get back into school.

Though the trip west ended far earlier than he had intended, the mere fact that Scott made it at all marked the teen indelibly and imbued him with a thrill-seeker's spirit. Too intense for him at this point in his life, the San Francisco scene still presented him with an invitation to live it up, with a vision of big-time fun he'd never imagined before. He probably didn't even think about the damage the speed freaks and acidheads were doing to themselves, he focused only on the Haight's kinetic energy. He wasn't hooked on drugs, he was hooked on counterculture partying. Like water seeking its level, he searched his home county for kindred spirits and found them in the artistic community around Nyack. There, in coffeehouses and people's basements, black lights were lit, pot was shared, acid was dropped, occasionally poetry was read. Scott floated through his senior year of high school high as a kite, playing a giggling Puck in the Midsummer Night's Dream that was 1967. By the end of senior year, young Scott was a full-fledged hippie, carrying an F in most classes but not a care in the world. He wanted to go back to California.

He was standing on his head in a corner of his parents' living room, tripping delightfully, when the idea came to him. His parents had long before absolved themselves of guilt about their son's behavior, or responsibility about changing it. A nice Jewish couple living in the suburbs, the Lanes had opted for a hands-off nurturing style. Scott's friends were always welcome in their home, Scott's comings and goings were his own affair. Sociologists were writing that just such unregulated parenting was responsible for growing student unrest: taking over the dean's office, they explained, was really a childish demand for more attention. All the Lanes knew was that Scott was weird but seemed to be happy. They wanted him to be happy.

I wanna try LA this time.

He's just trying to get our attention, his father grumbled to his mother.

What about summer school, she inquired, taking her son seriously even though he was upside down. You won't be able to go to Rockland Community if you don't finish summer school.

The possibility of no further formal education didn't really worry Scott at all. Besides, maybe he'd be back in time for the sessions anyway. With a thumb as his open ticket and the setting sun as his directional, the wanderer set out after graduation for a commune in Hollywood he had heard about through the underground grapevine. Riverendell, named after a Hobbit site, was a dilapidated house on Western Avenue, where, straggling in some three weeks after leaving home, he was greeted by a formless group of young men and women. Within minutes he had dropped some acid; within weeks, he says, he had had sex with a ghost.

Acid was cheap then, and with a little panhandling by day, Scott and his new household of hippies could all afford nightly trips to mind-melting outer limits. Sometimes he'd roam around Hollywood looking for excitement: one night, he remembers, Tommy Smothers picked him up as he was hitchhiking and took him to a posh celebrity party in the hills. Another night director and avant-garde filmmaker Henry Jaglom picked him up and told him he should go into acting. But his brushes with the famous were far less frequent than his encounters with the endless parade of drop-in freaks who passed through Riverendell. One night a self-professed witch wandered in, claiming to have been drawn there by the spirit of a young woman who still haunted the premises. She is stuck here but is still able to make love. We will call her back from the beyond and she will pick someone among you for sex. Coaxing everyone down into the basement, dimming the lights and exhorting the circle to try a little more acid, the witch invoked the dead girl's spirit. Titters died out as the jolt of the acid rushed into the brains of the seance members. Whether it was a matter of merely minutes or hours, Scott can't say. He knows only that sometime during the night the witch said, She's calling to you, she wants you. And Scott, horny and high anyway, made his way over to a couch where, hallucination or not, he felt something move under him.

Needless to say, Rockland Community College seemed a rather unattractive option in comparison to the absolutely otherworldly diversions Riverendell promised. Just the same, Scott decided he had had enough, and left Hollywood in time to make summer school. Knowing when to call it quits might have been the key trait that saved this sixties party boy from burning out like so many other thrill-seeking teens of the day. An internal thermostat of sorts yanked him back from the brink whenever the drugs and the wild times threatened to push him over. Maybe it was just common sense, maybe it was an inherent knowledge he and other high-life survivors possess. Scott Lane returned from the Coast yet again, haggard, hungry, partied out, but richer in experience than every other kid in that summer school make-up class.

Scott would cut school once more that summer—to go to Woodstock. For several years prior to the big one, a small folk concert series, called Sound Out, had been held there. It was the success of these gatherings that prompted the Aquarian Exposition's organizers to consider this town for their 1969 blowout. Peaceful, intimate, bucolic, Sound Out featured acoustic artists like Odetta and Pete Seeger in a setting that corresponded to the back-to-the-land sensibilities of the era. Scott went, smoked some pot, listened to some music, chased after some girls.

Scott returned to Rockland, majoring in theater at Jaglom's advice. College proved as poor a marriage for the young man as did high school: attendance, grades, interest in general sank lower each week. The draft, the war, the race tensions, the assassinations—the times conspired against frivolity, and yet in the face of it all Scott stuck resolutely to his pursuit of self-gratification. The war protests he attended, he attended because he could meet girls there. The classes he went to, he went to stoned. And while radicals burned down buildings and stormed government offices, young Scott may have been engaging in a subversive activity far more potent: he was thumbing his nose at the entire puritan ethic that ruled the country, defying the dictates of America's hard-work tradition. He was cruising, he was coasting. He was just having a good time—and a good laugh.

Others weren't as lucky. He knew guys who were drafted—and he went out with their girls when they shipped out. He knew guys who got busted for selling drugs—and he went out with their girls while they did some short time. Perhaps Scott wasn't the living, breathing embodiment of his decade's other-directed ethos, and perhaps he took advantage of the era's good nature, its heart. But Scott wasn't so different from a lot of his long-haired, peace sign–throwing peers. The energy and exhilaration of 1969 arose as much out of young people's feeling that they could right society's wrongs and make a difference, as from their unalterable belief that they could make society meet their demands, hopes, expectations, whims. Scott saw opportunity everywhere and it charged him up. He unquestioningly expected the world to deliver, to come through, to satisfy him.

Woodstock, you mean the Sound Out?

He was yelling to his friend Barry from the bar they had been hanging around all summer. The year before, the summer of '68, he stole Barry's girlfriend when Barry left to play an out-of-town gig with his band. Scott talked his way out of it, the girl had been forgotten, and he and Barry had become best friends. And now, yelling to him from his car, Barry beckoned him over.

Forget that Sound Out thing. This is the Woodstock Festival. You know, a billion people, a half-billion chicks. Like, drugs all over the place. Like, the biggest party ever designed on this green planet.

Oh yeah, Scott said. The biggest party ever.

BETHEL, SULLIVAN COUNTY

THE QUICKWAY—officially Route 17—connects New York's densely populated southern urban sprawl with the state's northern cities, curving around hills thick with trees and deer and forgotten villages. Ever since it was completed in the 1960s, countless city kids have driven along this road, en route to the large universities and prestigious colleges nestled around Binghamton and above, in through the Finger Lakes and farther up to Syracuse, Rochester and Buffalo. They notice the trees, whose leaves will soon turn the hills into fantastic bowls of color. And they notice the deer; occasionally they hit one. But few of the speeding collegiates who seem determined to make the Quickway live up to its name ever discover much about the towns just off the highway, the people just beyond the exit lane, and why should they? The landscape is merely that pretty, bucolic blur that separates Mom and Dad's house from the dorm room and the future. That one August, however, the Quickway caravan slowed down, and the familiar trek north veered off the highway and west for a weekend. An estimated 500,000 cruised into the small valleys and through the corn farms that had whizzed by in trips past. With the self-involvement of youth, and particularly youth in the 1960s, the invading Woodstock hordes presumed it was their presence that had brought life to those villages and residents off the Quickway that summer. Before they arrived, they thought, nothing had ever happened in the hamlets of Sullivan County. When they left, nothing would ever happen again. About that they were wrong.

Burt, this festival is crazy enough, why do you have to work at it?

Anne Feldman was getting her two girls ready for summer playground, the last week of which had just begun. She usually agreed with her husband's decisions, but she was not happy about his signing on to work security at the Woodstock Festival, which was going ahead as scheduled on Max Yasgur's farm that week-end, against the town's protests. The Feldmans lived less than five miles from the site and already youngsters looking for the festival had straggled by their home. It's going to be disorganized, a complete mess, she said to Burt. I'm nervous.

Nervous about what? He laughed, reading the morning paper. Anne, we're the last ones in the world to worry about a few wackos.

Indeed, the Feldmans might welcome them as kindred spirits. Hardworking, rustic homeowners of Bethel, the couple nevertheless were in their own way counterculture exponents, delightfully out of sync with their surroundings, their peers and their neighbors. In the welter of media scrutiny that came to surround the festival, constant mention would be made of the disparity between the straight locals and the flower children who came to play. But among those supposedly mundane, everyday middle Americans, there were at least two nonconformists who fancied themselves, perhaps rightly so, avant-garde. Well into their forties by the time of Woodstock, with kids of their own, the Feldmans shared in the apprehension their fellow townsfolk had felt since the concert site had been moved to their backyard in July. What would it do to their village? But unlike many of their Bethel brethren, the Feldmans tempered their fears with excitement, anticipation. The Quickway might actually back up, a festival naysayer had told them. There are going to be all sorts of kooks here. Anne and Burt thought about that and looked forward to the visit.

If nothing else, the couple had one thing in common with the kids that many of their neighbors did not: like the majority of the festivalgoers, the Feldmans were city folk originally, which may explain why they were viewed as slightly different by the townspeople. Burt grew up in the Bronx, Anne in Manhattan. She knows she had no affinity for the country as a young woman. Even her summers at camp in Vermont left dreadful memories of sunburn and poison ivy. She had an inkling during her engagement, though, that she might have to get over her aversion when her fiancé Burt made the unusual suggestion that they take a hiking trip along the Shenandoah Ridge for their honeymoon in 1952. No Bermuda, no Niagara Falls even. Hiking. She now shows with pride two wedding pictures: in one, she's in full satin and veils, her arm crooked into a dandy Burt in tails; in the other she's in lederhosen and walking shoes being led off by a smiling Burt to the hills of Virginia. It was an unconventional honeymoon chosen in a rather conventional way: the man decided. And it established a pattern for much of their marriage. Burt made the decisions, Anne made them work.

Because of a back condition that would continue to deteriorate, Burt wanted to get out of Manhattan, where reliance on public transportation aggravated his physical disability. When he found a job in 1957 as an editor of a newspaper in Monticello, Anne at first refused to move up to the town about seventy-five miles northwest of the New York she loved. She had a job—as a biochemistry lab assistant—and wasn't certain Burt's new position would last. Besides, she was well over thirty at this point, having gotten married at what was considered a mature age in the 1950s, and didn't relish a move. Eventually she joined him there, all the while fearing that small-town exclusivity would prevent her from making friends and finding work. Instead, she found an even more challenging situation, one that brought out her resourcefulness and forced her to accept and then love her new living conditions. No sooner had the Feldmans moved up to Sullivan County than the area started to go under. As the sophisticated existence in Manhattan receded into memory, the couple realized they had plunked themselves down in the middle of a big depression hitting a tiny town.

Since the early part of the century the Catskill area of Sullivan County had prospered on the annual summer influx of sun-and-fun-seeking New York vacationers. Bungalow colonies for families, more expensive hotels for upscale tourists, elaborate resort complexes—without destroying the area's natural beauty, the development of the county into a rural but not too remote retreat sustained a boom economy that hummed along right through the early 1960s. With the increased availability of airplane travel to more exotic places than Monticello, however, hard times crushed down suddenly on the thriving towns the Quickway had been designed to preserve. Motels were shuttered and bungalows fell into disrepair, setting off a chain reaction of financial failure first affecting the immediate leisure industry—restaurants and theaters—but soon enough dragging down the entire local economy. When Anne and Burt first arrived in Monticello, his newspaper was one of three serving the toddling town. Within a year of his arrival, it had folded.

Now what do we do, they asked each other, facing the swinging sixties jobless and isolated. We just do what we can to get by, Anne reasoned. College trained in biology, she knew that her expertise and experience weren't going to help her much in the low-tech, high-unemployment Catskills. But home trained in sewing, Anne began to take in stitching work, hemming skirts and letting out seams for the townsfolk newly interested in making old clothes last. The cottage industry grew, and she eventually took on an assistant. But it didn't provide enough income, so she started an even more unusual business: making earrings. She noticed the fashions of the day featured by hippies who started to filter into Monticello in an effort to get back to the land. While the feathered and beaded earrings many of the young women favored dangled down to their shoulders, no one seemed to wear the same sort of decorated jewelry made shorter. Anne saw a fashion need: modish feathered earrings that hugged the lobe rather than dangle. She remembered there were several bird farms nearby, where pheasants and quail and other exotic foul were raised to service the gourmet needs of the hotels in the past. She made regular rounds of the farms and collected plumage in large paper bags she hauled home. When she wasn't turning an old prom gown into a party dress, she was fashioning feathers into stylish earrings the distinction of which was their short, round shape. They flattered short, round-faced women, like Anne herself. Being about as far away from a hippie craftsman as a Monticello housewife can be, Anne Feldman was just the same sharing the experience of many young flower children: she was using her manual skills to produce trendy goods and services that were all the more desirable because they were homemade.

Burt's job search was less colorful, at first. Because he was familiar with the newspaper business, he found work selling advertising space to hotels. Since those were exactly the spots hardest hit by the depression that closed his first Monticello employer, the potential in his new post was extremely limited. With the fall-off in hotel work, the itinerant population in the county began to swell, and with it the incidence of crime. The prisons required additional staffing, and Burt reluctantly took a position as a warden, hardly the sort of work the gregarious and literate man had envisioned for himself. So when a moonlighting opportunity came up that promised both extra cash and a diversion from the jail, Burt leaped at the chance. The former editor of the Monticello newspaper became the spotlight operator at a burlesque theater in nearby Fallsburgh. And because his wife didn't like his driving all the way back from the theater alone, or maybe just didn't like his being there alone, she became his chauffeur. Since she had nothing better to do while she waited in the wings, she started to mend the strippers' costumes and decorate them with feathers. The couple's life was becoming a cross between *The Egg and I* and *Gypsy*.

While the Woodstock Festival would turn out to be the biggest entertainment event Sullivan County ever witnessed, it was by no means the only show in town. For decades the hills had been alive with the bad jokes of Borscht Belt comedians and the tacky tunes of strip-circuit dance girls. In the major hotels like Grossinger's, of course, big-name talent performed to audiences in sharp summer wear. But throughout the rolling valleys, in little roadhouse gin mills and converted movie houses, burlesque in all its vulgar glory thrived as robustly as the tomatoes in the fields. Working men from Brooklyn splurging during their one-week vacations took their wives to the show, which combined stand-up with take-off in a perfectly acceptable combination. In a way Woodstock was just another big burlesque show, where strangers from the big city descended on the locals expecting to find in the country entertainment that suited their urbane tastes. That was the Catskills, one of vaudeville's final outposts. Cows chomped cud in the idyllic serenity of Max Yasgur's farm, the same peaceable kingdom the hippies would sanctify as their Aquarian wonderland several years later, and the Feldmans drove off to the theater. Says Burt, spotting a deer on the roadside, They got a new girl on tonight. She wants the pink spotlight.

The new girl showed up, the stage manager that night did not. Burt was in his usual place in the back of the dingy hall looking for the pink gel, and Anne was in the wings stage right sewing a tattered leotard together. Well, Anne knows all the routines, she's here every night, said one of the strippers, pointing at the slightly frumpy seamstress in the corner. And so for the next two summers, Anne joined Burt as the Feldmans of the Fallsburgh Burlesque. He'd light the stage for the gals and the hams, she'd dart out in the darkness to change the set. Make do, everything's a new experience, learning comes in unexpected places. . . . They adopted the do-your-own-thing rhetoric of the day to rationalize the fact that they had come to the country looking for a better life and ended up working in a strip joint.

In a way Anne and Burt's life in the mid-sixties was a study in the sort of creative response to adversity many others in the area were experiencing during the same period. Derailed from the careers they had envisioned when they moved to the country, the Feldmans were free agents, embracing the new and the extraordinary as a survival tactic. Of course they didn't know it at the time, but the unexpected twists their career path was taking would lead them, as it would other locals, directly to the Woodstock Festival and beyond. Such was certainly the case with Paul D'Amico, native son and now town physician, who would have been just about getting up for early rounds one morning as the Feldmans drove home after a particularly late show.

Happy Birthday, honey, his wife said groggily. And congratulations, you beat the draft.

A year earlier, at thirty-four, the father of three had actually received an A-1 draft notice, much to his disbelief and shock. It was 1967 and the Vietnam War was in full swing, and he remembers hearing of physicians being drafted up to age thirty-five. Aside from the enormous disruption military service would bring to the family life and career he had established, he also thoroughly opposed the conduct of the war. If they're going to fight this thing, he told anyone who would listen, they should fight it all out, not in fits and starts. Use the bomb if they have to, but win this thing or get out. He was that weird sort of dove that this particularly ill-run war created: a hawk at heart whose support of withdrawal stemmed not from any pacifist beliefs, but from his disgust with what he saw as American pusillanimity. But now on this July morning he had achieved his own victory over the war: by knitting together a frail string of deferrals, D'Amico had managed to beat the A-1 classification simply by turning thirty-five. He headed off to his office breathing more easily.

Elated because he had avoided the Army—that notion surprised the patriotic doctor. An ROTC undergraduate for part of his years at Georgetown, he began his osteopathic medical education in 1956. Upon its completion in the early 1960s, he returned to Livingston Manor, a town about fifteen miles up the Quickway from Monticello. He had been born there and his parents still resided there. Having set up a practice down the block from his home, he was surprised to find how much the summer vacation business had shrunk. He remembered a time when thirty buses from the city would pull in and out of the town a day during the height of the resort season. And that had dwindled to a trickle. In place of the wealthy New Yorkers, the town began to attract the poverty-level workers laid off from the struggling hotels. And as the income level spiraled downward, the incidence of alcoholism and drug abuse increased. He hadn't been trained for it, but because his was the newest practice in the area, and simply because he wouldn't reject these outcast patients, D'Amico began to treat more and more substance-abuse cases. Slowly but surely, the good doctor became one of the area's only experts in the then still hush-hush problem of addiction.

His self-education, coupled with his own growing body of observation, allowed him to develop unorthodox theories about the physical, psychological and social aspects of substance abuse. His concept of addiction as a disease rather than a character fault coincided with new ideas evolving in the greater medical community at the time. But his thinking about culture's complicity in fomenting addiction—rock songs were stimuli to taking drugs, he believed—put him on the fringe. In addition, on the basis of his own firm adherence to his Catholic upbringing, he strongly advocated the inclusion of spiritual training in drug and alcohol rehabilitation, an approach most of his more secular counterparts shunned. Still, his theories were not so outrageous that they precluded him from developing a reputation for tough but successful treatment, and eventually he was even asked to serve as consulting physician in a respected detoxification facility in the area.

For all his experience with the addicted, D'Amico still assumed drug use and drinking excess were limited to a small part of the population: serious medical problems, but confined. Occasionally he would see an overdose case in the hospital that troubled him: typically a young hippie type, camping out in one of the Sullivan County preserves, who had taken too much of some "recreational" drug. He'd treat him and release him. Isolated incidents, he assumed. But the incidents increased, drew closer to home. "Three Monticello Students Felled Taking Drugs, LSD, at Their Final Exams," read the headline of the local paper in June 1969. This is bigger than I thought, he said to himself. I wonder just how prevalent drug use is among kids today?

* * *

George Neuhaus had a horrible feeling everyone in and around Bethel was going to find out real soon, like it or not. "Yippies, SDS Reported Bound for Rock Festival," he read in the paper before tossing the weekly edition aside with disgust. The Yasgur fiasco and its half-million kids were just a few days away. If he had still been in power, he vowed to himself, this would never have happened. And yet, exactly because it was going to happen, it might not be too long before he was back in control.

Control, in the former Bethel town supervisor's eyes, was exactly what was missing in this crisis. After getting kicked out of Wallkill, those fast-talking, deal-making, palm-coating smoothies from New York crawled into our backyard the way the fog comes over the hills and can't be stopped. But hadn't Neuhaus spent his two years in office, from 1966 through 1967, developing a zoning code that would have been airtight against just this sort of invasion? The elaborate network of regulations was designed to allow farmer and homeowner and commercial developer to live in harmony, but it was full of nooses and hurdles sufficient to halt the Woodstock Ventures chicanery. Still, small-town politics is a world where efficiency and common sense don't have a chance against emotion and personality conflict. And back in 1967 Neuhaus's opponent, Jerry Amatucci, had defeated the incumbent on an antizoning platform, and Amatucci wasn't about to rely on his predecessor's legislative legacy to overpower the festival promoters. The rules are there, Neuhaus told a committee of concerned citizens gathering for an eleventh-hour crisis meeting. Jerry Amatucci just doesn't want to use them.

This is the worst thing that could ever happen, hippies running amok in our cornfields. This is the worst thing, don't you think, George?

No, Neuhaus didn't think this was the worst thing. In his fifty-odd years, he had seen worse. Born in Queens, George first came up to Bethel during the 1920s to spend summers with his grandparents, whose hotel and dairy farms were riding the crest of prosperity the entire area enjoyed. It was a relaxed, Tom Sawyer-esque existence. That dreamlike youth ended suddenly in 1932, when, within a period of several months, both his father and his grandparents died. His mother relocated permanently to Bethel to manage the resort, leaving George with other family to finish school in Queens. Now summer trips up to the country meant working vacations, helping his mother out with the crowds that still came for holidays even though the Depression had settled across the nation. Then, when the war broke out, George enlisted and saw active duty in Europe, through four separate campaigns. After the war he married, built a family, and became a leading real estate broker in the Sullivan County area. It seemed almost inevitable that this burly, self-assertive man would enter politics eventually, but that didn't occur until the 1960s, when he won the town supervisor's seat his first time on the ballot.

Between the early hard knocks and the latter-day successes, Neuhaus certainly had the correct philosophical perspective to get through the anticipated invasion of the hippies. And the timing of the event couldn't have been more serendipitous. It was an election year, nominating ballots for the November town-board vote due barely a month after the festival. Although he wasn't actively campaigning, Neuhaus wanted his position back. First of all, the family hotel, now more an albatross than a lucrative business, had burned down the previous year. His real estate operations had supplanted the resort as his major source of income, and the loss of the hotel actually freed him to pay serious attention to his political aspirations. Then, too, he had been surprised himself at how personally rejected he had felt when voted out of office two years earlier. Proud, hurt and determined, he played possum during the Amatucci administration, waiting for the politico to screw up. And now, like a gift from heaven, the Woodstock weirdos were at the doorstep, the almost certain disaster of their hippie folly his unexpected free ticket back to power.

This is the worst thing that could happen, don't you think, George?

Yes, he said from his front porch, it's pretty bad.

How bad do you think this will be, Anne asked Burt.

Oh, Anne, it will be fun. The Feldmans' burlesque days were far behind them, and adopting two school-age daughters had reined in some of their eccentricities over the last few years. Still, even in their seemingly normal existence, they maintained a certain flair. Anne still did some craftwork at home, but always with a distinctive novelty: she was clipping the hair from her poodle and spinning it into wool, that sort of thing. Burt was working as a security guard pretty much full-time now; he'd be working at the festival as part of the contingent of locals who were assisting in crowd control. Residents of Bethel now for over a decade, the Feldmans had become blissfully countrified. Anne couldn't even drive a car when she arrived in Monticello, and now she tooled around the back roads of the county in a four-wheel-drive jeep. Burt had set himself up as something of the unofficial historian of the area. And this festival, he suspected, would certainly make history.

The couple had made several trips over to the Yasgur place, as had most of the locals, during the past few weeks. The progress there was amazing: a stage six stories high had risen miraculously in the hollow of the field, and tractors crisscrossing the hills had fashioned the land into a beautiful amphitheater. Ever since the hippie crews had arrived, the small country provisions stores up and down the main road had been doing business reminiscent of the nearly forgotten boom times past. They're hippie communist bastards, Burt recalls a neighbor saying. Local kids, no longer able to find summer work in the resorts, were hired on for day labor, the first honest buck they had earned all summer. They're dope-smoking, fornicating weirdos, a friend said to Anne. Aside from the money the Ventures representatives were spending, they were also giving cash away: $10,000 had just been donated to the Bethel Medical Center. The economic impact aside, the excitement was thrilling, at least to some of the residents. For Burt and Anne, this was the most energy and activity they had seen since leaving Manhattan.

Let's run the hose up to the road, Anne, said Burt on the Thursday morning before the festival. And let's put out some sandwich things. The kids won't be able to get anything to eat in there.

Look, they've already arrested a hundred fifty kids on the way to that festival, Dr. D'Amico told a nurse that Thursday afternoon.

Look, this thing is out of control. There are cars backed up all the way to Seventeen, said George Neuhaus to his wife on Thursday night.

And on the Quickway, a half-million kids pulled off the highway into the sleepy towns they've sped by before. Before this festival, they thought, nothing ever happened in the hamlets of Sullivan County. When it's done, nothing will ever happen again. About that they were wrong.

It took several months for Penny Stallings to drop her hippy chic for genuine funky garb. But in this photo, taken in the last days of the festival preparation, the SMU grad has mastered the unkempt look that was de rigueur among the organizer elite.

One of the few women in the Woodstock Ventures executive ranks, Lee Blumer was not above toting and fetching with the lowliest employee. She was one of the few organizers to stay in the rock-and-roll business throughout the two decades following the concert.

For thousands who followed what faulty directions were available, getting to the festival along clogged farm roads became a day-long process. Local townsfolk, though, knew back roads that allowed them to drive in and out easily— spreading the word that the "Aquarian Exposition" was a sex-and-drug orgy.

Hippy capitalism flourished in the impromptu, psychedelic casbah that sprang up in the wood around Yasgur's farm.

Most memories focus on the crowds, the bad weather, and the lack of shelter, but ingenuity and independence played their part as well. Backstage, John Sebastian constructed a waterproof lean-to out of a few pieces of canvas. This camper resorted to more primitive materials.

Sacrilege, profanity, and wit mixed in equal measure in the ethos that spawned Woodstock. Even if these revelers had known that several of their cocelebrants had died during the weekend, it probably wouldn't have changed their youthfully brazen attitude.

Between drug use and the boredom that set in between performances, it was inevitable that the concertgoers would turn to the inviting lighting scaffolding for fun. Amazingly, no one fell off. In fact, the greater risk came from the threat of items falling off the towers onto the crowd below.

By rhetoric and gesture, many who attended the concert expressed disdain for and distance from American ideals. Still, as revealed in their later recollections, a number who were there—on stage, behind stage, and in the crowd—felt secretly uncomfortable about the event's seeming disloyalty.

Half a million strong—or so the song says, and by best estimates that seems to be the most accurate figure. But between police downsizing their numbers and the media exaggerating theirs, head counts that appeared in immediate press reports varied from 350,000 to 600,000.

Country Joe McDonald wore headband and shades along with his Army jacket during his solo set. Contrary to that jaunty look, though, he was uncertain about his performance, his future, and the concert's eventual impact on his career.

John Sebastian painted rainbows all over the crowd's blues, and it looks like some of the color slipped onto his clothes. But for all his well-documented enthusiasm, the singer grew to regard this performance as a low point in his then-still-young solo career.

Carlos Santana had created the band bearing his name in 1967, but their following remained limited to their Bay Area home up until 1969. Their Woodstock appearance introduced the cult group to a much larger audience, and earned them a Columbia Records contract and fame that would last through the next decade.

Arlo Guthrie was at the height of his popularity when he
appeared at the Woodstock Festival. His most influential record,
Alice's Restaurant, was two years behind him; the movie based on
the tall tale was to be released in 1970.

Several observers who had known Janis Joplin earlier in her career recognized she was in trouble when they saw how she looked backstage. Little over a year later, in October 1970, she would be found dead in Los Angeles.

Joe Cocker's appearance at Woodstock was part of his first American tour, following the release of *With a Little Help from My Friends*. Many in the crowd remember their shock upon seeing his idiosyncratic gyrations and shakes as he performed.

Tom Constanten, known by the other Grateful Dead members as TC, left the band several months after the festival performance—which he remembers as one of their worst.

Most concertgoers weren't as fastidious—or prepared—as this skinny-dipper shaver. The ponds around the farm were transformed into mass wading pools, but many of the then-hippies were uncomfortable with the nudity, and equally uncomfortable with keeping clothes on.

The ample rains found most festivalgoers unprepared. In their giant plastic garbage bags, groups huddled into moist cocoons on Sunday afternoon. Already the crowd was thinning out; for the third and final night of the show, the audience was significantly diminished.

For those who decided to stay behind, the last day was marked by comradery and high jinks. Among the organizers it was felt that if drugs had not been so prevalent, the youthful exuberance would quickly have turned into ugly rioting.

Jimi Hendrix closed the festival at sunrise on Monday morning with his own unmistakable version of "The Star Spangled Banner." Though many had already left by this time, those who witnessed the guitarist say it was the highlight of the weekend.

The devastation of Yasgur's farm. It was out of this compost heap of old sleeping bags, milk cartons, and tent canvas that the next two decades of personal histories would grow.

Part II

GLORY
DAYS

AFTER MONTHS of delays, setbacks and blunders that threatened to keep it from ever taking place, the Woodstock Festival started long before anyone expected.

The first official guitar blast on Friday the fifteenth didn't occur until about an hour after the scheduled four-o'clock kickoff, when folksinger Richie Havens was thrust on stage, substituting for a scheduled performer who had not yet arrived. But the official festival amounted to something of a sideshow by the time it got off the ground. Not exactly an afterthought, but an extra attraction for a crowd that didn't much care about official anything, and certainly not about official party hours. The ever-rising din from the national and local press, coupled with the lavish advertising the Woodstock Ventures promotional dollars bought, succeeded in turning the start-off date into the counterculture's own D day. FM radio, the over-the-air underground network of hip information, seized upon the festival as if it were the second coming, although in fact it was just one of a dozen major outdoor festivals occurring that summer. DJs hyped it and every hippie, would-be hippie, music lover, freak, commune dweller, party animal and outnik isolated in his or her bedroom heard the call to regroup. This was no military maneuver, however, and the precise date signified little. Rather than just inform the public about a curtain time, the media blitz gave the youth of America a sense of place: Woodstock, their own Brigadoon, which would appear and evaporate in the course of several days. It was appropriate that the festival wasn't even taking place in the eponymous village in Ulster County, but in the Sullivan County township of Bethel, about forty-five miles southwest in the state. Running on hippie time and in Aquarian space, the event didn't have a real address or a real itinerary. Regulating fun, restricting it to given hours—that defied every notion of spontaneity and individuality the event had come to symbolize in the minds of the youths who looked to Woodstock as a spiritual venture. A happening like this ran on its own internal clock, ticking and tocking to the beat of the moment. Responding intuitively to the lure of the festival, kids didn't check their watches or calendars for the exact time; many of them didn't even check a map of the area. They just went—en masse. For days before, beginning with a trickle and then growing into a stream and then erupting into an unstoppable flow, the disciples of the zeitgeist began to assemble for the ultimate coming together.

For the hitchhikers and Volkswagen bus riders, for the bare-footed and barebreasted, getting to the festival at midweek simply meant starting the decade's biggest bash a few days early. But the unexpected midweek crunch of concertgoers took on quite a different aspect to the crew members, shocked by the first arrivals—and their own unpreparedness. For the Woodstock Ventures personnel, those initial revelers were surprise invaders crashing the private little community they had created in the Catskills. Before fences could even be completed, interlopers by the thousands settled onto the fifty-acre bowl. Unable to remove the early birds, management frantically tried to block off access to the field, realizing too late that the biggest disadvantage to a natural setting is its resistance to imposed control mechanisms. By Thursday, when the first amplified voice from the stage greeted the assemblage, 65,000 were already estimated to have waltzed into the amphitheater without a single ticket collected. At that point the organizers silently concurred that for all intents and purposes it would be a free concert.

For Penny and Lee and Rufus and Henry, seeing those first long-haired heads dotting the hills was like waking from a dream. This thing was real, it was happening, right here in the rolling cowfield the displaced band of city folk had been treating like their private backyard. A band of hippies camped on a knoll, a gangly kid and his "old lady" rolled out their sleeping bag near the stage. And suddenly the four small-time players understood the enormity of the endeavor in which they had been distracted participants for the last few months. Up until that Thursday when people began to arrive in droves, Woodstock had been a private adventure, a sexual romp, camp. Remote and cut off in their Catskill oasis, these scruffy learn-as-you-go organization kids had mostly forgotten the real reason they were there. The blur of their busy days and the bliss of being together obscured the seriousness of their goal.

All along they had been convinced that the reputed experts and bosses behind the event were incompetent know-nothings. The last-minute site change to Bethel, the impossibility of adequately transforming Yasgur's cow farm into a suitable venue, the new protest suits filed by disgruntled locals, the constantly changing roster of artists lined up to play: each day brought its new wrinkle of stress. But then, the nearly daily screw-ups of the higher-ups were just that afternoon's joke. Even at their most despondent and frustrated, the Woodstock workers floated through the summer in a dreamlike, adolescent haze. Their meals were taken care of, their rooms arranged for them. In essence, they were an isolated, self-sufficient community with no one to worry about but themselves. Then suddenly they weren't alone anymore. Their idyll had gone public and they feared the disasters the coming weekend might deliver down upon them.

A fire at the Diamond Horseshoe Thursday night left them all shaken. The troops had retreated to the bungalow colony for the final night of rest, frazzled by the overwork and the knowledge that it had left them underprepared. Suddenly, in the crisp mountain night, sparks began to leap from the corner of the rickety Catskill motel. The dinner gong rang through the darkness, rousing sleepers and ending this last chance for a romantic walk in the woods. Even as they managed to douse the flames, the fire's searing reality shook them from the reverie that had been their summer. It brought home the specter of cataclysm at least the lowly workers had seen dancing around the edges ever since they moved to Bethel. Just that morning the company contracted to run the food concessions had threatened to walk out on the deal. It wasn't even the weekend yet, and already traffic congestion made it clear that parking and transportation would develop into a major problem. Yet oddly enough, the fire served a purpose: controlling it, banding together and refusing to panic, the Woodstock lowlies received early proof of the mettle they would have to demonstrate throughout the weekend ahead.

For Penny perhaps more than the others, the fire has come to symbolize the first clear sign how much the summer had changed her. The flames sparked a response she barely recognized. And now in her memory her reactions to the fire stand as the first clue to herself that the beauty queen from SMU had grown during those weeks upstate, toughened up, learned to believe in herself. She had left Texas and her protective family environment several years before, but New York had only stymied and daunted her. It was not until the Woodstock Ventures job relocated her—separated her from Barry, and the cocoon he had created for her in Manhattan— that she truly became her own self. Penny was learning new ways to be a woman. From Jean Ward she had seen for the first time the strength of character and confidence a truly feminine personality could maintain. And in successfully carrying out the million mundane but essential tasks she had taken charge of during the preceding months, a transformation had come over her. The Hog Farm wanted goat's milk, she found goat's milk. New housing was needed for the Bastard Sons, new housing was found. For the first time, she sensed the competence that would stay with her the rest of her life. In Max's field a couple of miles away, the biggest coming-out ball of the sixties was getting under way. At the Horseshoe, as the fire raged, Penny was realizing just how grown-up she had become. Instead of running the other way, relying on the expertise of others, she without even thinking just addressed the problem and its solution. In her pajamas, she ran from her room out to the bucket brigade and joined the hippies trying to extinguish the blaze.

> It turned out the fire was in the basement, an electrical fire. There were these macho guys, the maniacs, fighting the fire, because the firemen couldn't get there. And I stood down there in my flowing pajamas, in my baby-dolls, with the hose, with those guys. Until I said, "What am I doing, this is an electrical fire. This place is going to blow any minute. It's going to vaporize in a second." At which point I fled.
>
> Barry called during the fire and someone answered the phone. The guy said, "Man, I can't get her now. There's a fire here." And Barry said, "Well, is she out?" And he answered, "I don't know, man. I really got to go now." So Barry got in the car and came up here immediately. He was here at three and stayed through the weekend. Barry was a grown-up, and there was a certain amount of distance in watching the "kids" make this insane mess. Not that he's much older, but he hadn't fallen for any of this at all. He just saw it as a potential catastrophe. He stood over on the side and said, "Look at these dorks, what are they going to do. They're going to kill everybody."

Penny and Lee, who had called themselves the Ethel and Lucy of Woodstock, found each other outside the Horseshoe after the fire and could muster little of the humor that had gotten them through the months of preparation. They looked around them as the bushed coworkers sat on the wet grass, silently pondering the fire and the future. For Penny, there was terror of the unknown; for Lee, terror of the all-too-familiar. From her years in the music business, she knew the mentality of rock-and-roll entrepreneurs and had a far better understanding of just how badly the weekend could go. She had seen this carelessness before, the insensitivity promoters exhibited to talent and audience alike. She herself had been its victim, fired from jobs because of the same sort of shoot-from-the-hip management style that was being practiced here. Only now, hundreds of thousands stood to be hurt.

Brainy, but cut off from the male-controlled decision-making process, Lee could see clearly the forces converging to make this the biggest rock festival to date. She suspected Michael Lang had been lowballing attendance figures all along, making provisions for 100,000 when in fact he secretly anticipated half a million. The momentum from a summer full of successful outdoor concerts would sweep music lovers and event groupies alike to this climactic happening. Plus, proximity to the enormous population centers in the northeast corridor positioned millions of youngsters only a hitch or even a hike away from the site. But Bethel was just remote enough from any major city to prevent immediate reinforcements for the woefully limited transportation, health support services, security, and food and water available locally. What Lee didn't foresee was the resilience, decency, affability and generosity the invading hordes would bring along with them, virtues that would save this historic weekend from disaster.

She laughed again as always when Penny broke the postfire tension with her Lang imitation, the love-and-peace-and-money routine her friend had perfected by this point. But her experiences immediately prior to the weekend were causing her enormous concerns. Oh, great, she thought to herself, ribbing Penny for trying to put out the fire, the firemen aren't coming either. She already knew the cops were staying away.

The fact that the stage hadn't gone into construction until three weeks before the festival would be a problem. Lee would tense up every time she heard Lang say, It's fine. It's great. We're building. She was always the person to say, But . . . But . . . And everyone else would say, It's fine. She perfected a survivor's attitude: I am doing what I can do, and there isn't anything more I can do.

The organizers' ability simply to ride the wave amazed Lee, as sheer willpower and arrogance bulldozed through seemingly insurmountable odds. Water, electricity, food supplies, building materials—each one of these necessities had been secured and not a single one through the anticipated or routine methods. And each time Lee thought the final blow had fallen, the dumb luck of Lang and company turned defeat into triumph. Finally, though, in early August, she thought they hit an impasse that couldn't be circumvented with BS and positive thinking. Lee had traveled down to Manhattan with some of the security managers to interview New York City cops for the site force. Off-duty policemen, paid $50 a shift, were planned to bolster the nonprofessional staff of non-threatening "people managers" who would do the bulk of the security work. Picking the policemen for the job was like screening potential jurors, but Lee felt comfortable with the interviewing since she had dealt with cops during her work at New York rock clubs. She saw roughly five hundred New York City officers at the Fillmore East, asking them the same things: "What do you feel about hippies?" "About marijuana?" A surprising number of the city's finest expressed admiration for the festival's ideology and a personal interest in participating that went beyond the desire to make a few extra bucks. Lee came back with a list of names that promised a laid-back but competent peacekeeping and crowd-control force, a safety net for the chaos she saw pending. *At least when all hell breaks loose, there will be enough pros to keep order.*

In the end the screening was unnecessary: just days before the concert was to begin, permission for New York City personnel to participate in the Aquarian Exposition, even during their off-hours, was officially revoked. That left nothing but the undisciplined battalions of T-shirted kids who had signed on more or less as tour guides through this freak-show Disneyland. Faced with insufficient policing, Lee envisioned the worst: *When the state realizes the size of the crowd and if there isn't adequate security, the National Guard will be sent in.* Cops she had learned to respect: they used to fix parking tickets when she was working at the clubs downtown. But soldiers! Her own rupture with her Green Beret boyfriend intensified for her personally the animosity her whole generation had toward the military. *Imagine what would happen here if Army personnel showed up.*

I was much more concerned with soldiers than cops. In 1967 I met a man who was a Green Beret. It was a great passion, but not for a long time. I didn't know what a Green Beret was. Nor did I have a very high understanding of what was happening in Vietnam. He had already been there for two terms when I met him. He spoke Vietnamese fluently. And he killed "gooks"—whatever he called them. I didn't really get it at first, until he became more up-front with me about what he did and had been doing, about his dreams and his nightmares. He wanted me to get married and move with him to Laos! Eventually he joined the CIA. The more he talked about what was going on, the killing, he actually brought me to a new consciousness.

Determined to prevent the military from intervening, she used the interview list to put out feelers to the hippie-friendly cops to find out if any were willing to staff the event despite the ban. A loose underground network sprang up, but Lee was finding that the really desirable officers wouldn't break with the official ruling, and the cops who made themselves available turned out to be crooked. They were willing to ignore department rules, but only for almost double the price. Hired on the sly, they wanted $90 a shift and the money up front. Lee's admiration for cops disappeared as they reported for duty. With their gung-ho redneck politics, they reminded her of her Green Beret. And she worried how long it would take before one of these "peace officers" destroyed the peace they had been hired merely to oversee.

The final week before the festival was further marred by a growing mutinous rancor among the grunts whose unskilled labor was the major power source during the frenzied site preparation. By Thursday the pleasurable elements of the Woodstock venture had virtually disappeared for Rufus and the rest of the land crew, replaced by the fatigue each fourteen-hour day instilled. Chasing local skirts had decreased, and even bedding Hog Farm girls was reduced to a minimum. The torrential rains of that summer— eight inches were recorded in a single twenty-four-hour period the last week in July—aggravated the already back-breaking tasks of turning the cowfield into an amphitheater. And what Mother Nature didn't do to irritate the grunts, Michael Lang did. He became the focus and object of the Bastard Sons' anger, the butt of their jokes, and, as Rufus recalls, the release valve for their frustrations.

> Michael Lang was the most hated guy, he was a total asshole. We had very little to do with him, but we hated him. He was an elitist pig, and we were the little guys on the bottom. There was a fucking hierarchy a mile long. And we were the best of the bottom.

Despite the hard work and the lowly position he held in the hippie hierarchy, Rufus continued to enjoy the manly camaraderie he had discovered on the farm, though his colleagues couldn't have been worse examples of masculine fortitude. Surrounded by burn-outs and basket cases, Rufus still believed he was in a sweaty macho world where a diminutive city teen could prove his virility. He led the others in putdown sessions aimed at the more genteel groups of workers, the stage crew or the artsy Children of Light, a troupe of designers hired to turn a stand of woods into a crafts fairground. Eventually, Rufus found himself working for that troupe: Thursday he spent the day decorating the food concessions with Indian tapestries the designers ordered him to hang over wooden frames. But even that reversal—and the overall disdain shown him by the power elite—couldn't undo the new sense of potency swelling within him. When he heard the call "Fire" that Thursday night, he leaped at the opportunity to demonstrate the fierce new virility that had taken root inside his scrawny self.

Photographer Henry Diltz didn't share in the disdain Rufus felt for Lang and the rest of this egalitarian experiment's elite. Nor was he privy to the tribulations Lee and Penny witnessed every day. In fact, if there was a single person whose real experience in any way coincides with the peace-and-love mythology the PR for Woodstock promulgated, it would be Henry Diltz. Paid to observe and record, he passed through Thursday distanced from the panic and resentment by a lens. Frenzy settled in, and he drifted above it all. He remembers hippie carpenters banging away and describes Lang as "very much in control." He remembers long naked swims in the pools around the bowl in the company of Hog Farm commune members. He remembers sun-dappled Catskill days and star-filled nights. As with any mythology, there must have been an element of truth to the peaceable-kingdom image Woodstock presented: at least for Henry the final days leading up to the festival were every bit as loving and joyful as the weekend itself was promised to be.

> Behind the stage there was a lake and everyone would go nude swimming. They were really like gypsies. All these ladies with their little naked kids, that's how they were used to it. Suntanned. Ladies had all kinds of beautiful-colored cloths wrapped around them. It seemed to me this seemed right, on the natch. What was a hippie anyway? Let's get back to nature. I felt that too.
>
> I remember riding down there. And they all took off their clothes and went swimming in the pond. Then I got out and went up to the wharf and started taking photos and nobody cared. And I took this one beautiful photo of one girl kind of bobbing around in the water with lily pads. Looked like a pre-Raphaelite painting. Little water nymphs. Then I took a series of pictures of one lady who was very, very pregnant, and she had a little brown-skinned child, maybe three years old. He had kinky hair, and a coffee-with-cream color. This was her son. She was blonde, Scandinavian-looking. She was sitting on this weathered wharf, and in this first picture she's reaching down to the water, grabbing the hand. Next picture she's pulled him up. And in the third he's sitting next to her. It's a beautiful series of pictures.

If the delirium of putting on a show had temporarily blinded the Woodstock team from the stunning reality of half a million bodies, Sullivan County residents suffered from no such delusions of a grand old time. By Thursday, the naysayers around Bethel saw their worst fears materialize into an unrelenting stream of longhairs who clogged the country roads, trampled through unharvested fields of corn, and ransacked porch-front stores for bread, beer and Hostess cupcakes. By midday August 14, the two lanes of 17B—the main access road into Yasgur's farm—had locked into an impassable four-car-wide steel-and-chrome wall, blocking all vehicular movement from White Lake to the main intersection with 17 and the goods and services in Monticello beyond. Pies were being baked up and down Sullivan County for the fair in Grahamsville that Saturday—would anybody be able to get there? The same fire trucks that had been prevented from rushing to the Diamond Horseshoe would be kept from attending any other emergencies that weekend, as would any ambulance that might have been needed. The residents of the hamlets around Yasgur's land felt trapped.

Resentment caught on early. Opportunists were already preying upon the unprepared kids, charging a dollar for a slurp of hose water, more than that for a raw tomato from a garden. On the highways, cops were hassling hippie travelers, arresting more than a hundred kids wending their way upstate, for minor drug infractions. But by equal measure, county locals were themselves preyed upon. A preacher went down into the basement of his church on 17B one morning, only to find the cellar turned into an impromptu commune, complete with naked cohabitants. A farmer whose land bordered Yasgur's crawling acres couldn't believe his eyes when he found a hippie girl riding his cow— without a blouse. An elderly resident nearly fainted when she stumbled upon a young man using her backyard rose patch as a toilet.

Former town supervisor George Neuhaus took a secret delight in the disruption, even though he himself was personally put out by the congestion. The traffic made his regular visit to his aging mother impossible. But he was far more outraged at the corruption he suspected had permitted this clearly illegal event to bypass the laws and courts. Earlier that week he had been approached by young men whose scruffy looks immediately linked them, in his mind, with the disorganized organizers. They offered him money to lobby for the Ventures interests now that the event was going to go ahead as planned anyway. He felt a moral superiority to his turncoat fellow townsmen when he shooed the hippie palm-greasers off his land. But his satisfaction with the way things were turning out grew out of his keen political ambition as much as indignation: the more disastrous this weekend turned out, the more assured his return to office that November. Every cornstalk uprooted, every lawn pissed on was another plank in the platform he stood silently building for himself Thursday night.

As the crowds grew ever thicker Thursday, even those townsfolk who had been intrigued enough by the novelty of the event to support it experienced profound doubt. A few weeks earlier a local chamber of commerce had actually voted to back the festival, citing the economic advantage the otherwise depressed area stood to gain by it. So far that summer the only financial boost in the area had come from the newly renovated racetrack at Monticello, where a revamped lighting system made day and night betting a reality. Still, the region's primary resort business was in a slump. Despite the clear economic needs of the area, the influx of psychedelic bucks dismayed loyalists as well as long-standing adversaries. Thursday found few Woodstock supporters left among the once divided populace—at their forefront, however, stood Anne and Burt Feldman, delighted witnesses to the dawning of the Age of Aquarius.

Burt's first half-week working on the security detail had already produced its share of counterculture revelations, all of which he brought home to share with Anne. Typically, he tried to make the job sound important and demanding, but his wife saw through this immediately. After all, what kind of security could there be at an event this massive and this disorganized? And during this heyday for anarchy, what sort of authority could bumbling Burt Feldman hope to wield? An incident that morning had under-scored the absurdity of his position. Assigned to keep hippies off some heavy equipment, Burt asked a pair of young ladies to stop playing on a tractor. City kids fascinated by the machinery, the girls had devised a game that involved throwing themselves off the engine casing onto a pile of hay below. Using the paternalistic logic he practiced on his own two daughters, Burt explained the dan-gers: because their blouses were loose-fitting, a sleeve might catch on a strut or prong and yank their arms. This benign approach, he figured, would meet with better results than a hard-line do-what-you're-told directive. But his tactic was couched in establishment think, as ineffective in the face of new-age reasoning as traditional law and order would prove unnecessary in the ensuing weekend. The two girls, unfettered by the cultural restraints that boxed in Burt's logic, just stripped off the risky tops and continued to play, braless and unencumbered. Burt shuffled away silenced and amazed.

Back home that night he marveled with Anne at the freedom the kids exhibited, an openness that made their own unorthodox living seem Republican. The fact that members of their community were thwarting this good time convinced them they had to do all they could during the weekend to help out. Neighbors had warned Anne against keeping the hose out and visible to the roaming festivalgoers during the day. The road in front of their houses was still free of abandoned cars, but any kindness extended to the Woodstock barbarians, she was told, would just attract problems. Instead of heeding their cautions, Burt and Anne decided to make an all-night kiosk of their lawn. First they set up a folding table and brought out all the baked goods they could find. To make sure the kids and not animals got the food, they put the breads and what sandwich makings they had in tins and plastic containers. They hooked the hose to the table and even put out paper cups. Then, as a beacon to passersby—and a goad to the whispering neighbors—they hung an extra-bright bulb from a nearby tree to illuminate the oasis. "As a result, not only did I get a lot of awfully nice young people, but this road was policed from the top of that hill to the bottom of that other one," said Anne.

Local politics, backstage anxieties, upstate parochialism set on its ear, rock business double-dealing run amok—the kids who flocked to Woodstock knew nothing of the behind-the-scenes dramas in Bethel. They knew only what the promoters had worked overtime to communicate to them: the Woodstock Music and Art Fair: An Aquarian Exposition was the must-attend event of the decade. There were political implications to the gathering, proof to a disbelieving world that the new generation's lifestyle worked. But behind the rhetoric was the irrefutable magic of sex, drugs, rock and roll: the weekend would be the most phenomenal blast in history. The notion that Woodstock was going to be a big deal helped make it a big deal: you went because everybody else was going. It is remembered now for its magnitude, but even before it happened the anticipated size was what made it irresistible. Like a supernova, it generated its own gravity, tugging and pulling America's youth into its force field. But despite its mass, the significance of Woodstock lay in how it served each kid's needs in a unique way. It was the giant Rorschach test of the time, an event filling the specific, very personal dreams of the thousands who went. That Thursday, in overcrowded cars, in Day-Glo buses, on Harleys, on foot, kids embarked on an odyssey the media would see only as a mass migration. For each traveler, though, the road to Woodstock was a personal voyage of self-discovery.

For Scott Lane, the trip was short: some fifty miles between his home in Spring Valley and the Catskills. Spontaneity governed the life of the nineteen-year-old. Holding down a part-time summer job at a local pharmacy presented him with just about all the responsibility he wanted or could handle. He directed the bulk of his energy in the pursuit of good times: ladies, drugs and music. The festival upstate promised healthy amounts of all three; he decided to go the minute he heard about it.

That didn't mean, of course, that he was ready to depart when his buddy Barry showed up at the bar they frequented that Wednesday night, car running, pointing north. Scott had figured he'd just hop a ride with somebody the next day, since everybody he hung around with was planning on going. But with the simple impromptu decision-making by which he made all his moves, he ran out to the parking lot without so much as a jacket and said, Let's go. After all, in the past he had left for Los Angeles with scarcely any more elaborate planning. Scott didn't pack a toothbrush, a sweater or even a wallet when he traveled: he carried his wits and his charm. They had served him well before. Confident of his ability to make out successfully in any new situation by pluck—and chicanery if need be—Scott was an unabashed opportunist.

Although Scott took off for the country without so much as a sweatshirt, he had made sure his buddy took along some provisions. According to Scott's recollection Barry had nine ounces of hash, forty-five tabs of acid, some Lebanese pot, enough mind-expanding substance for their own use, with leftovers for spot sales. They weren't dealers per se, but they never passed up a perfect market opening either. It would be very cool to possess that amount of drugs at the festival, but dangerous to transport it. Anticipating possible harassment from the police en route to the festival, Barry showed Scott a foolproof method of smuggling contraband. Trunk, glove compartment and even the space under the backseat were all known stash places. Barry unscrewed the headlight lamp of the car and stuffed the bags and envelopes between the heavy wires.

Barry and Scott got up to Bethel late Wednesday night, when 17B had yet to back up and access to the farm was clear. They slept in the car. When they woke the next day, through the woods and adjoining farmland the flow onto the performance field was well under way. Realizing that no tickets were being collected and that in fact he had walked freely across the bowl without ever passing through a gate, Scott circulated among the festivalgoers already firmly ensconced in the field, asking if he could have the tickets they wouldn't be needing. He was going to make a collage, he explained. Many told him to drop dead, but others were convinced enough of his artistic bent and that the event would be free, and turned them over. When he had about a dozen, he left the farm and walked out beyond the festival site to the road where newcomers who had abandoned their cars miles away were arriving. Offering the tickets for a reduced rate of $10 for all three days, he quickly sold them to people who hadn't yet seen the gateless grass amphitheater. With a duplicity he labels honor, the born *macher* sold the tickets only to those he took for squares, weekend hippies who in his eyes merited the fleecing. The accepted disdain his peers held for money legitimized Scott's money-making schemes. Having left Spring Valley Wednesday night penniless, by Thursday afternoon Scott was carrying $120.

At about the same time, Elen Orson arrived at the small dude ranch in Swan Lake where the Woodstock documentary film crew was staying. She checked into her room—and never saw it again.

If Scott's trip to Woodstock typified the come-as-you-are nonchalance of many festival participants, Elen's getting there represented the other extreme: the last forty-eight hours had been a hectic, exciting, breakneck dash that amounted to fantasy come true. All week long in the Manhattan production facilities where she worked, the craziness that had taken root upstate was re-created. For the last few weeks she'd known that her bosses, Michael Wadleigh and Bob Maurice, were negotiating for the film rights to the festival. And when, that Monday, the deal had been finalized, everyone—except lowly editorial assistant Elen—was drawn into the frenzy of preparation such an enormous location shoot would take. Insurance needed to be arranged overnight, miles of raw footage had to be found. And staffing—this shoot would require everyone on the payroll to drop everything and head up to Sullivan County pronto.

The idea to film the weekend not for posterity but for a future movie release had been a part of the plan all along. A popular documentary of the 1967 Monterey Pop Festival proved that audiences were willing to buy tickets for a filmed concert, if the primary event drew enough attention when it happened. Woodstock had been created as a media event, so certainly it qualified as movie-worthy. Still, no money interests could be found to back the filming, and the major studios were unwilling to purchase distribution rights for a movie of a festival that rumor indicated might never even occur. In a late desperation move, a deal was struck with Wadleigh-Maurice, a virtually unknown company with only a few documentaries to its credit. Necessity was destiny for the producers—and for their lowliest employee.

> Three days before the show, which is about three days after I started to work for the team, they got some kind of agreement from Warner Brothers. In three days they put the whole show together. They got film stock, the crews, the insurance, the trucks, the typewriters. And they got me. I was feeling miserable that I was working with people who were actually going to go.

And then my phone rings, and it's Thelma Schoonmaker, the editor. And she says, "Look we're up here at the site and we're trying to put together the crew. Maybe you might want to do it. We'll pay your way, we'll get you a hotel room. We don't know if we can pay you anything." So I got up there.

The scene at the bungalow colony reserved for the crew immediately communicated to the seventeen-year-old the chaos that would characterize her weekend. But just as the chaos among the festival organizers had presented Lee and Penny with learning experiences, so, too, would the unpreparedness of the film crew open up opportunities for Elen. It was still unclear what role she was to play, but given her youth and the fact that she was new to the company, she assumed she would find herself in the office pushing papers, ordering food. She hoped that every once in a while during a lapse she'd be able to dash off to the concert site and catch a few performances. Her skills, especially in location filming, probably were superior to those of many of the designated production assistants. The two summers working with the French filmmaker had taught her how to move quickly through agitated crowds, how to second-guess the cameraman's needs, and how to react to an ever-changing environment. But here, on this professional shoot, with so much riding on capturing the right image even as it disappeared, she would never be given the chance to demonstrate those skills. Besides, being production assistant was a man's job: it involved lugging heavy magazines of raw footage to wherever your cameraman wandered. Once you tracked him down you exchanged the new magazine for the used one in his camera, hauled that one back to the production facility, and began the process over again. The usually back-breaking work was going to be even more difficult at Woodstock. Aside from the crowds, which would make transport difficult, several cameramen were to be assigned to the eighty-foot sound towers to record aerial shots. The production assistants who drew that assignment would have the additional strain of lugging two fifteen-pound magazines up the shaky skeleton of the towers.

A meeting was called Thursday afternoon, a last-minute reconnoitering before the big day. Elen listened as the drill was run: it still wasn't clear which groups were going to appear and in what order and when, so there would be no running schedule to follow. It still wasn't certain which groups had given the go-ahead for filming—another uncertainty. The weather report looked dismal, and there could be hazards with the electrical photographic equipment if wet. Also, if a storm blew, the towers could sway. Access to and from the site had already become nearly impossible. The list of cautions and warnings went on and on, Elen half listening, thinking the office staff would not be involved in the excitement and risks of coverage. Then suddenly she heard the guy with the clipboard say, Okay, we need camera assistants.

She raised her hand, and no one even blinked. If she could load a magazine she had the job. Within minutes she was hustled aside by a middle-aged hippie cameraman with whom she'd be working Friday. On the towers. We'll be doing lots of crowd reactions, but also stage stuff, he told her. She was ecstatic. Just a week earlier she had assumed that because a boyfriend couldn't take her she wouldn't be going to Woodstock. Here it was, the day before the concert began, and not only had she gotten to the festival on her own, she had landed a job traditionally reserved for young men. Tomorrow, the towers.

Bill Pelligrini was watching as the final feet of scaffolding for those towers went up that afternoon, giant manmade outcroppings against the verdant natural landscape. Around him pot smoke from the crowd was beginning to drift into a deliciously ripe cloud over the field, which by Friday would wear a halo of marijuana smog so thick you could get high just by breathing. Perhaps slightly buzzed already, the nineteen-year-old high school dropout grew philosophical. High tech serving the needs of the people, electricity facilitating this ultimate back-to-the-land happening, capitalism funding the dreams of his brethren. The sun glinted off the tower into the young man's eyes, which were lost in a vision on which he could not yet quite focus. He was miles away from the street life of the Bowery, and sensed his future was quite close.

Bill had arrived from the Atlantic City musical weekend about ten days earlier, joining the ever-widening circle of hangers-on that the activity in Bethel was drawing. Like day laborers during the Depression, young people would wait near the Ventures offices prepared to head off into the fields on a minute's notice if work came up. After the panhandling months on the Bowery and then the cramped work in Greg's crafts loft, he heartily embraced the outdoor work available on the site. Bill spent a few days on an ad hoc security detail, assigned like Burt Feldman to keep hippies off heavy equipment. Another day he was handed trash bags and told to clean up an area that would be used later for parking. Although he doesn't remember being paid for his time, Bill enjoyed participating in this work force of young, like-minded people. After a high school career in which every day of class drove him further into isolation, he thrived on the casual camaraderie of Woodstock. Rather than alienate him, his long hair and hippie affectations provided him access to those around him. All his life he had associated work with soul-numbing drudgery: his mother had been a waitress, his father cut hair. Like many of his generation, he had hopes that somehow he'd find work he believed in. Up until now his only real experience had been in Greg's attic. Here he was witnessing a massive enterprise that married good old-fashioned perspiration with counterculture values. It didn't occur to him, as it did to Penny and Lee, that all the flower-child talk in the world wouldn't undo the shifty, unethical and just plain incompetent economics behind this project.

> Already the spirit of Woodstock was affecting people. No bad moods, no grumps. People were just very loose. A guy came with a clipboard and wrote your name down on a badge, a little cardboard badge, and you were working for the festival. Then the clipboard would get lost. We're not talking the U.S. Army here. We were supposed to get paid after the festival, but the shit hit the fan and they didn't ask anybody for tickets. I thought, How can I ask for wages, then?

Thursday would be Bill's last day working with the staff; Friday he was expecting Greg, who would be setting up his small crafts

stand in the exposition area. Although most people think of the
concert portion of the weekend, in conjunction with the musical
entertainment a large fair was set up in the wooded areas surrounding the amphitheater. Great care had been directed in the
design and construction of the booths to be operated there, since
no taint of exploitation was to creep into this money-changing
center. All building was compatible with the natural sylvan karma
the event was to embody. Another entire performance area, ironically designated "the free stage," was built with the expectation of
an overflow crowd which would still need to be entertained. The
Hog Farm compound Henry Diltz had discovered and fallen in love
with during the weeks leading up to the festival stood in the
middle of this tie-dye and macrame bazaar. A puppet theater, a
playground for hippie kids of all ages, an information center:
Yasgur's woods teamed with Aquarian diversions. Native Americans, imported from the Southwest for "authenticity," were
installed just across the road from the stage; with their rough-
hewn expertise they had already built a small village. Dominating
the area, however, were head shops, craft booths and art stands,
each an example of the same hippie enterprise that on a much
grander scale had created the festival itself. Bill wandered among
them, absorbing the atmosphere hungrily. The ingenuity he
detected here impressed him. On one counter lay paraphernalia
bags created from red, white and blue burlap potato sacks, a
technique Anne Feldman had seen and marveled at weeks earlier.
Drug booths were in abundance, but Bill inspected with greater
admiration the down-to-earth crafts of smiling, content young
people. Here at the fair even more than on the field, he felt there
was a community he could connect with.

> It wasn't billed as a concert, it was billed as an Aquarian Exhibi-
> tion. There were booths being constructed for incense and
> leather goods in the woods. It was real peaceful in there with a
> dapply pine kind of light. They had goats and they were building
> structures without a single nail. This whole gymnasium thing,
> that might still be there today. And they moved a rock and carved

a hole in the middle, and just suspended it. It was a mysterious object and I didn't question it. I just went and said, "Wow." I was like a newborn baby there.

The purity of self-sufficient manual labor—presented to him in the rusticity and arboreal light of these transformed woods—struck a chord. A bearded man, about twenty-five, with strong, proficient hands, used tools Bill had never seen to create a moccasin out of an animal skin. A pregnant woman, sitting with her legs extended in front of her, wove a shawl with a sunset pattern on a device he didn't recognize. On that Thursday evening Bill began to come to terms with a reality his entire generation would grapple with as it moved into the 1970s: How does one coexist with capitalism without compromising one's values? The air was heavy with incense and the loamy smell of country night, and Bill wondered if money could ever smell this good.

Out on the highways, the migration to Woodstock hit full force. As far downstate as the Tappan Zee Bridge, which crossed the Hudson and connected the metropolitan area with northern counties, normal rush-hour congestion gnarled into even tighter knots, aggravated by the pilgrimage to the country. Dr. Paul D'Amico expected a smooth, uninterrupted drive back to Livingston Manor when he set out from Manhattan at six that evening. When he began to hit snarls at the Tappan Zee Bridge, he knew something unusual was up. The customary two and a half hours required for the entire ride got him no farther than halfway. "I remember I was coming from New York City when that festival started. I thought, 'Where in the hell is all this traffic going?' "

It's possible D'Amico was the only man in America who at that point was not aware the center of the universe had shifted to Bethel. For others heading to the festival, traffic started much earlier—and was welcomed as proof positive they were indeed heading to an event of preternatural significance. Ron Stone, who had to convince a friend that the festival would be a once-in-a-lifetime thing, remembers seeing Woodstock-bound cars and getting charged up:

> Thursday night I ran into Georgetown to get the tickets; there was some question about whether or not we'd be able to get them. Paid this outrageous amount, fifteen dollars apiece, for them. An ungodly amount of money for students.
>
> We left and drove up the parkway. I remember the first stop was one of those islands in Delaware or lower Jersey, a lot of cars were there, it was midnight. We met other people our age driving up. "Going to Woodstock? Oh, it's going to be a great festival." They told us it was in Bethel not Woodstock. They were coming from North Carolina or something. That was important: it confirmed the fact that an event was happening. I had sold my friends on the fact that an event was happening; they just believed I knew where the action was. They just took my word for it, and got ready to spend the weekend in the middle of nowhere in New York.
>
> By the time we got near the site, both lanes of the highway were filled with cars going north, so we had to go on the shoulder. Then a police car got right in front of us with the light going and siren, so we just followed it. It looked like a mess, but to me that's where I wanted to be. Where the action was.

All along northeastern roads, encounter among those going to the festival reinforced their sense of the greatness ahead. Many experienced in advance the magical oneness that awaited them on the field. The sixties was a time of enormous mobility for the young: gas was cheap, hitchhiking was considered a most respectable and dependable transportation alternative. Being on the road had mystical meaning for the sensation-craving generation. Add to that ongoing romance of movement the element of quest inherent in the Woodstock journey, and the trip this Thursday amounted to a peak experience.

Susie Kaufman left Morristown in a surge of external enthusiasm, and the high from the drive to Bethel suppressed whatever internal confusion she felt about herself for the moment. Accompanied by three male friends, she embraced the weekend as a chance to escape the confines of her small town, where rumors and doubts about her rape lingered. Encouraged by her psychiatrist, the young woman was intent on leaving herself open to the images and impressions she would encounter. Like so many others, the experiences started with the journey to the farm.

As you got up there all you saw was more and more hippies, wherever you looked. I had never seen so many hippies. And I was a hippie. I had long straight hair all the way down my back. It just got more and more exciting. Less straight people and more people like us.

We stopped in a town up there somewhere. I was friendly with the locals, ladies who wore housedresses. If they didn't respond, I'd drop it. It was a little uncomfortable the way the villagers looked at us. I was not wearing a bra. There were hippies all over the place. I was wearing jeans and a nice purple shirt. No big deal. There were people nodding their head negatively. Others who brought out garden hoses for us to drink from, the kind of thing my mother would have done.

We ended up parking three miles away from the site. By the time we got to the concert, the fences were already broken down and I was disappointed because I had spent all this money and they didn't want the ticket. What a gyp! I paid for this and everyone else was getting in.

One of the biggest problems, besides the traffic, was the confusion over the actual site for the festival. Everyone was calling the thing Woodstock, so off to Woodstock, New York, headed thousands, much to the dismay of that town's residents. "The Aquarian Exposition presented by the Woodstock Music and Art Fair has nothing to do with Woodstock, N.Y. Neither the fair nor the business office is located here," reported the *Ulster County Townsman* that July. Earlier, the local paper had carried endless series of stories fretting about "the hippy problem." "During the day and into the night, they sit everywhere. Our citizens are afraid to go shopping in the village, and our children are intimidated or corrupted by them. The flood continues and will grow, detracting from our lovely town." By the time the August festival rolled around, Woodstock's titular connection with the event in Bethel was a thorn in the community's side. One boy, part of the horde passing through Woodstock Thursday expecting to find the promised land, was even arrested for trespass. Instead of posting a fine, the local magistrate consigned him to the Ulster County Jail.

By the thousands the children of the sixties drove on in the night. August 14 slipped into August 15, Yasgur's acres set the stage for as many stories as there were souls in the field. It was Day One of the Woodstock Music and Art Fair, which had been under way for a good twenty-four hours already.

FRIDAY

W HAT HE saw below him that bright Friday morning as the helicopter swung lower over the green field blew John Sebastian away. The reports had been legitimate, the accounts on TV and in the papers hadn't exaggerated. The crowd estimates varied, the traffic bulletins differed—here he was witnessing it firsthand, from a privileged bird's-eye view. It was Wonderland, Oz. Like a gigantic cradle full of sleeping children, a colorful ocean of bodies in repose stretched out forever down there on the sun-drenched grass. Thousands of lovers coupled in sloppy camp gear, thousands of hippies just waking to the insistent buzz of the chopper, thousands of music devotees willingly waiting for the concert to start—an audience like none he'd ever dreamed of.

And yet it was no audience for him, for the singer had flown to the farm concert that steamy August morning not as a performer but as an observer, a fan, a face in the crowd. The call to commune had gone out to the famous and the anonymous alike, and like so many others he felt compelled to respond. The organizers hadn't ever put a feeler out to him for a slot on the program; still, Sebastian wanted to be part of this event. But as the helicopter hovered for a moment—waiting for another shuttle copter to clear—the former Lovin' Spoonful heartthrob must have felt a bitter pinch of regret. Provided aerial access to Woodstock because of his past connections to the rock mainstream, he was to be denied, he thought, the unique experience of performing here himself. He could attend this gathering, but his absence from the roster of billed acts suggested his own moment had passed. Simply "being there" would be painful. The helicopter touched down on the makeshift plot behind the stage—and all around him he saw the show biz frenzy he loved. He got out, immediately greeted roadies, techies and managers he knew, and gamely emulated the upbeat attitude permeating the area. Behind him the behemoth stage stood, a wall. Like so many of his fellow Woodstock initiates, Sebastian couldn't have imagined at that point the surprises and revelations this simple weekend in the country would serve up. The reports had been true, he thought to himself. Anything can happen here.

Although the backstage area was teeming with activity, there was a noticeable and disturbing absence of one rather crucial ingredient: rock-and-roll stars. It was noon of Day One, and a record-breaking crowd of youngsters were waiting for their minds to be blown with music. The same helicopter pad on which Sebastian's chopper landed awaited the arrival of any one of the half-dozen acts scheduled to appear that day beginning at four. According to the official program—there actually was a playbill of sorts available—the opening night's folk-inspired roster was to include Joan Baez, Arlo Guthrie, Tim Hardin, Richie Havens, the Incredible String Band, Ravi Shankar, Bert Sommer and Sweetwater. None had yet reported in. And with the traffic conditions worsening, concern mounted over the possibility that somewhere out on the highway, caravans full of guitars and stars stood immobile. Country Joe McDonald was already backstage, but he wasn't scheduled to go on until Sunday! As the day went on, however, all arrangements went out the window, replaced by the simple show biz rule of the day—whoever is ready goes on next.

Despite the confusion and anxiety—or maybe because of it— Sebastian immediately felt comfortable among the rock professionals. He recalls an egalitarian environment in which everyone pitched in, a universe of harmony among the workers that paralleled the overlapping circles of peace establishing themselves on the field. If his musical expertise wasn't going to be of any use here, he would make at least some contribution.

> I ended up backstage in short order mainly because I knew everybody, these were all my contemporaries, people I had played with, hung out with, sat around tables smoking dope with. I knew everybody in that backstage area. This was not like TV talk shows, where all the people have to pretend they know each other. This was absolutely a community. And it was a community that had endured some difficulties together, not going to war, or any of the enormous traumas that draw people together. Simply the traumas of being on the road together, and experiencing the oppressions for having long hair in the era before it was fashionable and accepted. I felt very much at one with the whole group.
>
> I was quickly given all the passes I would ever need, and started wandering around backstage. Everyone was coping simultaneously with the fact that it had become or was about to become a free festival. The mechanics about getting people on and off the stage had been thought about, in an attempt to make this all logical, but it was a monumental task. So all those who weren't onstage found themselves helping with food or helping with lodging, helping any way they could.
>
> I wandered around and found an eight-by-eight Volkswagen bus tent that had become a dressing room. I felt like I was right at home. I swept out the tent and began to batten it down a little bit. It had been put up very fast and people obviously had bounced around inside of it a little bit and shaken its moorings. So I started to fasten it down and Chip Monk came along at one point, and the famous voice of Woodstock says, "Geez, you know

about this." And I said, "Well, I have been living in a tent just like this for the last couple of months." He said, "Terrific, you're in charge of this tent." I said okay.

The entire Incredible String Band put all their instruments inside. Now the Incredible String Band, if you recall, was an all-acoustic band when electricity was becoming really the main menu for musicians of this type. So they had an oud and a twelve-string, and a sitar, and mandolins, and banjos, everything is there in the open. Here we're hiding this stuff in the extremities of the tent so none of the moisture would get in. There we were the first night.

It was still early, so I decided, I'll make a circle around that crowd . . . just to see what's going on. It was a long walk, took three hours. I wandered up into the wooded area where there was a jungle-gym area, various craftspeople had set up their little worlds. Incredibly magical to wander through this area and see the various factions of this community of souls who had come together.

I was not recognized at all.

In addition to the talent hassles, the organizers were confronted with a barrage of unexpected problems, all of which required immediate solution. Feeding the fans was one—although the Hog Farm free kitchen was handling that for the moment. Feeding the crew backstage was another. During the planning stages, it was assumed the staff would continue to use Diamond Horseshoe as their base. But with the traffic conditions, trips back and forth to the site would be impossible. Before leaving the Diamond Horseshoe Friday morning, the stink from the previous night's fire still pungent, Penny asked the bosses about making arrangements to transport supplies to the site. Her Cassandra's warnings were dismissed by the more seasoned concert organizers, who asked her how many festivals she had run. We'll manage, she was summarily told. All the provisions she had stockpiled for the weekend stayed in the Horseshoe pantry—where no one was able to get to them again.

Lee's foresight was better heeded. Having realized early that morning that helicopter transport in and out of the site was going to become the festival's lifeline, she got on the horn and began a frantic search for extra choppers. Up and down the Hudson Valley she called, looking for anything with a propeller. She located a half-dozen through aviation schools in the adjoining counties, and with that problem solved moved on to monitoring the tides of shifty security personnel. Over the radio, she heard DJs warning people not to head up to Woodstock, to turn around and go back home. The phrase "disaster area" kept cropping up, and all she kept thinking about was the National Guard. One military uniform and this powder keg might explode.

For both Lee and Penny, the opening day of the concert brought a sickening awareness of how tentative a peace reigned at Woodstock. Aware of the sloppy calculations, improvised construction and fudged figures, they walked to the site that morning with a sense of profound dread. How would they ever justify the frivolity of the last few months, if this volcano exploded? And yet they were just bit players in a comedy their actions couldn't prevent from becoming a tragedy. Penny recalls:

> We were all afraid that many people were going to be killed. Someone said it looked like the scene from *Gone With the Wind* with all the bodies. I can't tell you how frightened we were. This was really a jerry-built operation. The stage was sinking every day. I was afraid to go on the freight elevator onto the stage. It plummeted down. It was hair-raising. The main electric terminal by our trailer was so alive you had to jump into the trailer, not touching any of the metal steps. According to the electricians thousands of people could have gotten electrocuted. Maybe they were trying to scare me, maybe they were being melodramatic. All I know is, once I stepped by accident on the step and I was thrown on my back.

The morning sun streamed down on the Woodstock Nation, the newly formed independent state whose constitution was a shared state of mind. Its motto: Do your own thing. It's bill of rights: Sha-na-na-na, live for today. With a glorious Catskill setting for a playground, the assembled multitude easily managed to squelch whatever negative vibes circulated. Rumors that the concert would never start, that serious food and water shortages lay ahead, that crowd control might get ugly certainly persisted throughout the long afternoon. But it was simply too nice a day to worry about it. Getting off on the weather, the plentiful drugs and the proximity of so many like-minded freaks lifted the crowd of 500,000 to nirvana.

Nowhere was the delirious charm better captured than in the reed-framed ponds that dotted the farmland. Within walking distance of the now overheated field there were five different ponds, to which the hippies gravitated like otter cubs—taut young bodies, glistening, naked. Here was the freedom of spirit, the sensual delight, the lusty oneness with nature the generation celebrated. You shook off your pants, your bra, your tie-dyed T-shirt, and left behind you on the shore the small-mindedness of the establishment. In the cleansing waters uninhibited hedonism found its element. If somewhere uptight people were worrying about impending disaster, here sunburned butts were the major concern—although for some the very freedom that drew them to the pond created a problem.

For Justin Anthony, a seventeen-year-old high school gymnast, the situation at the pond was fraught with a whole new set of etiquette questions. He wandered over to the lakes with his older brother, and was torn between the responses years in the locker room had programmed into him and the proper Woodstock consciousness. The candor between the sexes he witnessed presented a heretofore unequaled learning experience.

> I remember going to the pond, where nobody was supposed to swim, and I remember being embarrassed, because I didn't know how to react to being seventeen and naked around all these girls. Might be real embarrassing. I think we left our shorts on. It's not like I had never been naked before, but being naked in a coed crowd! All different ages—mostly older. Most of the people were real relaxed about this thing. A year later I was too. But at this point in time it was uncomfortable. They weren't all ugly. It certainly would have been an embarrassing thing to have a boner right in the middle of this crowd. They'd all look at you.
>
> People were extremely outgoing. No distinction between older and younger. Even before the concert began, people were there to

really have a good time. I was a wide-eyed seventeen-year-old kid. Most of the people who showed up had been hippies for at least a couple of years. They came in their buses. This was stuff you only heard about before! Communes started to show up, made it all the way from California. It was hippieland. All these long-hairs, and no straights to hassle us.

The fact that swimming was prohibited in the ponds meant nothing to the sixties sprites convinced they had found the new Atlantis. Water belonged to the people, that was that. All this scenario needed to realize its potential as pastoral romance was a kindly old truant officer, whose vain efforts to enforce the no-bathing rules could produce comic relief. And who else to fit the bill more perfectly than well-intentioned, misdirected Burt Feldman. Again pulling a no-win assignment with the floundering security detail, Burt reluctantly meandered over to the ponds knowing full well his jurisdiction over the water nymphs would be negligible.

He headed toward Filippini Pond, one of the larger artificial lakes in the immediate area and one which because of its size had attracted the most flesh. He had been told by his fellow workers that skinny-dipping was the norm of the day and wasn't too surprised when he saw clusters of dripping hippies crossing the road that separated him from the pond.

Filippini Pond was a short way up from the crossroads, West Shore Road and Hurd Road. Filippini Pond is fairly extensive. An artificial pond. The deepest point in the whole pond is, I think, about four and a half feet. To be generous, five in the dead center, but I doubt it. I hear twelve thousand at a time were bathing there. It could be, as I said it's shallow, but extensive. And everybody went skinny-dipping, because it was an awful hot day. Muggy. There's a boat rental for fishing there. Boats were dispensed at a two-story building, a very small building. On the second floor, there was a balcony, where the livery man, the man who rented the boats, could stand and survey the lake. This was his job. It so happened the man's name was Ben Leon, and he was over ninety. It did not require anybody spry. All they had to do was sign the boat out and generally keep their eye on it from this little porch or balcony on the second floor. Here was this damned old fool, and this I can remember so vividly. He was on that damned porch with a gigantic pair of Navy binoculars, they must have been the kind you scan for submarines. I didn't think the old fool had enough strength to lift them. I could hear him quite a distance away. "Heee, hooo. Haaah." He was having himself a time. I think he was ninety-two, if I remember correctly.

At about the same time, Burt's wife, Anne, was also smiling: a dopey, unexplainable, wide grin her two kids couldn't understand. They couldn't have known what she was so happy about, since Anne herself didn't understand why she was feeling so sensational. This was, after all, the first time the Bethel housewife and mother had gotten stoned.

Given the hassles of the day, there had been no reason for Anne to experience such elation. Although the whole world seemed to be revolving around that damn festival up the road, that's not what her two daughters cared about. Friday was the last day of summer playground, the day for the season's-end swimming contests. At Yasgur's fiasco, sanitation and security might be the worries of the hour; here at the Feldmans' the backstroke still held sway. Anne checked the folding table with the goodies in front of her house, rounded the two girls into her four-wheel-drive jeep, and headed off for playschool.

Situated on the shores of White Lake, not yet invaded by the marauding nudists, the girls' summer camp was easy to get to despite the traffic. The jeep traveled the back roads not yet clogged with abandoned cars. Anne deposited the two girls at camp and decided to kill the few hours before they were dismissed with an excursion to the local supermarket for more sandwich makings. While she was there, neighbors gathered around and of course the discussion focused exclusively on the ruination of their town by the hippie invasion. Anne, having had no problem getting around that morning, retorted, perhaps too loudly, that she knew the back roads, knew how to come and go without hitting traffic. After leaving the store, she soon realized a motorcade of buses and

motorbikes were following her, incorrectly assuming she was heading to the festival via a secret path.

Even with her mastery of the back roads, the trip back to her
kids' camp took two hours longer than she anticipated. She
arrived, trailing a caravan of scruffy tag-alongs, to find her daughters shaking on the beach. By this time the Woodstock skinny-
dippers had located this bit of prime Catskill waterfront, and
Anne's nine- and eleven-year-olds were taking none of the delight
old Ben Leon had in the show. And when they saw their mother
arrive with the love parade behind her, they thought life as they
had known it was over. Assuring them she hadn't converted, she
was reluctant to expose the two kids to the freak show of the
festival proper. But Anne had no choice now, delayed as she was.
She had told Burt she would pick him up near Filippini Pond at
three, and it was close to that now.

> I had absolutely no trouble getting to where he was. Took old
> back roads nobody knew about. But there was a blockage, just at
> the crossroads of West Shore Drive and Hurd Road—just people
> on the road. So we stopped, and I said, "I wonder what that
> sweet smell is?" It was just about nose level if you were sitting in a
> jeep, which of course I was. And my eleven-year-old said, "Well,
> Mommy, that's pot." And I said, "How would you know about
> that?" And she said, "That's what the kids in school said it was."
>
> If I had just been standing flat on the ground the cloud would
> have been over my head. But it was about seven feet up, and so
> was I. I had no idea what was happening to me. I was feeling no
> pain. Everything was the funniest thing in the world. The kids
> were under it, I was the one getting it all. It was great.

Anne's contact high gently nudged her into the fuzzy edges of
another dimension to which many here were going to abandon
themselves entirely. Once she drove out of the cloud, her mystery
euphoria quickly dissipated. But for many others, Friday signaled
the beginning of a weekend-long drug binge. The cloud of
exhalant covering the field formed a visible canopy. Under it, the
hearty partied—and the not-so-hearty tried to cope.

Scott Lane's psychedelic headlight amounted to a pinhead fraction of the illegal goods that found their way into the festival area. In the woods, tailgate salesmen offered the widest array of mind expanders conceivable, openly and without interference from security. Pharmacological exotica competed with everyday pot in a market where clearly the buyer was given choice. Even if you didn't want to buy anything, hippie courtesy demanded that those who had, shared. If you stood in one place long enough somebody would pass something to you. In such an uncontrolled environment, controlled-substance bummers were frequent. Bad-trip cases started to pile up, and neither the Hog Farm nor the inadequately staffed infirmary could handle them all. By Friday afternoon an auxiliary hospital was set up in a school gymnasium with 150 beds, and a call was put out to local physicians for volunteers. Dr. Paul D'Amico heard the request and agreed to a shift Saturday.

Anne and Burt were both surprised at the drug use, but shock at its extent wasn't limited to the "square" locals. Among the young-sters in the crowd, the generation that had grown up with drugs, the amount and type of drug use were perceived as worrisome by many. Hardly anyone in the crowd objected to pot and its mild high, but harsher drugs were common too. Kids who had been long-standing potheads were suddenly shocked by the prevalence of amphetamines, psychedelics and downers. Media reports tended to universalize the acceptance of the drugs by the kids, but indeed discomfort with the effects drugs were having on the crowd became a major worry for some. And among the closest of friends, differing drug habits became a point of friction.

Ron Stone felt discredited by the catatonic revelers around him. He had convinced his buddies from Washington that Woodstock would be a major political event. In fact, the mass law-breaking the dope smoking amounted to could be considered an implicit politi-cal statement. Ron didn't see it that way. Instead of consciousness raising, all the former page and lobbyist saw was brain frying, with everyone acting like a juiced-up addict. Virtually naive about drugs himself, he was not so much threatened by the excess as disappointed in his peers.

The drugs that were being done at Woodstock just made zombies out of everyone. No insight was coming out of it. They were letter drugs I had never heard of. Everyone was doing drugs that had three-letter names: MDA was the drug of choice for the section of the hillside we were on.

If they passed out joints, that would have been a wonderful thing. But that wasn't where it was at. It was chemical, chemicals was where it was at. People were burning out left and right, big holes in the brain. I wasn't shocked, just disillusioned.

There was nothing political about the people that were there. The only political action that crowd was willing to make would have been anger if anybody had stopped the drugs. If somebody had stopped the drugs to that crowd, there would have been a riot. That would have been the only action you could have gotten this group to agree on.

Jimmy Jordan felt more comfortable with drug use: he often got high to bolster himself before heading out to gay clubs in Manhattan. He and Evan occasionally smoked dope together, but at Woodstock he didn't feel the necessity. He purposely avoided any drugs that Friday because he didn't want the numbing he knew he'd experience if he got high. College-age Evan, however, was fascinated by the variety of highs possible and wanted to experiment wildly. He accused Jimmy of being a bore when he passed up some pot. Their disagreement over drugs was just a symptom of the fundamental rift between the two that would result in tension throughout the weekend and beyond.

I saw Woodstock as something very special for us to share. I didn't know it would be a breaking point in our relationship, or have that kind of an effect. It's kind of hard to pinpoint any one thing. It was always what Evan wanted to do then: "I want to do this. I want to do that." He was smoking grass. I didn't feel I needed to. I was a stick-in-the-mud because I didn't do it. I didn't see it that way. You wanted to, you did; you didn't, you didn't. Depended on what you felt like.

When I smoked grass, it would blur things for me. I wanted to see and hear without being numbed by drugs. I didn't need it to get high, I was high.

In large part, though, getting high on something—even if you didn't know what it was—was the accepted norm for the afternoon. The gentle buzz shared by most everybody may well have been the crowd's salvation. Without the sedation, it's quite likely the heat of the afternoon and the absence of creature comforts would have agitated this love-in into an ugly riot. Instead, unified in the glow of their highs, the members of the Woodstock Nation remained at peace. After years of undercover smoking in dorm rooms where they stuffed towels below the door and in parks where they had to dart furtively behind bushes, the heads of America found themselves the ruling class. Fear, anxiety, paranoia evaporated at this joyfully unpoliced pot party. The openness allowed to their once secret habit added enormously to the aura of celebration that hovered over the afternoon, as real as that cloud of pot Anne Feldman inhaled. Dope had long sealed the unspoken covenant between counterculture followers. It was the communion by which the hip recognized one another. Here at Woodstock, the downtrodden cultists enjoyed an unprecedented freedom. You got high, and because everyone else was getting high, you got even higher.

That atmosphere wasn't limited to the festivalgoers; the staff and crew, as nervous as they were, relied on pharmaceutical assistance in getting through the tension-filled day. In fact, a general air of lightheartedness flowed through the backstage area that afternoon, mirroring the calm out front. And because of that sense of security and openness, those who had long avoided drug experimentation decided to jump into the void. John Sebastian was one of them. While circulating unnoticed through the crowd, he picked up on the infectious soaring spirit. And once back with his fellow rockers, he found a similar exhilaration—and a similar source.

I made my way back into the stage area. There were people whose job it was to keep people off the catwalks. Most of these people had in their pockets large quantities of mysterious-looking pills. Every time I made that trip I was offered these pills, and I asked, "What is this?" The first time someone said, "Well, it's sort of like acid, only it's more like mescaline but it's not, really. It's kind of like THC." Nobody would give a clear generic pharmacological description of these pills. And after about the third or fourth time I was offered the things, and I had noticed that everyone in the stage area who wasn't onstage was coming on with these pills and nobody seemed to be having ill effects, I accepted.

I had spent the first six months with the Lovin' Spoonful smoking three or four joints before we went onstage, but once we became known and we were doing concerts that counted, it became something I could no longer do. I did not feel I could do anything even as mild as smoke pot before I went on. It's just the wrong moment to be feeling wildly introspective, the moment before you go on in front of a crowd of people. Here I was, in a different situation now. There was no indication I would ever be asked to perform. I was enjoying the situation immensely. It was rather a psychedelic afternoon and it was, in fact, the first time I ever took acid.

Well, I circulated a few more times and I began to feel the intensity of what I had taken. I said to myself, This is not like mescaline. This is much more intense. And I began to feel the cathartic euphoria a good acid trip produces. I decided that the best thing I could do rather than try to fight this was to retreat, lie down and let this wave roll over me. Which I did. Went back to my tent.

I found out earlier than this particular experience that Timothy Leary had been using Lovin' Spoonful music in his lessons as a good example of psychedelic music. But the Spoonful were very down-to-earth people. We felt like we could knock off nine-tenths of these California bands by not falling for this whole drug-culture psychology. I really was a stranger to the psychedelic experience. But I had watched many other people go through with it, and I knew that the best thing I could do was to be something they talk about in a lot of Eastern philosophies: Be one with this experience. Let go. Don't fight it. Which I successfully ended up doing and the actual whammy of it subsided and I found I could walk around.

So widespread was drug use at Woodstock that it rendered law enforcement impossible. How do you arrest 500,000 people, where is the net big enough to throw over them, where is the jail large enough to hold them? It was a different story out on the highways leading to the festival, though, where no crowd protection prevented harassment of individual hippies. Up and down the roadways of New York State, troopers and local patrolmen had their eyes peeled for cars that carried the telltale signs of Woodstock: peace-sign insignias, rear windows crammed with long hair, radios blasting rock music. Pulled over for some minor vehicular infraction—a missing taillight, an unsignaled lane change—festival-bound youngsters were asked to step out of the car while highly questionable searches were made of their automobiles and possessions. More often than not, some trifling amount of pot was discovered. And the officers, incensed by the reports of flagrant disregard for the law in Bethel, would make their small step toward stemming the tide of national decay. Suddenly kids found themselves manacled, hauled off to jails in remote Catskill hamlets like Hurleyville or Callicoon and held for bails as high as $15,000. The savvy, habituated to such redneck harassment, knew the charges were inflated and wouldn't stick. Their biggest concern was missing the party.

For Scott Lane, the party had a distinctly sexual edge. He remembers Friday—and the festival in its entirety—as a series of encounters that involved his love life, in one way or another.

First he ran into a buddy named Fred DiRosa, who was upset because the woman he had come to the festival with had already dumped him for another guy. Sympathetic, Scott invited him along to go looking for girls, but he didn't reveal his own secret about the girlfriend.

> And he tells me this girl he came up with left him and was staying on this fucking bus with somebody. I couldn't believe she was going out with him. He wasn't very attractive but a wonderful, wonderful guy. The girl was this beautiful redhead, really alluring. I had had an affair with her. She was older. I was nineteen, she was twenty-six. I found out subsequently that I had

gotten her pregnant and she had an abortion. DiRosa was told he
was the father and paid for the abortion.

Scott doesn't remember now anything about how he met and
wooed the woman with whom he would spend the night. He
simply remembers doing so successfully.

> Friday I picked up some girl who had a tent. I don't remember
> the circumstances. But she was with some girl who had a real
> nice tent. It looked like an African safari, a major tent. I don't
> remember much about her.

Snug within the canvas confines, Scott was oblivious to proceedings near the stage that the eager crowd took as signals that final
preparations for the concert proper were under way. Amplification
levels were tested, circuits checked and rechecked. Backstage, of
course, there was still no word from any of the first acts, although
Richie Havens at least had shown up. To the thousands who had
spent the day playing in the sun, though, the activity suggested
that their long wait in the heat was to be rewarded. Among the
crew and staff, confusion mounted: the security system, for example, was becoming increasingly disorganized as the color-coded
pass protocols disintegrated into chaos. Henry Diltz, who was to
be given total access, was told his credentials were out of order and
was temporarily barred from the stage area. Meanwhile, a tripping
hippie managed to wander right into the performing area and
began an impromptu striptease.

Elen Orson's credentials gave her access to one place few others
were permitted: the towers. Friday morning she went out to inves-
tigate the structures with the cameraman to whom she had been
assigned, and both of them looked nervously at the perches where
they were to spend their precarious evening. The plates upon
which the towers were built had no underground foundation, no
anchoring below. This meant the scaffolding balanced only on
large slabs of iron, the sway steadied by cables running from the

midpoint of the column to the plates below. She and the cameraman decided to climb up to survey their vantage point and lay out
the shots they'd be able to get from the elevation. Terrified at first,
Elen followed behind the cameraman, forcing herself up despite
her fear of heights. She was amazed to find that she experienced
nothing of her familiar phobia when she reached the top.

Back on terra firma her cameraman told her there really wasn't
anything to do until the concert started, as another team was
gathering crowd shots. He suggested they regroup at four. She
wandered around watching everybody get high, delighting in
being part of this generation of free spirits. But over this garden of
earthly delights, her tower loomed ominously, reminding her of
her responsibilities. This would be a test for her, a chance fortune
had sent her way. She fingered a tab of acid in her pocket: the
friends she had driven up with had given it to her as sort of a
welcome-aboard token. If she had come up here as she originally
planned, with Brian, maybe she would have taken the hit and
gotten into the mood of the event. But this was work now, an
opportunity to prove herself. She ran into a friend she knew from
New York and gave him the acid. She'd handle the towers straight.

By the time the concert started, she already knew she'd made
the right decision.

> I had to go under the stage, get two magazines. They weighed,
> loaded, about fifteen pounds each. I brought a diaper bag with a
> strap—my sister-in-law had just had a baby and I grabbed it for a
> gadget bag. It was just big enough to fit two magazines in. So I
> would go under the stage, get two fresh magazines, and walk
> through the crowd, which at the front was wall to wall. People
> were, like, hugging each other and didn't even know each other.
> There were no aisles, no trails. I would get to the base of the tower
> and climb up with these magazines and take the ones he had shot
> and go back and get more. It took about twenty minutes to get
> through the crowd and it was only a matter of thirty yards. On
> one trip, I was heading back with the thirty extra pounds and
> about a hundred twenty pounds of me, so that makes a hundred
> fifty pounds of big strapping woman coming through. I'm walk-
> ing through people and suddenly I lift my foot and realize the

only place to put my foot is on this man's balls. His girlfriend is
sitting next to him, sees my foot coming down, and screams.

She couldn't avoid that accident, but the damage there was
minimal. Later Elen skirted disaster with a smaller margin. Climb-
ing up the tower with two magazines in the diaper bag, she didn't
realize the seams were slowly giving way from the weight. The
bag, dangling off her shoulder, swayed over the crowd at the base
of the tower. As she pulled herself higher and higher, with each
move the bag ripped a little bit more, threatening to drop the
magazines onto someone's head. Finally, just as she swung herself
and her load onto the filming platform, the diaper bag gave way,
sending the two metal magazines crashing onto the landing, perilously close to the edge. Elen stared down and shuddered. It was to
be only the first of a series of close calls she would encounter
working Woodstock's towers.

By the time the music actually started—a little after five—Elen
had been up and down the scaffolding so many times she knew
each rung by heart. She was still too frazzled about the bag's
breaking to pay much attention to Richie Havens, who ended up
being the opening act simply because he was on hand. Elen may
have been concentrating on work, but the crowd responded ecstat-
ically to the concert's beginning. A black folksinger distinguished
by toothless grin, raspy voice and aggressive guitar-strumming
style, Havens presented material running from Afro-American
hymns to antiwar protest anthems. His energetic acoustic performance suited the moment perfectly: it allowed technicians an
uncomplicated test run for their equipment and gave the crowd a
gentle overture to the easy listening the evening would provide.
His wry "Universal Soldier"—about the duty men had to refuse
conscription—coincided with the political expectations some had
brought to the concert. And his jazzy version of "Here Comes the
Sun" was the embodiment of the afternoon's feel-good spirit. He
may not have been the scheduled first act, but he was a nearly
perfect one. As with so many things that amazingly blessed weekend, serendipity had stepped in when planning failed.

There was, inevitably, a downside to the stroke of good luck. So warmly was Havens received that backstage the concert organizers got nervous. Psyched by Havens, how would the audience react if there were too long an interval before the next act took over? And neither Sweetwater nor the Incredible String Band was around. Someone else had to go on.

Country Joe McDonald remembers the conflicting emotions he experienced when he was approached about filling in after Havens until one of the scheduled groups surfaced. The singer just happened to be backstage, there like Sebastian to enjoy the concert. But he had no intentions of going on Friday. He thought he was being kidded when he was approached about subbing next. There had been rumors that he was planning on leaving his group, the Fish. And he misunderstood the request to perform now as a dig referring to his pending solo career. Even after being convinced the interest in his performing was genuine, his reluctance continued. The audience knew him only as the front man for a group of electric-rock musicians, with a hard-driving psychedelic sound. There would be little appreciation of Country Joe alone, singing acoustically. Still, the thought of performing for that enormous crowd enticed and terrified him. It would be a once-in-a-lifetime opportunity. Besides, there was a possibility the crowd would riot without music. Like an unwilling understudy, he stood speechless as someone thrust a guitar in his hand and pushed him toward the stage.

> I said I didn't have a guitar. I didn't even have a guitar pick, just a matchbook cover. They gave me a rope for a strap.
>
> I just sang a mixed-bag folk set. Not too many people were paying attention to me. I was watching them and they were talking. They knew Country Joe and the Fish, so I wasn't really surprised. I was just Muzak or something. I knew my job was just to go up and kill time. But after about an hour I got more confident, I figured I had nothing more to lose. Boredom brings on confidence. I stopped playing for a minute and went over and asked Bill [Belmont, the road manager] if I should try out the cheer. I came back out.
>
> And I said, "Give me an F." And everybody turned and looked at me, and said, 'F.' "
>
> Then I said, "Give me a U." And they yelled back, 'U.' And it

went on like that. And I went on singing the song and they all kept staring at me. My adrenaline got really pumping. And I couldn't hear them singing because the sound went up all outdoors. That's why in the middle I said, "Sing louder." I didn't know they were making a movie, I couldn't see any cameras. I did see them filming when I was watching the other acts, but it never occurred to me that they had filmed me.

If Havens's set introduced the political tone to the festival, McDonald's sing-along version of the "Fixin'-to-Die Rag" stood as one of the most overtly antiwar statements of the entire concert. And typical of Woodstock, it was fun. If they didn't know the chorus before, the kids picked it up quickly, singing the words the way they would have latched onto the easily memorized lyrics of campfire songs. The crowd, excited by the audacity of the cheer, felt the high of group rebelliousness simply by joining in song. Ironically, it was really all just show biz. Sensing he was dying up there, Joe launched into a riff he knew would get the audience's attention.

A savvy showman responding to the entertainment dictates of the moment: Joe's decision to charge up the audience with his antiwar tune and his obscene cheer was merely the instinctual impulse of a stage pro. A whim, it was nevertheless witnessed by thousands and then recorded in a film seen by millions. Country Joe became the guy who sang the "FUCK" song. To a large portion of a generation, that Woodstock appearance was the only image ever associated with this versatile artist. A veteran himself, Country Joe in one evening's performance became linked with an antiwar song and an antimilitary ideology that represented only a small fraction of his self. This was Woodstock, though, and a gig like none other in history. Such was the impact of this event that the arc of an artist's entire career could be redirected by the songs he selected to sing, the patter he chose to deliver, the clothes he decided to wear. Joe had no clear sense of how his life would be changed by his time on the stage, but he did know he had finally connected with the audience—an entertainer's goal. Had he realized the shadow that would follow him from Woodstock into the

1970s, he might have been able to caution the other artists backstage that this chance of a lifetime might have lifelong consequences. He might have been able to say something constructive to
John Sebastian, who was just then getting ready to go out and
learn the same lesson for himself.

Stoned on a drug he couldn't even identify, Sebastian knew this
was not the appropriate time for a performance. Aside from being
too high to play, the composer-singer was extremely nervous about
appearing solo in front of so large a crowd. Like Joe McDonald, he
was known by everyone exclusively as a member of a group, not as
an individual act. True, he was trying to establish himself on his
own now that the group had broken up, but you just didn't break
yourself in before one of the largest crowds ever assembled. And
finally, maybe it was part of his drug paranoia, but he felt funny
dressed the way he was. Tie-dyed from head to toe, he might be
just a little too trendy to be taken seriously.

Knowing he was fried, Sebastian nevertheless couldn't help
accepting the chance to do his thing in front of this historic crowd.
As Country Joe was finishing up, the stage manager turned to John
and begged him to go out.

> I said, "I haven't brought an instrument, nobody ever asked me."
> The Spoonful had been disbanded. I really did not know
> whether the audience would accept me as a single performer.
> Certainly I had composed a lot of the tunes, and had a large part
> in the creation of the music. But as a performer I mainly kept my
> head down in between songs and tried to make sure I was in
> tune. I had been onstage as a solo performer only twenty or thirty
> times by the time of that concert, in small clubs.
>
> But I was also way too whacked to say no. And the oppor-
> tunity to play in front of that many people, more people than I
> had ever seen—I was very excited by the idea.
>
> In retrospect, it really is one of my least favorite performances I
> have ever given. Here was in fact what became for many years
> my highest-visibility performance and it's always been a sad note
> for me. Well, I spoke, I sang, I played. You can wake me up in the
> middle of the night and I can play and sing and speak better than
> I did that day. But I guess you can say I got away with it because it

was a part of this event. The sight of that crowd was so much more intoxicating than any drug I could have taken. That's what made it even harder to keep the thread of thought in the song. I forgot words, I felt I lost my train of thought several times.

This wasn't just an audience of people. The one thing I did manage to get out was that this felt like a culmination of something that had been happening in smaller groups: people getting together around little low tables all over the country and passing a joint around and talking about how this world was changing as a result of the culture that was growing out of music and a lifestyle that was growing out of a culture.

And tremendously misleading. Preserved in memory and then on film, the tie-dyed, spaced-out Sebastian became linked in the public's mind with a hippy-dippy lifestyle out of sync with the real musician. Wow, man, like far out—kids did impersonations of the singer that made him sound like a sixties burn-out. Trying to express the sentiments he had about Woodstock while tripping, the expressive young man became a parody of drug-induced inarticulateness. Genuinely and understandably moved by the experience, which had both personal and professional significance, he prattled on goofily between songs. Still, as unhappy as he may be with the aftereffects of that performance, it is well remembered by many of the audience members. Henry Diltz particularly recalls photographing him.

I got behind him on the stage and took a shot of this lone figure in this colorful jacket with this sea of humanity in front. John Sebastian and his tie-dyed jacket, yellow and brown, standing there and giving the peace sign. All little bumps of heads off into infinity. All the way over to your left, and all to your right. And the hillside totally covered with camps and tents. Huge sea of heads.

Susie Kaufman remembers both Country Joe and John Sebastian as highlights of the first night.

I adored John Sebastian. He was great. I'd seen him at some concerts smoking joints backstage before he went on, so I guess he was always stoned. Up there he was more high, like everyone else, getting this heavy natural high. Everybody was stoned so I didn't notice. Now I would notice something like that, but back then I didn't. I was wondering what they were feeling like performing for the largest audience they would ever perform for.

Sylvia Greene remembers Friday night as special for several reasons. First, her friend Rebecca had not yet wandered off into the crowd, leaving her alone. By Saturday her friend would be gone, Sylvia abandoned and feeling deserted. But on Friday she and Rebecca shared the performances as they had so many other concerts together. She remembers Sebastian, Havens and Country Joe, but what lingers in her mind the most is the performance by little-known folksinger Bert Sommer. Hardly recognized at the time, and not included in the movie, Sommer has dropped out of most people's memories of the weekend. But Sylvia had a special reason for recalling his act. Sexually competitive with Rebecca, Sylvia found something in his performance that gave her a temporary advantage over her friend.

> Bert Sommer was a friend of mine. He did a Simon and Garfunkel song, and I knew he was singing it for me. He even said he wanted to marry me, on the radio once. He had been in *Hair.* He was older, but he had his own way about him. If I had gotten into it, I think he would have definitely had a relationship with me. But I was not ready to be sexually active yet. The feeling wasn't strong enough.

Whether or not Sommer actually intended the song for Sylvia made no difference. Rebecca knew she had had a brief affair with the singer and the mere fact that he was performing on that stage fed into the jealousy that always boiled beneath the surface of the girls' relationship. As Sylvia glowed in the assumed dedication, Rebecca silently fumed. She might have gotten up and set out on her sexual foray that first night if the skies hadn't suddenly opened up, dousing her anger.

Without any warning, as sitarist Ravi Shankar strummed his Indian meditation music, a thunderhead rolled over the hills surrounding Yasgur's farm. For a quarter of an hour rain beat down on the thousands, who refused to let the shower dampen their spirits. Many of those who had set up tents didn't even bother to retreat under their protection, joining in the pagan rain worship all around them. Resilience and good-natured acceptance of adversity had become the operative virtues at Woodstock; rain or no rain, the festival would remain festive. Ron Stone remembers one particularly graphic example of just how undeterred the good-time seekers were by the storm.

> It started to rain, and still next to our tent there was a couple making love all night long. They had wrapped themselves in plastic, in something like a Slip 'n Slide surface. Even though they were in four inches of water, they were oblivious to it. They were stoned out of their minds. Regardless, they really enjoyed themselves. The noises and the groans they made kept us awake, but it was sort of fun. That personified the best of Woodstock to us. In all the rain these people were still making love in the woods. The joke then when you met someone attractive was, "Didn't we ball once at a festival?" Well, someone was actually doing it next to us.

As quickly as it had started, the storm stopped. The cloud bank rolled off, revealing the starry night sky. Burly stagehands rushed out onto the stage to dry it as best they could, and the concert continued, the scheduled performers now all in the backstage area. Arlo Guthrie, Sweetwater, Melanie—another unscheduled appearance—and Joan Baez, closing off the night. The green and welcoming blanket of Yasgur's farm had turned into acres of mud, but the dampness lifted off the ground as tired children curled into their bedrolls. Country smells filled the air, tinged with the acrid odor of incense, pot and humanity. Recalls Bill Pelligrini:

> I remember the first night after the music stopped. We were walking back down Yasgur's road, and there was no moon. It was pitch-black, one of those Catskill nights when you could put your hand in front of your face and not see it. We used the old candle-in-the-can trick. And when you got down to a little rise in

the road you could look back behind you and as far as you could
see the land was dotted with campfires.

A strange silence fell over the field, not exactly quiet, but still.
Penny gazed out over the muddy field and the thousands lying
down to rest. As insignificant as her bosses sometimes made her
feel, at this moment she felt responsible for those thousands of
kids. And with the responsibility came a sense of power. Penny
had spent the day in low-profile execution of the thousand minute
tasks that had kept this miracle alive. She had just finished her
most demanding chore of the day: converting the staff cafeteria
into a twenty-bed hospital room. At the request of the medical
team, dismayed at the growing number of cases they were handling, she commandeered the only available space, over the objections of the cafeteria manager. Somehow she had found the
supplies and directed laborers in fully servicing the quarters with
electricity and plumbing. And all in two hours. Delivering orders
to the men, making decisions as she went along, filling out the
black jacket that designated Ventures management, Penny barely
recognized the competent person she had become.

Now it was calm, yet somehow ominous too. The unpredictability of the day seemed to subside, but the sheer presence of so
much humanity in one place generated a palpable energy, even in
repose. Penny sat down for a moment on one of the bunks, still
empty but soon to be filled with a hippie on a bad trip. A helicopter buzzed overhead, and the electric whirr—it seemed almost
insectlike—that filled the stage area was oddly peaceful. She had
gotten used to those sounds and they receded into white-noise
oblivion. Penny looked over the giant bowl and thought she heard
the very countryside emitting a sigh of relief. She had almost
finished the sigh before she realized it was coming from herself.
They had gotten through the first day.

SATURDAY

Eᴀʀʟʏ Sᴀᴛᴜʀᴅᴀʏ morning, while thousands of kids rested safely, if somewhat uncomfortably, in Yasgur's fields, a tractor rolled over a young man curled up in his sleeping bag in a pasture down the road from the festival site, crushing him to death. The Woodstock Nation had its first casualty.

News of the accident swept through the Diamond Horseshoe more swiftly than the fire with which the weekend had begun. The chilling reality of the seventeen-year-old's death threw a pall over the crew, many of whom had slept the night before convinced they had gotten through the first day by some divine fluke. Deceived by the good luck they had encountered so far, the workers had lapsed into a false sense of security, invulnerability. Penny and Lee, satisfied with the accomplishments of Friday, woke up on Saturday more confident. Rufus, who had been working as talent escort, was looking forward to meeting the day's stars, including Janis Joplin, whom he knew vaguely from his days in the SoHo rehearsal studio. Henry Diltz was happy—he had been getting great shots.

All of this seemed suddenly unimportant in the face of the boy's death that morning. While the organizers bore no legal liability for the accident, guilt couldn't be avoided. And if not guilt, then sadness. This was just supposed to be a party, a summertime outdoor fling. Nobody was supposed to die. Or OD, for that matter, or miscarry, or get sick, or even go hungry, all of which had been happening. Faced with this ultimate tragedy, the staff again realized the million things that could go wrong, the million ways events could conspire to tilt this party over the edge into calamity. Deprivation was one thing, they could handle that. But death had made a visit to Woodstock, unannounced and uninvited. It could come again.

Unaware of the accident, many of the kids were spending the new morning making love. Sex and death both played their part at Woodstock, and at this point sex was winning. Staged at the height of the sexual revolution, the weekend festival saw hippies in pond and tent, in woods and on horseback groping and humping with glorious abandon. Young men and women settled down together in the tall grass, high on a seize-the-day attitude. Described now, the sexual excess seems animalistic, licentious. But in 1969 such public lovemaking carried a whole different meaning. It epitomized the generation's rejection of American values—as presented most directly to them by the monogamous and uptight domesticity they grew up with in their parents' homes. Released from that captivity for this weekend at least, the kids were determined to dump the artifice of social interaction they characterized as puritanical, and get back to nature. Seeking pleasure, they firmly believed, was a treasured goal in itself, no longer the vile, unholy or debasing thing they had been told it was by religious instructors. Make love—and you made a statement. Neatly, the rhetoric of the day legitimized the horniness adolescents have always felt, making screwing in the countryside seem politically correct.

Henry Diltz took a photo that summed up the ethos of Saturday perfectly: "I remember one shot of Max's red barn. Rock fences around it. I remember this couple, a guy lying on top of this girl right in the middle of this field. The cows were looking at them."

For many the lusty celebration of youth turned this Saturday morning into a magical moment of intimacy and connection. Scott Lane, emerging from the tent where he had shared a night with a girl he can't remember, set off looking for the next encounter. Yasgur's farm may have been the site of the biggest singles party of all time.

Not surprisingly, however, to the outside world the love-in was an assault on all that was decent and good. Nudity and open fornication challenged the very notion of civilized society, and to the local gentry the idea that a bacchanal was in full swing in their backyard was appalling. Compelled by curiosity to see for himself if the reports he had heard could possibly be true, George Neuhaus wandered up to the site Saturday morning; the long-married father of seven was shocked.

> There was open sex. They didn't care if they stopped on the side of the road. They didn't care if you were walking down with your mother or grandmother. They didn't care. It was a wild orgy.
>
> My wife didn't go up, I didn't want to expose her to that. She doesn't enjoy orgies and things. She's not that kind of person. I guess what people do behind their own closed doors is their own business. But it doesn't belong in a public area. If you have young children, a daughter, you wouldn't want her exposed to that kind of thing. This is what they were trying to promote. It just don't go. If that was what they were going to have in this country, it wouldn't be long. . . . Anybody could come in and take us over. Russia would be here tomorrow; "Hey, we'll straighten youse all out." In a sophisticated society, living together, we have to agree to have controls and laws so we can live in a peaceful society. Everybody has rights, but we formulate laws so we protect everybody's rights.

Looking on from outside, the men and women of Sullivan County couldn't understand the new style of relationship being practiced in the muddy bowl of the concert site. But then, many of the young settled down in that sexual theater were themselves confused by their generation's still-unclear code of behavior. In this great libidinal dance of the flower children, wallflowers were many. If for some the day brought uncomplicated and easy bouts of lovemaking, for others it merely intensified confusion created by sexual redefinition.

Susie Kaufman came to Woodstock looking for answers to questions she didn't quite realize related to her sexuality. Months of counseling had barely reconstructed the sexual identity crushed during her earlier violent encounter. Ironically, she didn't harbor hatred of men as a result of the incident, but rather had turned her rage inward, now doubting her own confidence as a woman. She carried all that baggage upstate with her, but didn't expect to have it unpacked. The weekend was to be strictly a cultural foray, her reentry into the with-it crowd she preferred but had largely shunned since the rape. Surrounded by men with whom she had no sexual relation, she felt protected enough to take these first steps outward. She hoped to find a nurturing environment, but not one as rife with sexual activity as what she was witnessing this Saturday. Simply by exposing herself to freedom and self-acceptance, she was able to let go of some of the pain she had been holding in for over a year. Even though some of the openness other women enjoyed offended her modesty, she became intrigued by the panoply of female role models here.

> Women were taking their tops off. It embarrassed me, I wasn't ready for that. But you got used to it quickly. You didn't see a lot of guys falling over themselves to get a better look.
>
> I remember a woman who had a white Afro, a black woman. It was really unusual. A white robe and big gold jewelry. Very African-looking and very modern. I was fascinated by her and looked at her for hours. I thought, I'm not alone, and these people are not going to stare at me or look at me any different. If they do look at me, it's because they like the way I look. It's okay after all to look like this.
>
> I was so happy. I had always felt very insecure about my looks, very homely as a teenager. I went up there thinking I was not a pretty girl. But being able to look across a hundred or so people

and catch the eyes of a girl who was really beautiful and not being jealous. For the first time in my life, which is hard because girls can be jealous. And just smiling at her the way I'd smile at a man. The looks you exchanged with people across a hundred bodies were never just glances or glimpses. You looked at each other and it was almost a psychic experience.

Even for women who weren't facing the psychological hurdles Susie contended with, the sexual freedom at Woodstock caused uncertainty. Old-fashioned gender differences were supposed to have broken down, and now girls were expected to want sex as much as boys traditionally did. But for some, the license celebrated in the field that day actually amounted to a new form of oppression: according to older morality, you were damned if you did; the new order damned you if you didn't. Despite ample opportunity her first year away at college, Sylvia had not yet had sex by the time she went to Woodstock. And she certainly wasn't interested in losing her virginity here in the mud with a stranger. But Rebecca was much more adventurous, and scoffed at Sylvia's uptightness. Their friendship had confronted this difference before, and here at the festival the difference again divided them.

Upon waking Saturday morning, Sylvia realized her friend had left her.

Rebecca would come and go. We were together and apart. A lot of time together, then she would be doing her own thing. When she would go off, I would just accept it. I got bummed out there after a while. It was wet and cold and muddy and at some time I just said, "Is this fun?" In the day, when nothing was going on, it wasn't fun.

I didn't ask her whether or not she was off with somebody, but I pretty much figured she was. Just someone she met up there. I didn't always want to be putting her on the spot. There were times when I wished she would just hang out with me instead. I tolerated a lot from her that people wouldn't tolerate in a friend.

Sylvia patiently waited for Rebecca's returns, perplexed by the fact that the supposed sexual freedom the Woodstock Nation held dear wasn't broad enough to include her choices. Doing your own thing really meant having sex, regardless of whether or not you felt ready. Others in the crowd were realizing just as piercingly that 1960s sexual freedom was a rather restrictive code of ethics. If it rejected celibacy between man and woman, it imposed it on men and men. Being gay was not cool by the group standards practiced that Saturday morning.

Jimmy Jordan wasn't so naive as to think he could actually make love to Evan out in broad daylight here. But as all around him he beheld embracing couples, he wanted to share some moment of togetherness with the young man he had come to the festival with. Certainly the liberal orientation of the crowd permitted two men to exchange a brief hug. But like so many others groping with the upended sexual norms of the day, Jimmy didn't know how to read his partner's reaction when he rebuffed his advance.

> What surprised me was the openness that was there. I mean, you would see people doing it on the side of the field or when you went to take a crap. When you went to the lake to swim nude, everyone was hugging and kissing. And it's funny, because I have always been the opposite, not comfortable with public display. But I just wanted, when we were lying on the blanket, to feel close to him. And some sense of intimacy. He totally rejected that. That kind of threw me.

Meanwhile, conditions at the festival site were growing worse. Sanitation facilities, limited as they were, were overflowing to the point of being unusable. Service trucks were impeded from hauling away the waste, and raw sewage was dumped into an enormous open trench. Still, the portable toilets were so foul-smelling and unclean that most kids just headed off into the cornfields and woods surrounding the area, turning the entire area into an outhouse. The plastic tubing used to bring drinking water into the various refreshment outposts kept sprouting leaks. And staff disorganization and frozen-goods spoilage at the concession stands seriously jeopardized the availability of food. All that lovemaking was fine, but eventually everybody had to eat.

For all the problems the Hog Farm had caused during the weeks preceding the festival, the commune filled a vital vacuum in the weekend's fractured food chain. The Farm's enormous vats filled with gut-sticking vegetable goulash provided the only reliable nutrition for many of the thousands who had come here without so much as a can of tuna. And with the staff cafeteria converted into a hospital, even crew members took their meals over at the Hog Farm's pavilion. Elen Orson recalls this as her first exposure to natural cooking after years of eating at her mother's table.

> I got to the food concession stand, to the Hog Farm, and I hadn't really eaten. I went over to the brown rice. I never ate it in Clifton, where my mother cooked the steak by putting it in a pan with water and boiling it. That's how her mother taught her to cook beef. That's what you do. I've been eating brown rice ever since. It had corn and lima beans. I hated lima beans, but with the brown rice the flavor was great. For a while after that I went around making brown rice and succotash for people.

The pavilion, which also housed the commune's own drug-overdose facility, became the heartbeat of the festival, perhaps even more crucial to its success than the stage. It was here that all the volunteering and sharing for which Woodstock has become legendary concentrated, and those who wandered into it often adopted for themselves a personal sense of mission in making the weekend work. John Sebastian, having had the night to sleep off his drug trip, took a walk to the Hog Farm on Saturday afternoon.

> Distributing the food was a monumental task. If you weren't doing something, you could go and shovel brown rice onto plates. Just do anything to make this thing work. There was a tremendous sense that if this thing was a catastrophe, it would be a blot on our record. And to me the greatest stab was when I came back to civilization, and to see *The New York Times* and other reputable newspapers reporting it as drugs and mud and catastrophe. What had happened was so very, very different.
>
> I had a feeling for the way everyone wanted to be those three days. I had wanted to be that way myself in my own private way.

And here was a communal attempt at this. I felt in some way that I was back to another early role, that of a camp counselor. I had spent a lot of my earlier life as a camp counselor, and here I was again in the same position. We had to show the kids how to keep the mud out of the cabin and then they'd be all righty. Give them the foundation and they'd enjoy the experience.

Pitching in and putting up got you by—or you could just pull out. By Saturday, as the odyssey onto the field continued, despite media warnings to stay away, the exodus away from the festival had already begun. Many of those who wanted to get out couldn't, unless they wanted to leave that new car Daddy bought them for graduation in the jam somewhere. But for the disgruntled who didn't dig the deprivations of the day and whose transportation out was available, it looked as if this were as good a time as any to quit. Ron Stone woke up Saturday and, with still no evidence of the sort of overt activism he had hoped to find here, packed it in. The festival was becoming a freak show, complete with noisy observers, all of which made him extremely anxious to leave.

The memories strongest to me are the constant flight of one- and two-engine planes right over the crowd. Not a block high, whatever number of feet that is. If one of those planes had crashed it would have taken out an awful lot of people. There were all these planes that wanted to fly in to see all these people. They were a menace to themselves up there, and they made me nervous. There were more than there should have been. There shouldn't have been any planes flying over there at all.

Morning came and we decided, The music is nice, but is it really worth putting up with this nonsense? We were worried about problems that might arise. This may sound selfish, but we knew they had already run out of the food in the concession area and we knew we had the only food in our area. And we wanted to eat too. We were worried about to what degree we would be able to share food. Somehow people had figured out the same entrance as we did and the cars were starting to back up on the road in. We thought we ought to get out while we could before our car got blocked in.

The rain had definitely turned us off, but we felt we were smart. Like the people who cleverly leave in the seventh inning, when they know it's not going to be a turnaround. We decided to drive back to Washington. Listening to the radio station made it sound like they had been invaded from Mars.

At the same time Stone was leaving, Saturday's airlift of rock stars to the festival had begun. If Friday's gentle folk lineup had sent the weekend sailing on a soothing, mellow wave, the roster for the second day's performances promised to crank the excitement level up along with the decibels. And while medium-range greats like Joan Baez and Arlo Guthrie adorned the opening night, Saturday's attractions featured some of rock's most luminous stars: Janis Joplin, Jefferson Airplane, the Grateful Dead, the Who, Sly and the Family Stone and Creedence Clearwater Revival. If they all showed, the audience knew they would be treated to a collection of contemporary recording talent like none ever assembled before. If that lure didn't hold Ron Stone in place, it certainly rooted thousands of diehards to their soggy blankets.

As on the preceding day, the anticipation out front was matched by jangled nerves backstage. Again problems abounded, and since Saturday's talents were bigger talents, the problems were enlarged proportionally. Lee overheard several management disputes concerning up-front payment, with agents demanding cash before the performance. At this point everyone knew the concert had been opened up and there would be no gate. So it wasn't all that surprising that rumors circulated about Ventures bosses bouncing checks and their pending bankruptcy. On the other hand, how could demands for cash be met on a Saturday afternoon in the middle of the country? Beyond money matters, many of the performers were skittish about the volatility of the crowd, the weather, the intensity of the media scrutiny and the condition of the stage. The more electrically oriented groups scheduled for the afternoon and evening required more precise technical assistance than the acoustic performers Friday, and they questioned whether or not they were going to get it here. They complained about the inferiority of the backstage facilities and the unacceptability of the amplification equipment.

For Tom Constanten, the whole situation was fraught with unhappiness even before he arrived. For the last few months it had become more and more obvious that the Grateful Dead keyboardist was having problems meshing with the band, and he sensed a growing rift between himself and the others. The group's fanatically devoted cult pretty much ignored Constanten, focusing on the more colorful members, especially lead singer Jerry Garcia. To the audience Constanten was superfluous. And the increasingly improvisational style evolving among the others tended to cut him out more and more. Little about this rustic gig, for which they might not even get paid, boded well.

Constanten remembers flying into the site that Saturday afternoon, picking up vibrations he didn't like. He sensed none of the awe and wonder expressed by Sebastian as he circled the field, but then when Sebastian was arriving he wasn't contemplating what it would be like to play to this crowd. Tom knew right away, looking down at that stage in the middle of the great outdoors, that its limitations would merely exaggerate all of the existing problems. What he did share with the former Lovin' Spoonful singer, however, was a gnawing doubt about his professional future, specifically his place in the group.

> A lot of other bands in the sixties, their charts were a lot more tightly arranged than the Grateful Dead's. You knew where you stood, because it was set. It was like a high school band playing from the music, in terms of how much improvisation was going on. Whereas with the Grateful Dead there was a great deal of improvisation going on all the time.
>
> When you add amplification, certain problems increase exponentially. It was difficult for me to be sure the mix I heard was the same as the mix the other members of the band heard, or the audience heard. Very seldom were they the same. I would hear myself coming through the amplifier superfortissimo, blast myself out, and someone would say they couldn't hear me. Or vice versa. I can ascribe a lot of things that might have been taken

as disagreements as based on that. There were acoustical reasons for it.

A lot of the big outdoor gigs were the worst. I guess having walls encircle you closed the system and made fine-tuning easier. But without those walls, the sound went off in space. A passing breeze can wipe out a section of sound. And you couldn't see members of the band. We would segue to one song right in the middle of another.

For Constanten the technical hardships at Woodstock coincided with the more abiding and personal ones he brought along with him. In that he was not alone. Rock and roll, as the festival itself proved, had ascended to the very forefront of pop culture during the late sixties. Celebrity, quick money and self-delusion, the unholy trinity that stalks the American Dream, concentrated a seductive power on this native talent. The dizzying whirlwind that the swift rise of rock music had created was already beginning to suck the life out of some of the very figures who had fueled the rocket ride. Many of the young men and women who would perform at this celebration of sixties rock would be dead before half of the next decade had passed. Among them Janis Joplin, perhaps the biggest attraction of the festival's second day and surely also the most troubled.

To most of the rock personnel gathered backstage, Janis's haggard appearance and disorientation came as no surprise. Her disintegration from drink and drugs was well-known. And while her foul temperament put off most of the crew, two different men from very different times in her life took great interest in the great lady's presence. Rufus, the lowest of the low on the Woodstock pecking order, looked at this disheveled queen of the blues as she grappled vainly through her fog to open the door of the helicopter in which she had just arrived. Cussing and spitting, as always, he thought. He had seen her like that before and knew she needed him again. He thought about their first encounters.

Baggies was a studio on Greene Street, in SoHo before it was SoHo. Everyone would rehearse there. Jimi Hendrix used it,

Bonnie and Delaney used it. Janis used it regularly. One of my gigs there was to go find Janis. "Where's Janis?" someone would say. Yeah, yeah, I knew where she was. I would find her in St. Mark's Place with the actor who was in *Bonnie and Clyde*, Michael J. Pollard. She'd be ripped drunk on the street, just lying there giggling away. I'd get her into the cab.

During the festival we geeks became sort of rangers. No assignments, really. The idea was, we were the guys who would pull it together. That's the way I was with Janis: it wasn't my job to pull her out of the helicopter. But I was there.

Such was not the attitude of the other man who drew near Janis to see for himself the ravages the hard life had wrought on the woman he had once loved. Country Joe McDonald shook his head as she shuffled in front of him.

Janis and I knew each other very, very well. At one point Janis was my girlfriend. We lived together for six months in Haight-Ashbury. At Woodstock she was not in a very responsive mood and we had grown apart by then. There was a problem with her and drugs, and it was getting between her and some of her friends. That was a problem. The relationship had ended a couple of years before Woodstock. At this point I knew she had a bisexual sexual life. That didn't bother me. What bothered me was the drug part. It was almost as if Janis wasn't there.

Hard drugs were just starting to make the scene. It bothered who it bothered and not others. The initial counterculture was fueled by psychedelics, which are essentially hash and marijuana. Organic psychedelics. It wasn't until 1968 that speed became a problem. And amphetamines and heroin. We didn't have much time to respond. It split people apart. The people who would tolerate the harder drugs became one camp, and those who wouldn't tolerate them became another camp. And if you're around people who use hard drugs and you don't allow them to do it, or you get in their face about it, they just leave. And at that time Janis was stoned on heroin at Woodstock. And that's how it was, so she stayed by herself. Stayed pretty secluded.

High-strung stars, even more tightly wired by drugs and nerves, milled around backstage. Things were tense, even though everyone tried to cover up the anxiety with forced camaraderie and happy talk. Today the music was set to begin around noon, and Lee looked sympathetically at the poor slobs in the band who were going to be sent out there to open the show. With the audience expecting top-drawer entertainment, the schedule called for the no-name act Quill to break in the crowd. Lee knew how daunting opening was: she remembered Jimi Hendrix being booed off the stage when he opened for the Monkees several years back. And she felt doubly bad for the guys in Quill because of all they had gone through that summer. Though they were heading out to perform for one of the decade's most freedom-crazed audiences, Quill—with Lee as their promoter—had spent a good part of the previous six weeks playing for convicts, reform-schoolers and juvenile delinquents.

In order to stem local opposition to their activities, the festival organizers had early on decided that a certain amount of goodwill needed to be spread through community outreach projects. By extending their good vibrations throughout upstate New York, they hoped to promote cooperation as well as the festival itself. Along with her other duties, Lee was quickly assigned the task of setting up charity gigs for Quill, a band with ties to the management, at penal institutions. No ulterior motives could be attributed to playing there; security for the hippie entrepreneurs would be guaranteed. If there was any cynicism behind the plan, it didn't shield Lee from the emotional impact of actually visiting the institutions, where offenders too young to shave were locked up. The recollection of broken youth would shadow her Woodstock experience forever.

> Probably none of the experiences I had was more frightening. In doing this tour, I got to know why they had an eighty-five-percent graduating class from Warwick to Elmira, which means these little boys get started at twelve and eventually wind up in prison. They didn't have any rehabilitation. To discuss activities

and help for these people . . . even in those days it was really
outside the realm of the prison official. They just wanted to
contain them because these were bad kids.

Just as unknown as Quill, Jocko Marcellino walked around the
backstage, not believing he was actually here. Sha Na Na and Janis!
Sha Na Na and the Grateful Dead! For the stagestruck Columbia
University undergraduate this proximity to the stars was more
than a dream come true, since he had never had the audacity to
dream this big. A couple of times earlier that year when they were
playing at the Steve Paul Scene, a celebrity would come in and pat
them on the head. Their nostalgia vaudeville was still perceived as
a novelty act, one most of the audience had never heard of before.
Still, their fluke inclusion in the program meant a certain degree of
acceptance into the rock fraternity. Sort of. Still struggling to
finance costumes and equipment for their new act, the members of
Sha Na Na were no doubt the beggars at the banquet. On this eve
of the glitter era, the superstar elite could demand perks usually
associated with Hollywood personalities. Among this collection of
coddled demigods, Jocko's dungarees and T-shirt signaled his status as poor boy parvenu.

> We rented a locker on the campus for our equipment, and we'd
> rent a van for our gigs on the road. So this is only, like, our
> seventh gig. We're the only ones who set up our own equipment
> at Woodstock. I remember my biggest regret was not being able
> to fly into the site. We went through the backwoods. By then
> everyone had been warned it was a disaster area, but there were
> ways of getting in with the police. Just follow them in. I remem-
> ber following in seven trucks of Sly Stone's equipment. And
> here's my little U-Haul van with a sign "Sha Na Na" that we made
> ourselves on the side.

Quill finally took the stage, and the opening-act curse main-
tained its grip. Nobody paid much attention; they were dismissed
as the warmup band. It wouldn't be until later that afternoon,
when Santana took the stage, that music would again claim its
position as number-one attraction at the festival. In the meantime,

the epicenter that Woodstock had developed into continued to send shock waves farther and farther out into the world at large, which stared in amazement at the throng through the probing eye of the ever-present media. Even before it began, the Aquarian Exposition was almost guaranteed greater scrutiny and fascination. Set just eighty miles away from the media capital of Manhattan, the festival immediately upstaged similar events that summer simply by being an easier beat to cover. Crusty wire-service and national magazine editors, who had read with only passing interest scattered reports about huge weekend concerts in Atlanta and Seattle and elsewhere, suddenly directed their attention to this backyard happening: after all, their kids had gone to this one, their summer homes were in the Catskills. Their personal stake in the concert perhaps coloring their editorial judgment, bosses finally agreed to assign the Woodstock story to those twenty-five-year-old reporters who'd been yipping all summer about these happenings. A little traffic tie-up never stopped a dogged journalist from getting to the hot spot. And by Saturday afternoon the festival grounds were alive with reporters.

Like so many other cultural phenomena, the blooming of the new youth community became a "story" only when the New York–based media were forced to take a subjective interest in it. Because of their oblique connections with and simple proximity to this festival, it became the focus of an unprecedented amount of mainstream press attention. Nobody bothered to point out that similarly drug-infested, sexually promiscuous happenings were occurring all over the country. Nobody bothered to find out how the festival touched the individual lives of the participants. The mass media jumped on Woodstock as a grotesque mass event. And it was that intense coverage which transformed Woodstock almost overnight into a cultural cliché. There's no better way to become a "Tonight Show" joke than by serving as the subject of a *Life* magazine special issue. The *Life* photographers had arrived Friday night.

If the long-term effect of the media circus would be to reduce the event to cliché, the immediate upshot was far different. Moralists were outraged, parents worried about their children who had gone, and kids stuck home seethed with jealousy. Footage from the farm, as shocking to some as it was enticing to others, was being broadcast across the country on TV. Inflammatory reports in hometown newspapers emphasized the very real health and security threats without communicating the generally tranquil mood of the event. Always informative, *The New York Times* ran a sidebar to its coverage explaining to its readers exactly what "being stoned" felt like. Alarmed parents wrung their hands and did whatever they could to establish for sure their children were all right. One, an unidentified writer for *The New Yorker*'s "About Town" section, accompanied his kid there, and promptly lost her in the crowd. He recorded his experiences later for the stuffy magazine, writing, "We were in a mass of us." Sylvia Greene later found out that her mother had actually called Leslie West, her distant cousin and lead singer in the group Mountain, to ask if he would take a minute during their performance later that afternoon to announce that she should come home. He ignored the request.

Reporters, eking out every possible angle of this multifaceted three-day wonder before it disappeared, cornered the locals for insights and experiences. For some residents the moment in the media glare almost made the whole thing worthwhile. They basked in the attention and freely expounded on the meaning of it all. Others, genuinely disturbed by the disruption and decadence, turned away from the inquiries. For folks like Dr. Paul D'Amico the events and their implications were too confusing and upsetting to bear quick analysis. Instead of a passing retort, the physician considered what he experienced at Woodstock deeply, so much so that it reoriented his career. A novice in the field of drug use as he walked among the cots set up in a high school gym that Saturday afternoon, Dr. D'Amico was taking the first steps of a path that would lead from this Woodstock OD unit to the major rehabilitation facility he would head.

This weekend's invasion of hippies to his native Catskills absolutely shocked the doctor, whose family practice had rarely brought him into contact with drug-abuse cases. These trippers in the gym that afternoon were not strange, inscrutable beings, but regular kids, high as kites on something. A man who barely knew the high a couple of glasses of wine bring on, he had signed on Friday for an emergency detail at the hospital in the high school never imagining the intensity of mental derangement he'd witness there. He was mad at colleagues who refused to help out because of personal or moral aversions to the hippies' habits. Once he got to the gym that afternoon, he understood the repulsion his peers had voiced. But the pharmaceutically induced agony also triggered his concern, and he became darkly fascinated with this exposure to drug ordeals.

> I had thirty-five people overdosed all at once. My main job really wasn't too difficult. I had to see whether or not they should go into the hospital or sleep it off. Knew nothing about drugs at all. I took blood pressure, heart and respiration; if they were stable and not going deeper in, I left them alone. Made rounds of the thirty-five people. I was saying to myself, "My God, this is what it would be like if it were atomic casualties. And here I am." You'd question them about what they took and they might groggily say this or that, but you didn't know what they really got, or how pure it was. It was a miracle that more didn't die.
>
> It was, as I recall, mostly guys. My impression was that about a third was girls. That was to me devastating. All through history in all the cultures women have been given greater respect because they are the creative aspect of society. Men are not. And when you lose the creative element of society you end up in the destructive mode. And when you see women in that position, totally helpless and, I'll say the word, degraded, you start to wonder, you start to wonder.

Though only the worst cases were sent down to the high school, the infirmaries on the festival grounds were attending to their share of freak-outs as well. Henry Diltz passed by there hoping to get the show on film and remembers one shot typical of the discordant images. "A guy standing on his head with another guy running by, and in the background somebody on a motorcycle. Looked like a Fellini movie." A boy with wild eyes grabbed a passerby, shouting over and over again, Communication. Communication is key. Communication. Communication is key.

Nearby, at the Hog Farm food pavilion, Bill Pelligrini was strain-
ing to hear the afternoon's most sensational act, the salsa-psyche-
delic "Soul Survival" set by Santana. Most of the East Coast kids
hadn't yet heard the San Francisco–based group's Latin-inspired
rhythms, and they were responding enthusiastically to the first
really hot music of the day. Turned on by what he could hear, Bill
wasn't ready yet to join the crowd of turned-on fans. Instead of
wending his way over to the stage area, he returned to the woods,
to the cool colony of artisans who were gainfully devoting the
afternoon to their crafts.

Here, the rantings of drugged youngsters and the roar of rock
were silenced, replaced by the hum of hippie commerce. Between
the trees, smooth-talking salesmen peppered their pitch with hip
slang and comforting buzzwords. Step right up, man. Just looking?
That's cool. The announcer on the stage had earlier said this was to
be a free concert. And rowdy revolutionaries were already threatening to "liberate" the food remaining at the concession stands, meaning they were going to steal it and give it away. But here Bill sensed
that the cash-for-profit economics being practiced were one with the
atmosphere of the weekend. Peace, love and money: Penny had
turned that into the mock motto of the Ventures operation. Without
articulating it in exactly the same way, Bill was considering those
same ingredients, but in more harmonious arrangement. He con-
templated the booths of handmade quartz and jade jewelry, tooled
leather clothing and simple smoking paraphernalia.

> I remember thinking, When this is all over, I'm going to have to
> go back to stringing beads. Here are people from all walks of life.
> Not everybody at Woodstock was living with their parents. There
> were people there who were venturing out in society and starting
> to pursue alternative lifestyles. They were here at this giant
> festival and they were here to sell their wares.
>
> I was pretty good with my hands. I always loved shop and they
> always threw me into science classes. They said, "Bill, you're not
> living up to your potential." I was condemned by my potential.
> The idea that I might want to be a builder or a construction
> worker—the school couldn't handle it.

I realized I didn't need a diploma. Up until that point I had been feeling a lot of pressure about dropping out. I had heard there was no way you could make it if you didn't have a diploma, you were going to earn so much less. I said, Wow, if I were a good leather worker, I could build this up. Start small, and with my own hands I could get as big as I want to be. You can start with ten bucks on the street corner, the classic Horatio Alger American dream.

There's nothing wrong with capitalism in my book. It's the poor slob who's not participating in the capital system, the guy who doesn't understand the value of his capital, the guy who rents his capital—which is usually his body and his mind—out for a wage who is really losing it. He's become labor, which is part of the capitalistic tool. So I said, Look at this process here. These people can raise the cow, butcher it, tan the hide, form it into leather and belts, and sell it. I mean, I don't necessarily go that far in it, but I said, Whoa.

For the first time in my life I understood what the marketplace was. And I didn't get it out of economics class.

It was, then, an afternoon of epiphanies in a weekend of revelations. Bill stumbled upon the beginnings of his future calling, Dr. D'Amico felt the stirrings of a new medical concern, Susie Kaufman sensed the rebirth of her deadened womanhood, Jocko Marcellino looked incredulously at the stardom that might possibly await him. Sylvia Greene and Jimmy Jordan were realizing painfully that the sexual revolution had passed them by. John Sebastian recognized that as his fame faded, a door opened that gained him entry to that larger community of American youth from which his celebrity had separated him. On her tower, camera magazine in hand, Elen Orson felt a surge of self-esteem, which, clipboard in hand, Penny was sensing too. Lee's cynicism crumbled as she compared this outdoor love-in to the prison concerts of the summer. In one of the medical tents a baby was born. Though it had started out with death, Saturday was fast becoming a day for new beginnings.

The sun began to set and, with some abatement in the heat, the kids began filtering in from the shade of the woods and shores, swelling the bowl for the night's performances. When twenty years later they were to think of Woodstock, for many it would be this magical evening that was remembered, with the back-to-back star appearances, the balmy Catskill air and the peaceful fraternity that wafted from blanket to blanket. Individually, each participant harbors a particular set of memories of unique happiness, sadness or transcendence. But the collective memory—where a blurry, shared image identifies the whole event—focuses on Saturday night's peak Woodstock experience. Or at least many say it was Saturday night.

In fact, however, in tribute to that evening, many now remember not what they actually saw that night, but rather a conglomerate of sounds and images from the entire weekend. Jumbled together over twenty years, the impressions collect around one night when no rain came to interrupt the spell, when no hassles disrupted the harmony. It was simply the most pleasant night of the weekend, but has thus become representative of the entire event's best moments. Interestingly, the movie Woodstock has heavily influenced the way people recall the night; it seems to have supplanted their own recollections. Many remember the groups in the order they appeared in the movie, which does not correspond to the actual running order. Others swear they recall Crosby, Stills and Nash singing the song "Woodstock" that Saturday night at the festival, even though the composition by Joni Mitchell—used in the credits sequence of the movie—wasn't even written at the time and the group itself didn't appear until Sunday. None of these out-of-sync souvenirs invalidate the uniqueness of that Saturday night. Rather, they prove its special place in Woodstock lore. The selective memory sought subsequent images to augment an already pleasurable experience. The film provided the Woodstock Nation with a mnemonic aid that helped embellish the memory.

If the folks in the field were gathering grooves to last them a lifetime, for the most part the feelings backstage that night were less positive. A distinct borderline divided the good times shared by the "people" and the continued war of nerves and egos under way behind the performing platform. As at any hit show, the audience witnessed little of the tension: with each subsequent act, the intoxicating high of starlight, klieg light and applause wove its magic on the performers, erasing whatever far from negligible concern had been spooking them just minutes before. From the audience's perspective—or at least for the majority of the stoned kids—the guitar licks were hot, the harmonies on target, the mere presence of their heroes and heroines enough to thrill.

But for Tom Constanten the evening's gig was a bust, exacerbated rather than alleviated by the actual performance. He remembers the festival appearance as part of an extended eastern tour that had included very successful shows at the Fillmore East, one of the halls where their cult following, the Dead Heads, could be counted on for devoted attendance and attention. At this point in his career with the band, when things were going right, they could still go very right indeed. But whatever confidence he had gained in New York had been dispelled since. The helicopter ride in had dismayed him: so many people, too many people. Looking out from backstage as Canned Heat's Bob "The Bear" Hite finished his set, the keyboard player eyed the crowd and knew right away that the almost ritualistic adulation the Grateful Dead had learned to expect from its following could not exist here. For all the radiance this audience generated, its size simply precluded the rapt concentration the Dead's sets required. There was too much space, both physical and metaphysical, between the audience and the group. And that meant, he knew, there would be too much space between himself and the other band members. Looking back now, he mentions going on late, technical problems, lack of audience receptivity. Darkening the actual experience of the night, however, may be the impact on his memory of his departure from the band, which followed Woodstock by barely four months.

You might recall how it had been raining, everything was getting doused. The effect it had on the stage was electrical to say the least. Guitarists were getting shocks from their strings. And as if that hadn't been enough itself, the stage was perceptibly rickety, you could feel the motion of it. There was that to think of also.

Of course the audience was nice and vinegary by the time we

got on—we got on late. They looked like one of those Hiero-
nymus Bosch paintings, with ten thousand grotesque bodies.

The electricity during the performance didn't bother me, but
because everyone else was so frazzled it made the tempo hard to
find a lot of the time. It was not an especially long performance as
they went. I think we played for forty-five minutes. There were so
many groups. It's like pizza when you order seven ingredients—
there isn't as much of any one as when you order two. Everyone
was glad to get off, we felt like an android jukebox. When it's
working, there's nothing like it and you know why you're doing
it. When it's not working, anything can seem to be a job. You feel
like the last-place baseball team: you got to show up and see
who's going to beat you that day.

Other performers carried on as if the biggest blowout of the
decade amounted to just another badly organized one-night
stand. From his tent in the performers' area, John Sebastian
watched some of the star tantrums and heard many of the gripes;
he was surprised that the spirit of the event had not touched his
peers. Hardly innocent to the rock world, he stood there in his tie-
dyed clothes, bewildered by the antics. He watched as the Dead
members, with unusual solemnity, marched off the stage and
quickly zipped away in station wagons. They didn't even stick
around to listen to Janis, who finally groped her way to the stage
after midnight. Few of his colleagues sensed the same community
Sebastian did. Few felt the same desire to remain a part of this
nation throughout the entire weekend. Still attempting to create a
new identity away from the limelight and the Spoonful, Sebastian
found new purpose at Woodstock, even if only for as long as the
festival lasted. His own trial by fire behind him, he assumed the
role of Saturday night's backstage guardian angel, backslapper—
and tent keeper.

At this point I was mainly engaged in keeping the tent dry.
Because of the rains Sly Stone was having trouble staying clean.
He had much more spectacular stage gear than other folks. I was
trying to loosen him up at one point and I walked over and his
sister was grumping about something. I said, "Gee, is there

anything I can do? Use the tent or something." And Sly said, "Oh, she just needs a little red meat and she'll be fine."

I thought about that remark for a half-hour. I often wonder to this day, was he just being as funny as I thought he was being, or did she actually want meat? I thought it was a funny remark.

At this point Creedence went on. People who only saw the Woodstock movie do not know how good Creedence Clearwater Revival was that day. I think Creedence Clearwater delivered a set that afternoon that was every bit as important and delicious as any of those other performers. I think they may not have had any other serious competition besides Sly Stone and Jimi Hendrix. Fogerty came off that stage and said, "Well, you guys really screwed that one up." I thought that was the most amazing demonstration by a three-piece band I had ever seen. I thought it was so tight and so wonderfully strong, particularly in my psychedelicized state. I think it really helped me have something to hang on to as the psychedelic experience washed over me.

Meanwhile, for the crew, frenzy charged the proceedings. Major crises arose and miraculously were solved—the threat of the National Guard had again been averted, and a sudden money shortage was overcome when a county banker agreed to cash checks in the middle of the night. Two days of narrow escapes were beginning to wear on the staff, though. As much as they tried to practice the flower-child credo of cooperation and mutual understanding, the inevitable stress of being together that long was building up.

Under the pressure, conflicts inherent from the very beginning of the festival planning came to a boil. As a counterculture megaevent, Woodstock had been divided since its inception between political and show biz realities. It was intended by its entrepreneurial sponsors as a massive entertainment and commercial venture, but one that observed and embodied the sixties generation's ideologies. The very fact that so many thousands would gather to celebrate a revolutionary lifestyle would be the statement here. The party was the message. More radical elements had all along been lobbying for more explicit political content, the sort of pamphleteering Ron Stone had expected to find when he drove up from Washington. For them the dozens of antiwar, anti-Nixon, antibomb, antivivisectionist booths that filled the woods around the site weren't sufficient proof of a politicized Woodstock. Envisioning a rally rather than a concert, and eyeing the stage as the decade's biggest soapbox, parties who had been calling for more speechifying grew desperate. This Saturday of Love was beginning to look as if it might not make way for them.

Country Joe looked over with disbelief when he heard Abbie Hoffman agitating for some time at the mike in between Sly and the Family Stone and the Who. Even if this were the place for a Yippie diatribe, this clearly wasn't the time: it was two in the morning and the last thing the hopping kids wanted to hear were the rantings of a self-promoting media star. It was little more than twenty-four hours since Joe had scored a hit with the "Fixin'-to-Die Rag," and already he knew that an antiwar jingle was about all this crowd could handle politically. Hoffman's demand to address the masses and raise their consciousness to his message was being rejected by the stage management.

Henry Diltz remembers hearing a brouhaha of some sort cooking backstage as the Who began their set. But the peripatetic photographer assumed Hoffman's continuing harangue was just another staff mistake. Even low-key, easygoing Henry had had his share of them. A catwalk of sorts had been built at the front of the stage, dropped about five feet below its edge, so that Henry, the handful of other authorized photographers and the film crew could work without interrupting audience sight lines. Nowhere, perhaps, did the hippie ethos stand more of a test than on that cramped, overcrowded, equipment-filled isthmus that connected Woodstock Nation, stage left, with Woodstock Nation, stage right. Underconstructed for the traffic it would eventually have to tolerate—like everything else at the festival—the catwalk was populated by men and women of a uniquely driven breed: the photographer of the moment. Here along the lip of the stage, cameramen and photographers competed to record that split second of perfection that once gone was gone forever. With animal-like rapacity, the catwalkers rushed into position and flashed, creating a concentrated melee of ambition, obnoxiousness and

pseudo-polite professionalism. Diltz lined up for a shot of the
Who's Roger Daltrey, his blond locks a halo against the lights. Just
as he was about to shoot, one of Elen Orson's colleagues from the
film crew pushed him aside, gruffly mumbling an apology. Decid-
ing life—as well as the festival—was too short to put up with such
hostility, Henry started to pick up his equipment when onstage a
far more shocking and violent encounter broke out.

> I was right in front of the Who, I was on the lip of the stage. There
> was Roger Daltrey, with his fringes flying. And Abbie Hoffman
> ran onto the stage and Peter Townshend took his guitar and held
> it straight out, perfectly, with the neck toward the guy, held it just
> like a bayonet, and went klunk, right into his neck. I thought
> they killed him. That was one of the most startling things about
> the whole concert. It was amazing. The Who were known as
> being very violent, these English pub-drinking musicians. They
> trashed their instruments. When these guys got in a fight, there
> wasn't a lot of prancing around and posturing. These guys were
> very earthy. I also thought they were right. Peter Townshend
> made quick work of him.

From his vantage point backstage, Country Joe looked with
equal amazement at the same incident.

> There was a pause, and Abbie Hoffman jumped up on the stage
> and grabbed Townshend's microphone and yelled that John Sin-
> clair, a political activist and poet, was in prison for possession of
> two joints while everybody in the audience was partying. And at
> that point Peter looked up and hit him in the head with this
> guitar. And Abbie jumped over the fence and into the crowd.
> Townshend didn't hit him over the head with his guitar. He just
> pushed him out of the way with the end of his guitar. There were
> only a few beats there in between songs.
> He was interrupting the act. I felt what Townshend did was
> justified. It didn't bother me. I was enjoying the Who more than I
> was enjoying Abbie.

Under different circumstances such a display of violence might
have triggered a mob reaction. Had there been enough people in

the audience who sympathized with Hoffman, or who even vaguely supported his right to a forum here, the sight of his summary ejection from the stage at the butt of a guitar would have been provocation to riot. Violence under such extreme conditions begets violence: and aside from scattered fistfights between drunken jock-hippies, this was the closest the festival came to visible hostilities. The incident was nothing less than the Woodstock Nation's invitation to disintegrate.

But this was not to be a community that followed sociological dogma. The domino effect of aggression was never played out; the unwritten constitution of harmonious accord remained inviolate. And preconceived methods of communicating ideological positions were to hold no sway here. Hoffman didn't realize it, but his self-appointed mission of consciousness-raising was entirely misplaced. With their silence, the people voted against Hoffman. With his pub-trained, teddy-boy bit of self-defense, Peter Townshend symbolically guillotined empty rhetoric so that the far more radical reign of abandon and mindless good times might continue. Here was an ideology iconoclastic even beyond the iconoclasts' ken.

But the clock was ticking. And the sun was rising. Jefferson Airplane followed the Who, ushering in Sunday, the last day for this particular visitation of Brigadoon. In town, the Feldmans, Dr. D'Amico and George Neuhaus awoke and could hear Grace Slick's screech piercing the Sabbath dawn. The residents washed their faces and fried their eggs, while in the field the boys and girls settled down. The magic night melted gently into sunrise—removing the shadows from the kids, still untired, still excited. The Airplane helicoptered away, and in parkas or bedrolls or each other's eager arms, young people snuggled then coupled. At the end of this perfect Woodstock day, the perfect political gesture: They were making love not war.

SUNDAY

THE WOODSTOCK love affair among 500,000 strangers that began with Friday's introductory party and saw Saturday's extended marriage feast and consummation faced its sudden and difficult period of adjustment Sunday. By Monday the romance would be over.

The intensity of the weekend compressed time, accelerating processes—both social and psychological—that usually take much much longer to run their course. A city came into being overnight and in a flash the whole cycle of growth, prosperity and decline played itself out. In fast forward the city's idiosyncratic culture and mores established themselves, its own forms of commerce and socializing evolved, and most important, the pride of belonging unified the populace. Then, overnight, it all began to disintegrate. That dizzying movement through life stages created a force that caught up the festival participants and hurled them along through unexpected personal changes. Bombarded with sensations, citizens of the Woodstock Nation passed through a full spectrum of human experience in four days. It was a civilization in miniature blessed with the acute awareness of its own beginning and its imminent end. A weekend in the country—after all, how much can that really change anyone? But this was no ordinary weekend, and no ordinary field in the country.

The fact that within twenty-four hours the entire cycle would be played out gave this Sunday morning its character. Endings always prompt reflection, and in the unique chronology of Woodstock Time, the festivalgoers woke up Sunday in an uncertain limbo somewhere between Saturday's orgiastic celebration of being and the finality of Monday's sunrise. Although another evening of music lay ahead, including the promised appearance of rock god Jimi Hendrix, the festival itself had entered its adulthood. With this maturity some of the earlier exuberance was replaced by a more sophisticated understanding of the true role Woodstock was to play in the ongoing culture out there. With the end near, things unique to this experience had to be savored quickly, assessed, sifted through. The intoxicating isolation of this protected paradise would not last forever, and already the castaways were thinking about what they'd be able to preserve of the utopia and bring back home with them. If Saturday was the ultimate day of pagan sensation and escape, Sunday would produce questioning, discovery and, for some, the joy of self-knowledge.

Scott Lane would continue his obsessive quest for pleasure through the festival's last hour, and beyond. For him the delirium of Saturday was not the passing promise of a perfect but isolated day in the sun, but an enduring code of ethics. Knowing well the proper etiquette of the moment, Scott rolled over, pulled on his blue jeans, and told the girl he had spent Saturday night with that it had been great. He had performed his well-rehearsed routines, both sexual and social. They may have missed much of the concert, but love ham Scott had created a show all his own. As with any performance, once the show is over, the performer goes on to the next one. Unashamedly taking the noncommittal leave his generation had adopted as cool, he set off for the next series of encounters. But even for this amiable narcissist, Sunday brought its moments when the piercing reality of life after Woodstock—or simply life after youth—caught him off guard.

As with most of the kids in the field that morning, the tug in Scott's gut was the most persistent reminder of the world as he had previously known it. In the preceding days at the festival the inverted infrastructure of Woodstock society had delighted him: sex and drugs, luxuries in the real world, were basic goods and services here. Meanwhile, the food and water he took for granted at home were becoming scarcities. At first that didn't matter to Scott or the other pleasure-seekers much, willing as they were to trade the occasional hunger pang for Woodstock's more available creature comforts. But by Sunday morning nature's basic needs were becoming undeniable, and suddenly the voluptuaries' fantasies of satisfaction focused on nothing more elaborate than a bagel with cream cheese.

While Scott would have been hard-pressed to find any delicacies quite so exotic, because of emergency efforts that had been under way through the night he would be able to find something to eat. Local hotels donated shipments of eggs and cereal, members of the ladies' auxiliaries in surrounding towns made sandwiches. Max Yasgur, terrified by the threats from his neighbors implicating him directly in the folly, and secretly pleased by the publicity he was receiving, donated milk and eggs from his dairy. The benign impulse to nurture that had been behind the Feldmans' roadside refreshment stand multiplied through the weekend, and by Sunday morning the food crisis at the concert was in check. While the charity of the surrounding townships ostensibly poured forth with no expectation of payback, the handout didn't come without implicit strings attached. None of the kids was expected to pay cash for the supplies they received. But the price of the well-intentioned sandwiches and doughnuts was something that had come to mean more than money in the emotional marketplace of the Woodstock Nation: that morning, the hippies traded in their illusion of independence for sustenance. No one mentioned it aloud, but the collective consciousness acknowledged it. The flower children were relying on the grown-ups out there to take care of them. While the innocence and openness of childhood were valued here, nobody felt comfortable with childhood's impotency and incompetence. Muddy rebels stood in soup lines for a handout, holding paper plates up like overgrown kids at a school picnic. And something changed. Perhaps it was during the Sunday-morning chowdown that the first wave of post-Woodstock awareness hit. After all, this antiestablishment slumber party was able to continue only because the older generation was working to keep it going. An unspoken irony hovered over the field as palpable as that cloud of law-breaking pot. The parental indulgence and security from which this weekend in the country had been an escape were the only things keeping the party alive. To its participants and many of its analysts, Woodstock stood as proof that a separate and extensive counterculture existed in pockets across the United States. The tending and nurturing of the festival by the simple folk of Sullivan County that Sunday suggested, though, that the whole event may have been merely the instinctive incubation one generation gives to the next, regardless of mutation. Saturday's feverish and contagious counterculture high was mellowing. Each sandwich swallowed, each burger bitten, each little brown egg accepted signaled another step away from insular make-believe toward the coexistence with the real world in which each citizen of the Woodstock Nation would soon be called upon to abide. It was Sunday brunch and the dreamers were waking up.

In line, Scott again spotted his buddy Fred DiRosa, his head sticking up above the crowd of long-hairs devouring a long-awaited breakfast. Fred, still down-spirited over being jilted on Friday, was in a sore mood and Scott decided he would try to cheer him up. He had heard about a spot in the woods where someone had hooked up some hosing for outdoor showers, and thought a little cleaning up would do them both a lot of good.

The showers were actually part of a well-designed campsite that had originally been intended as a controlled-access bivouac for festivalgoers who preregistered for a tent area. It turned into just another crash pad, overrun and unattended. Still, despite the lack of supervision of the plumbing at the campground, the showers were working when Fred and Scott finally found them. Like most of the structures that made it through the weekend, the shower facility had remained operational because it emphasized uncomplicated efficiency over design. Cinder blocks piled on top of each other about six feet high, wooden planks beneath and a series of spouts without nozzles. They stripped and joined the other guys cleaning up. Scott pranced in and out of the cold water, darting around the area like a demonic streaker.

> So me and DiRosa are taking naked showers underneath this waterfall—a cement wall with water dripping down. Suddenly, DiRosa says, "Oh shit, there's my dad." DiRosa's father was with the mounted patrol. He looked like Desi Arnaz, real sweet. But he hated hippies. The mounted patrol all came to Woodstock on their horses. His father was a real staunch conservative, and the horse had all these beads and flowers on it already. After the festival he was so moved by it he came back to help clean up, and came back a couple of months later too. Fred said after a couple of months he was back to his old scumbag self.
>
> So there we are, stark naked. Hi, Mr. DiRosa. Hey, did you say hello to the chief?

Dripping wet and stripped naked, the two youths stood in the woods and looked up into the stern but kind face of a fully uniformed, authoritarian man riding his festooned horse with dignity. By comparison, they looked small, powerless, shriveled. Scott, fumbling to figure how he could work this particular audience of one, was living out the universal actor's nightmare: suddenly realizing you are naked on a stage and don't even know what play you're in. The Woodstock crowd-pleaser ran smack into a critic he couldn't budge. It summed up that Sunday morning perfectly, when the reality of the world outside Woodstock began inexorably to crowd in on the good times. Caught at his most childlike and vulnerable, Scott could do nothing but mock the situation, by taunting the older man's position of power, becoming heckler to Mr. DiRosa's silence. Here in the Borscht Belt, where hundreds of standups had died before, Scott was realizing for the first time his act had a limited appeal. No matter how cool he tried to be, the absurdity of the incident could not be denied. As soon as

Mr. DiRosa arrived, the innocent pleasure of running naked through the woods seemed silly, dumb, infantile. Mr. DiRosa turned and rode away, leaving Scott to contemplate the meaning of the encounter.

In another part of the forest, Rufus Friedman went through an oddly parallel experience. Throughout the morning the all-purpose bantam of the Ventures team had been pitching in, mostly helping the film crew get through the traffic. At one point he jumped on top of the hood of the crew's car and pretended to be an ornament, barking and squealing at the meandering hippies to make way. Although he referred to himself as a cosmic fool when he carried on like this, Rufus was exhilarated by the sense of control and even power he had had this weekend. Whether he was escorting Janis through her haze or helping Penny build an infirmary out of a crew mess hall, each little task brought its own satisfaction. Yes, a geek he had been when he came to Woodstock, and as a geek he had been treated since he arrived. But now he was a geek with a Ventures jacket, a geek with a backstage pass, a geek who had built this thing and was making sure it stayed afloat.

And then he decided to take a break for a minute, a breather. A couple of friends beckoned him over for a quickie souvenir photo. It was the festival's last day, after all, time for such parting shots. Feeling like a big shot, he grabbed a female coworker and began to posture. Soon enough the two were engaging in mock foreplay, all for the sake of the camera.

> Then all of a sudden my parents showed up at the festival! My father decided to go have a look at it. He got through by telling the cops he was an investor. They didn't have backstage passes. They were just wandering around and bumped into me. There's my mom dressed in her finery. I was fooling around with this girl, getting our picture taken, she's making believe she's going down on me. I think I was a little embarrassed. You know how little kids are when parents show up at summer camp.

Such chance encounters with the older generation held mirrors up to the children that they didn't like. Just when they thought they had it all figured out, the intrusion of parents knocked them off their cocky surefootedness. Actors whose roles as lover and cowboy served them well in this fantasyscape, Scott and Rufus both faced sudden reminders that certain critical audiences couldn't so easily be suckered in. Master travelers through the Woodstock world, they were confronting the inevitable conflicts voyagers often experience: they return from exotic lands where for the length of their stay they felt completely at home, and feel queerly lost back with their own.

For completely different reasons, Dr. D'Amico was beginning to feel at home at the festival—or if not at home, at least connected by fascination. The renegade lifestyle Yasgur's farm hosted drew him in, obsessed him as it repelled him. He had finished his shift Saturday at the high school infirmary and, returning home, found himself thinking of little else but the scene in the gym that afternoon. Seeing the overflow from the festival as long-haired boys and braless girls streamed down the quiet main street of Livingston Manor, he tried to make sense of the self-destructive urges that seemed to control these kids. At night, watching the local news coverage from the site itself, he shared with his wife the feelings he had accumulated from his first encounter with overdose cases, flipped-out teens and deep-fried brain matter. Why would so many kids choose to lose themselves to the annihilation of drugs, he wondered. He associated the rebelliousness of taking drugs with an entire leftist lifestyle, as if smoking pot and draft evasion, antiwar protests and the peace movement were all inextricably linked as a single phenomenon. To a man of his unswerving Catholic mindset, the festival was the handiwork of the devil. The public sexual acts, the deliberate quest for intoxication were as compellingly and otherworldly profane as an apparition at Lourdes was supernaturally holy. His was an extreme reaction to the excesses of the Woodstock Nation, but one that points up the magnetism of the event on participant and observer alike. It was all an enigma that hooked into D'Amico's mystical orientation; he saw it as nothing less than a mass possession he needed to witness firsthand to decipher. The doctor decided he'd go up to the festival the next day, after mass. And unlike the kids in the field, he purposely brought his parents.

> I was so intrigued by this thing that I got my father, who was at this time seventy-some years old, and my mother and my wife and another friend in the seventies. And I said, "You want to see something that's going to be in the history books, you want to come with me. You won't believe what you'll see."
>
> You had to be there. The pot! I was disturbed about it. When I got there, I didn't know who the hell brought all the drugs in. To this day I wonder if there wasn't more to that than appears on the surface. All I knew was that the smoke was like a fog. It was a heavy, warm day. Close. And that smoke from that marijuana and the drugs they were taking, you could smell it all over.
>
> My wife must have looked a little scared, so many people and all high. One of them said to her, "You don't have to be ascared of us. We're peace people." And then he said, "Look at that helicopter. How beautiful." Apparently he was on psychedelics. He was having all these visions.
>
> All drugs are part of satanic influence in a way. Sex, drugs, and rock and roll, they're all related. If you have a spiritual outlook on life you have to get rid of the material or sensual. If you're spiritual you can accept people who are sensual. If you're a real Christian you condemn the acts of people, not the people. I felt they were being deluded. I felt the whole country was really being destroyed by the music and the implications of the songs. They were getting their spiritual experiences from drugs.

With his like-minded companions D'Amico strolled the farm and the woods, shaking his head. But whereas most of the residents of the county were just waiting this ordeal out, D'Amico was collecting impressions that would serve as a calling for a new mission in his life. Like a medieval saint who decides to devote himself to the conversion of pagans, D'Amico would eventually transfer his disdain for the drug users into pity and healing. It was far from his mind that Sunday morning as he shooed pacifist trippers away from his wife, but with time he'd become the county's top drug-abuse counselor and therapist.

As the doctor walked back to his car, mystified but intrigued,

Anne Feldman in her jeep sped by down the same back road. She had just dropped Burt off for another day of ineffectual security work, laughing at him as she watched him ramble off into the youthful crowd. What would he be assigned to do today, she wondered. Keep the nudists off the road again, keep the hippies from smoking pot, break them apart when they're making love. She smiled as she imagined her chubby little husband walking up to a strapping flower child and telling him to put on his pants. She laughed out loud as she thought of him standing far away from the stage, snapping his fingers to some nonsensical song he had never heard before. She knew it was not a sense of duty that compelled him to show up for this final day of bogus police work, but her husband's finely tuned sense of the absurd. He loved playing constable-on-patrol in this most improbable fantasy city on the hill, loved simply being with all these wackos. For all the media hype about the generation gap, many of the middle-aged folks keeping this youth event alive were getting just as much of a kick out of the proceedings as the hippies. The concertgoers were, Burt liked to believe, kindred spirits with him after all.

Because all pretense of law and order had been dropped by this time, Burt felt free to enjoy the morning secure in the knowledge that there was nothing he could do to improve the situation. The pressure was off. Anne, on the other hand, felt obliged to do something. It was fine for Burt to play the cop while really just taking in the scene, but Anne was a doer. Ever since she had followed Burt up here those many years ago, she had searched for outlets for her creativity and drive, vents to the frustrations life in the country presented. It wasn't easy but she always was on the lookout for opportunities to count, to matter. This, she sensed, was just such an opportunity. Burt got to join the security staff and have a conventional position at the concert. But as the festival turned all conventions upside down, that position became increasingly irrelevant. With no formal title, Anne was actually in a better position to respond to the real needs of the day. She drove sensing that a mission lay ahead.

Anne had become aware that some of her neighbors were taking great advantage of the festivalgoers, charging them astronomical amounts for telephone calls or use of the bathroom. Earlier that morning she had refreshed the water and sandwich material on the little roadside stand; she noticed the area was still parade-ground neat. Cruising the back roads in the jeep now, she saw a dismayed young couple sitting next to a handsome late-model car. Like many others, they had merely driven off the concrete and onto the dirt shoulder on Friday, when the ground was still hard and could tolerate a parked car. By Sunday the kids looking to get out early returned to their cars only to find them sunk in the mud created by the rain and pedestrian traffic over the weekend. Anne pulled up beside the couple and told them she could help.

With a knowledge of chains and axles she had acquired during her years in the country, Bronx-born Anne Feldman was helping the ignorant little city kids get back home from their weekend in her backyard. Other local women spread peanut butter and jelly. Some volunteered to help out at the infirmaries. And here was Anne, strapping giant links around Chrysler fronts, telling the hippies to back away, yanking 3,000-pound vehicles out of the muck. She'd wave good-bye to one satisfied customer and drive around looking for another. Like Penny and Lee before her, Anne was getting things done, using the skills she had never been asked before to demonstrate. When finally it was time to pick Burt up, she reluctantly detached her chains from one last car, gave the kids a wink and returned for her husband. In the distance she saw Burt coming out of the woods near the pond, strolling aimlessly among the hippies, the sun glinting off his little tin badge. He was snapping his fingers in time to some ear-splitting music from the stage. She was sure he'd be full of stories about what he had accomplished that day.

As she looked over at the stage, she saw a very strange man at the microphone. It wasn't his long hair or clashing multicolored clothing that startled her; she had seen all of that before. This fellow rasped with a voice most unpleasant to her ears, not at all melodic, and he contorted his body as if he were writhing in pain. His fingers flew around uncontrollably and his head lurched forward and backward as he slurred the words of his wretched song.

In the field, the kids were up on their feet swinging to the beat of the incomprehensible tune. She was catching Joe Cocker in full performance conniption, the first act to take the stage that Sunday.

At that point, most of the audience didn't know who Joe Cocker was either. The British blues singer's arc of popularity was just at its beginning when he landed this career-securing gig. But so eager were the kids to keep the festival alive despite the end they saw looming that they boogied robustly to whatever diversion came from the stage. Quill had opened the show the day before, almost as unknown, and they died, the sacrificial lamb of Saturday's unlimited expectations. Joe Cocker drew the point position the very next day, and because the atmosphere was so different—and maybe because he had truly durable talent—the performance set him up for life.

Without a really experienced eye but with a native intuition, Elen Orson knew then and there that the footage they were getting of Cocker would be a highlight of the festival film. He was so visual, so much more kinetic than so many of the other performers. Or at least from her point of view she could appreciate how much more filmic his contortions were. And now she could finally see the show. After spending Friday and Saturday removed from the stage in the remote towers, the production assistant had been reassigned to the lip ledge hugging the front of the stage. It was a prime position, just about sitting in the laps of the musicians. The dream job was delivering the perks: not only was she gaining incredible work experience, but Sunday put her on the stage for the most far-out concert of the year. Her job was still the same, running canisters of film back and forth to the cameraman, but ledge work was better than tower work: the distance to run was shorter and not cluttered with fans, and her diligence and efficiency were more easily noticed by the film crew's top personnel, who were clustered around the stage. There was one downer: the path to and from the ledge passed by the backstage Portosan area, and by Sunday afternoon approaching that area required fortitude, speed and an ability to hold one's breath. On one trip, she realized she had had it easy.

I think backstage there were four toilets for four hundred people. There were four Portosans in the back area. The Portosans were real bad, no paper left, and it was terrible. The smell was terrible. Someone was walking along and heard pounding in the Portosan. He saw that a van had backed up against one of the doors and somebody was trapped inside. It was something like being buried alive. I remember there were hippies handing out incense. That was their mission. Everyone found their niche and did what had to be done. Someone decided the bathrooms were unbearable and gave away all this incense.

Once she was back on the ledge, the cameraman asked Elen to give his shoulders a massage, therapy she had become famous for among the male crew members to whom she administered it. And as she began to knead the tense muscles in his neck, Cocker wailing away behind her, she felt a single wet drop on her head. And then another. Looking up at the sky, Elen knew the very position she occupied high above the crowd and free from obstruction might expose her to mortal danger. Massive black thunderheads, like a roiling and unstoppable fairy-tale monster, rolled over the treetops, their low menacing rumbles vibrating the platform she stood on as no artificial amplification could. She froze and looked into the sky with terror.

In the dog days of August, when the conditions are right, Catskills weather can get mean and dangerous. As if to remind the summer transients—city folk protected from real weather—who was the boss here, the region held certain meteorological surprises. In a period of an hour the visitor might find himself hiding from the overbright sun and then hiding again from treacherous lightning. The shower on Friday was a mild, refreshing baptism for the cocelebrants. Sunday's deluge was a Catskill Killer, a sinister freak of nature with a force most of the hippies in the field didn't even understand. Outside indulgence had taken care of the hunger pangs which earlier that day jeopardized the good times. But no surrogate parent or neighborly outreach program could protect the kids from an especially violent electric storm. Naked (literally, for some) and vulnerable, the Woodstock Nation turned away from the stage and watched as the simple and primal power of barometric pressure challenged their incredible self-assurance. Thunder and lightning hadn't frightened many of them since they were little. Many of them were frightened again.

The festival's decision-makers were facing a major conflict. Should safety or show biz be the first priority at an event where the show was the only way to ensure safety? Over the course of the weekend, the stage had become the major source of information, news, comfort. To curtail activity up there could trigger the breakdown of the tentative order that reigned over the 500,000. But if an electric storm hit, the platform could become a frying pan. It was a conundrum created by the sheer size of the event. In order to quell the riot the storm might bring, the public address system had to be kept alive. And beyond that, if the system were shut off as a preemptive measure against possible electrocution, would they be able to get it going again?

As camera assistant, Elen was facing a similar conflict. Should she weather the storm for documentary purposes, or should she run for cover and save her neck? A cautionary drizzle began as the winds picked up, hitting those stationed on the unprotected lip of the stage dead on. The cameraman with her kept on filming, whirling into action to capture the crowd's reaction to the oncoming storm: dumbstruck but entertained, they seemed to be accepting the possibility of a typhoon as simply the weekend's best special effect. Elen knew better.

> They had these big canopies over the stage, and when it drizzled, the tarps filled up with hundreds of pounds of water. That alone could have killed somebody. They had to lance them to let them drain. Then it started to get cloudy. I remember looking up at the sky, and being from this region, I know big black clouds coming over the hill real quick mean you better get inside real quick. How long do you think we're going to live with a hundred ten volts in our hands when this water comes down?
>
> "Let's turn off the power on the stage," we were saying. "But you can't stop this concert!" I wasn't sure what they should do. I was hoping it would just rain for a couple of minutes. It rained for over an hour. Very heavy rain.
>
> Just before they turned off the power, my cameraman realized

this may be the last shot he's going to get, so he starts turning around and around and around. Filming in a three-hundred-sixty-degree pan—the mayhem, the crowd, the stuff onstage getting moved around. At one point he caught me, got a nice close-up of me looking like, "Holy God, we're going to die." I wasn't aware they had a shot of me. They turned the power off and he ran out into the crowd. And I stayed in the pit. He was a little worried for me that everything was going to get a little nuts. He didn't know if the crowd would start charging. We were in a real good position to fry. I was holding an electrical cord jerry-rigged with tape, and my feet were wet. And everything was wet. If lightning had struck we all would have fried.

Meanwhile, the water was creating havoc with the foundations of the stage. As mud collected behind the pilings supporting the six stories of scaffolding, the whole edifice was actually sliding into the crowd. Sliding imperceptibly at first, but the tech staff was making rough estimates that the shifting would accelerate if the rain didn't stop. Around Penny Stallings, guys were making plans for what to do as soon as the rain stopped, admitting they could do nothing before it did. She turned away and looked at the field, now without a speck of green in the sea of brown. She watched as stoned kids climbed the sound towers, now swaying in the winds like spindly scarecrows. It was an amusement-park ride for them, she said to herself, as she heard a fellow Ventures staffer beg the daredevils to get away from the perilous structures. The stage, the towers, the possible exposed wires drenched by endangering torrents. She felt absolutely powerless; it was a sensation she had almost forgotten during the busy weekend. The other emergencies of the festival had involved human error, mismanagement, just plain arrogance and stupidity. But for the retribution of an angry rain god, she had no solution.

Pelted for nearly half an hour, the oblivious kids decided to take matters into their own hands. In tribal unison a chant of "No rain, no rain, no rain" went up from the field toward the unrelenting skies. And when the clouds ignored the incantation, the kids didn't despair: it was the group vocalization of protest as much as the protest itself that mattered. Never really acknowledging the danger they were in, the flower children viewed the inconvenience as just the latest insignificant deprivation of a weekend that wasn't about bourgeois comfort anyway. If it had been natural to make love under Saturday's sunny sky, it was just as natural to stand together, hold hands and chant through this mass shower. Luckily, the misbelief that no wrong could befall them in this special place kept the concertgoers from total chaos during the hour-long downpour. Nobody was thrilled, of course—and the downside of natural living was becoming an unfortunate theme of this final day in the country. Wet, and getting hungry again, the festivalgoers stoically tried to find hedonistic potential in the rain. Reverting to the impulses of youth, they slopped gleefully in the mud their parents had told them to stay clear of years before. Bare-assed, they took running leaps into oozing fields for slips-and-slides through muck. Standing up, they were spritzed clean by the rain pouring down. For all the peril the kids faced without being aware of it, the storm united them in a common feeling of resilience and goodwill, the benevolence engendered by sharing adversity.

Bill Pelligrini understood hard times, but sharing them was something new. An outcast who thought himself alone in his world view, he couldn't believe how many people like himself he had encountered this weekend. He wasn't the only one getting beat up for long hair, he wasn't the only one who wanted more from life than suburban mediocrity, and he wasn't the only one getting soaked on this last day of the festival. He thrust his face into the beating wall of water and opened his mouth to suck in the big, sweet drops. The danger and discomforts the storm delivered down on Bill and his newfound brethren were different from the hardships he—and so many of those who had journeyed here—had faced back home: here they weren't faced alone.

There was this milk truck, so I helped give milk away during the rainstorm. Then I took a trip down the mud slide. I was feeling good, I was ready to try anything. We were all wet. I remember sitting around campfires and all these people who were going through the same things I was going through were there. And for once we were in a lump of us that was so big they had to leave us

alone. It was such a big blob of people there, there was no
pressure point they could use. We can get along with each other
and enjoy each other, and respect each other's values. We don't
have to sit in the closet and be afraid of being different.

When the rain finally stopped, the organizers knew the clock
was ticking: if the show didn't start up again immediately, the
cooperativeness of the kids might be pushed beyond the limit. But
first, a major overhaul of the waterlogged electrical system had to
be conducted, the stage had to be shored up to prevent further
slippage, and perhaps most difficult of all, a performer had to be
found who was willing to go out and be the guinea pig for the
operation. As it turned out, adequate recircuiting of the system
required keeping it off for an unspecified time. Frantic, the stage
managers scurried about wondering how they could possibly keep
the crowd entertained until evening. Country Joe, one of the very
few vets backstage, did what a military man is trained never to do:
he volunteered.

After his unplanned solo debut on Friday, Joe had been joined
Saturday by the rest of his group; their performance together was
scheduled for Sunday. One of the few performers to stay the entire
weekend, Joe had by now passed beyond the nervousness so many
of the come-and-go musicians experienced during their visit to the
festival. Instead, the special aura of enclave, safe harbor, for hippie
rebels instilled in him a feeling of oneness with the crowd. Still not
completely happy with his performance Friday night, he was
dying to get out in front of them again, with or without amplification. When the stage stood empty that Sunday afternoon, he
couldn't resist the invitation. Accompanied by the Fish, he
charged the stage and launched into his act without the benefit of
sound-tower amplification.

We went onstage and did a little agitprop drumming-and-per-
cussing thing. We were chanting, "No more rain, no more rain,"
and passing out little treats from the performers' tent to the
audience.
    And everything was going really well until Barry Melton, who

was the lead guitar player of the Fish, brought two cases of beer in aluminum cans and started throwing them into the audience and hitting people in the head. Then they started throwing things back at us. They were getting in a very foul mood and we had to run off the stage.

But I felt completely at home, it was really an amazing free space. In 1969 the counterculture was not a secure place to be. A lot of people didn't like you and would just come up and hit you or arrest you for being a rocker or a hippie. So it was very refreshing to be in a totally free environment where you weren't going to be trashed for being part of the counterculture. And it became very obvious to me from the word go that this was our turf. The highway patrol was there, the police was there, the Army intelligence was probably there, but it didn't matter because we outnumbered them. And nothing bad was going to happen anyway.

The feeling that nothing bad was going to happen—a sensation very few of the organizers and staff shared—dominated the crowd in the aftermath of the rainstorm. It was as if each setback concretized the determination the audience felt en masse to stay cool. No doubt many were beat, uncomfortable, edgy. The departure rate was picking up, many believing the concert would never be able to get going again. But Joe correctly assessed the ruling emotion as he clowned in front of the appreciative assembly. Nothing bad was going to happen.

No feeling could have been more exquisitely tailored for Susie Kaufman at this particular time than the glow of security, protectedness, safekeeping. Dripping wet, she stood dirty and bedraggled and renewed. She had mockingly called herself the color-coordinated hippie because of her insistence on sloppy chic during the era of just plain sloppy. Now she didn't even care about the mud stains besmirching her fringes and white jeans. An inner joy she hadn't felt for a year surged inside, soothing the emotional wounds the rape had left. In her own hometown she had been violated and abused, and yet here among strangers she knew she couldn't have been safer. Instead of feeling weaker from the fatigue and dankness, she was energized.

Like most of the others in the field, Susie would attempt to remake camp in the soggy ground after the rain. While the organizers encouraged them to stick around, the show would go on, the diehards began wringing shirts out, removing plastic coverings and making peace with a remorselessly swampy earth. So deep was the mud in some hollows of the field that entire knapsacks sank into the puddles, there to remain hidden, some of them forever. Of greater concern were more dangerous objects—broken glass, can openers—that even more frequently slipped under the cover of mud, turning the amphitheater traversed by bare feet into a minefield of sole-splitting shrapnel. Susie picked her way through the puddles near her and stood carefully squishing her toes into the mess as she watched Max Yasgur, the owner of this now litter-strewn morass, take the stage. He was nervous and halting, but his craggy honesty reminded her of her father. She listened to his little speech, amplified through the one mike that had been hooked up after Joe and the Fish left the stage. She was taken by the elderly farmer's genuine enthusiasm for the peaceableness of the weekend, an amazing reaction given the condition of his cowfield. Then, as the old man went on, Susie heard a sudden yelp of pain from a young man not five feet away. From where she was standing, it was not difficult to focus immediately on the reason for the cry: amid the brown covering everything, the torrent of scarlet spurting from the bottom of his foot was like a signal flare against a night sky.

Blood and pain and fear, this boy was experiencing things Susie had barely resolved in herself. Yet the atmosphere of caring and concern at the festival had been so overwhelming that her own victimization disappeared from her mind. She rushed to reach out to the young man, the first boy she had felt strongly about since the rape. And as she helped take care of the wound, the intensity of this experience triggered an unexpected reaction.

> He was bleeding. It was impossible to get him to first aid. I was very pleased that everyone turned around and tended him. I remember asking for booze and someone contributed a bottle of brandy. He drank it and poured more over the foot.

I developed a crush. He was so sweet and dear and kind and gentle and soft. I just had a crush on him. He hung out for a couple of hours with us. Then he left. He was from someplace in the Midwest. Back then there were little personals in *The Village Voice* and you could write little notes. And I tried to find him. "If you remember getting your foot cut and getting it nursed by a bunch of very nice people, please get in touch." I didn't want to admit I had a crush on him, but if he wrote . . .

In the real world, when people don't eat, they get hungry; when it rains, they get wet; when glass shards cut into a boy's foot, the foot bleeds. Real-world intrusions were filtering into the fantasyscape that was Woodstock, reminding the Nation that its truce with time was running out. Enough Aquarian charm still lingered, though, to bend reality to conform to the idiosyncratic norms of the festival. Saturday's giddy notion that concertgoers could banish all demons seemed naive now. They knew the wolves could be kept at bay for only a few hours more, and so they treasured the interval all the more for the privileged and protected view of the enemy afforded them. From within the sanctuary of Woodstock, they could begin to make peace with the personal challenges that awaited beyond. Everyone had been doused by the rain that Sunday. But everyone had chanted together and, looking up, had seen it wasn't raining anymore.

Instead, from the sky, dropped by gently humming helicopters, a rain of daisies poured down upon their heads; the crowd-pleasing effect was thought up on the spot by the Ventures management. The same menacing green choppers the kids might see on TV every night in combat footage from Vietnam hovered benignly above, showering the faithful with love posies. Reality and make-believe were staging an eleventh-hour showstopper.

The rain delay had a mixed effect among the performers milling around backstage or just now arriving by helicopter. For those who had been scheduled for afternoon gigs—like Ten Years After and the Band—the hiatus was a blessing. It pushed them back to the more desirable evening hours, when lighting effects could be used

to accentuate the performance and the kids would be more atten-
tive. But more than three hours in all had been lost with the storm
and the subsequent maintenance work. And even without the
delay the night's roster would have been tight, including as it did
top-liners like Blood, Sweat and Tears, Paul Butterfield Blues Band
and Jimi Hendrix. This night had been arranged as the final bang
for the weekend, and the rain, oddly enough, hadn't scared off
any of the scheduled entertainment. Looking around at the superstars gathering in place for closing night, Jocko Marcellino sat
down depressed on a bench, watched as David Crosby, Stephen
Stills and Graham Nash walked in—he had forgotten all about
them—and said to himself, Shit, we're never going to get on.

The concert began, finally, with Alvin Lee and Ten Years After
opening Sunday evening on a wet stage under a sky that occasionally still drizzled. Jocko looked at his watch: it was eight
o'clock. The festival that had begun at its own pace without refer-
ence to calendar and clock was ending in a race against time, at
least for Sha Na Na. The least experienced act of the entire festival,
these novelty singers were also the most expendable. If somebody
had to go to make up for rain delays, Jocko knew who it would be.
He also sensed acutely what a terrific blow to Sha Na Na's future
being squeezed off the schedule would mean. He had heard the
griping from Saturday's acts, the reports from the Dead and the
Airplane that no worse performing conditions had ever been
endured. He had heard that the crowd was too zonked and just
too big to play for. But he also knew that for a band like his simply
to get a shot on the same stage as these rock superstars would be a
breakthrough no amount of touring or recording could equal.
While the more established groups could afford to complain, the
impact of appearing in this media-saturated encampment had
already been felt by the less familiar acts. A movie was being
made, critics you couldn't have paid to come listen to you were out
there taking notes, broadcasters from every station were hot for
footage from the most talked-about counterculture event of the
decade. A performance here amounted to an unparalleled spring-
board to success. Everybody was still talking about Friday night's
appearance by John Sebastian, his first before the media in nearly

a year; about Santana's session on Saturday, the group's first major gig on the East Coast. Careers were being built here, taking quantum leaps above the pack with an hour or even less on the stage. He watched as the members of the Dylan-inspired group the Band headed out onstage. It was already nearly eleven. Like everyone else in the crowd, Jocko knew the concert couldn't last forever and he shared with them the hope that somehow the dawn could be held back. He wanted the hours to stretch out just long enough to let Sha Na Na do its thing. He hadn't felt this anxious since his first varsity football game back in high school, and with the same almost automatic reaction he would have had then, the old Catholic schoolboy said a little prayer that he'd get to show his stuff.

Before tonight, Jocko had taken performing as one gigantic lark. The gigs at Columbia and then at the tiny clubs downtown had all been just so many small-time hotdog sessions. Playing football demanded more attention; he put more at stake on the line of scrimmage than he thought he ever did when he was playing a greaser in the nostalgia group. But now, when the possibility of show business success dangled so precariously but tantalizingly close, he was realizing for the first time how much he craved it. During those hours, keeping vigil through the rapid course of the night, he changed from a college kid with a hobby to a pro.

He listened attentively to the reaction each subsequent group received, reading in the applause the mood and, more important, the tenacity of the crowd. Even if they hated Sha Na Na, as long as the audience held in there the group could go on. The kids didn't dig Blood, Sweat and Tears, the jazzy, horn-and-keyboard-heavy quasi-orchestra fronted by David Clayton-Thomas. During their performance the applause was so lethargic that Jocko worried it meant the size of the crowd was diminishing rapidly. But the listeners perked up for Crosby, Stills and Nash. The unannounced appearance by Neil Young and the harmonies the newly formed quartet sent dancing off the stage prompted a huge, energetic surge from the crowd. Jocko's wish for each group was the same: a scintillating set that kept the audience in place but didn't require too many encores.

In the east, Monday's sun was already starting to creep over the

Catskills, and as he cursed it Jocko felt like a rock vampire who required night to make his kill. And then the young man saw something even more threatening than the sun. Like an ebony god, Jimi Hendrix walked into the backstage area. A legendary performer with legendary ego and quirks, Hendrix had been held until the very last because of his phenomenal charisma and intensity. For everyone else still left backstage—even some management officers had already beaten a retreat—the guitarist's arrival sent chills of excitement coursing up weary spines. Jocko looked at him and felt chills too. His presence meant there was very little time left now. Whenever Jimi wanted to go on, he would be given the stage. Meanwhile, eating up the precious minutes left before Sir Jimi felt the urge, the Paul Butterfield Blues Band just kept on playing, playing, playing. The light got brighter, the band kept playing. Jocko felt his spirits sinking.

Here we were, in the performers' pavilion. We talked to all these people. We were hanging with them, but we were ready to rock and roll. We were the little kids. But they gave us a certain respect. We were these college guys who had a real sensible idea. We were the first ones looking at the history of what all this was.

We were ogling all these people. I was an incredible Hendrix fan, and you could talk to him. And he would go, "Dig, I'd like to talk to you but I gotta go touch the sky." Sweet guy, but he was too high.

We almost didn't play. Butterfield played forever. We just snuck in. We were getting pissed. I love Paul Butterfield, but he went on forever. I didn't like him that day. When you're slated for any big festival, I've learned this now, get in near the beginning. And if Wadleigh hadn't gotten up his crew, we wouldn't have made the movie. They got only our encore. They were all sleeping, cooking up to get Hendrix.

So we got to play right before Hendrix. By then it was a refugee camp. We looked out at a refugee camp, most of the people were gone, not that many people were there. I met a guy, years later, who had been tripping the night before. Fell asleep and woke up when we were playing and had no idea what we were, and he thought he had gone on a terrific trip.

The trip, as it turns out, was Sha Na Na's. Of all the unexpected and fortuitous incidents of the weekend, perhaps the group's dawn set ranks among the most propitious. Because Hendrix was too skittish at first—or too high—to go on, because the film crew expected Jimi at sunrise, and because the Paul Butterfield Blues Band cooked until through the last remnants of night, a bunch of college kids got their shot on the stage, their act in the documentary, their foothold on fame. It was, in a way, fitting that Sha Na Na had this chance of a lifetime at this once-in-a-lifetime event. The only group that remembered the history of rock and roll at the history-making festival, Sha Na Na served as a reminder that good music and sweet memories need never die. It was a message with a particular cogency on the last night of the festival.

It had been a long and anxious vigil for Jocko, who would be rewarded by daylight with the breakthrough he had been praying for. Then it was Monday morning, and the sun climbed over the hills. Beyond, the real world was calling. Electric, wailing, scorching, the Jimi Hendrix version of "The Star-Spangled Banner" closed the festival with the reminder this had in fact been no Wonderland, no Brigadoon, but a corner of America, a real and troubled land that was now claiming the rebel colony back. A red-hot makeover of the national anthem, the black guitarist's psychedelicized solo was the country's anthem nonetheless. The kids in the field, for whom the illusion of independence was ending, stood up, saluted the anthem by brushing mud off their butts, and headed back to their cars, their lives. With the early-morning light streaming, illuminating the sweat on his brow into diamonds, Hendrix provided Woodstock with its final magical moments, before the Nation dissolved and the diaspora began.

Commentators, seeing only that the crowd was dispersing, dismissed the event as a three-day phenomenon: evanescent, transient, a thing of the moment. The festival itself ended, but what outsiders failed to understand was that, like the mud clinging to the sneakers of each of the kids trudging homeward, something stuck to the souls of these 500,000. And as they spread back out over the land, they each brought with them something personal: a gain, a loss, a lesson learned, a new path found. What you saw that morning looking down at the bowl was a black man caressing his guitar on a tottering stage and a bunch of tired hippies picking their way through the muck. More accurately, thousands of young people were returning to the real world to play out the individual dramas they had begun here in the country. In the end, the Nation disbanded even more abruptly than it had begun, fairly bursting apart like an incubating pod grown heavy with seeds. But the members of that Nation would carry forever an indelible stamp in the passport of their souls that they would cherish as a special brand of honor giving them the privilege to say, "We were there."

It was only as Jimi Hendrix wailed through "The Star-Spangled Banner" that Sylvia Greene saw Rebecca picking her way across the devastation of the nearly deserted field back to their camp. Whatever she had been doing all night, and whomever she had done it with, Sylvia's friend looked amazingly fresh and rested as she stepped over rolls of soiled clothing and heaps of steaming refuse like some teen angel haunting the site of a nuclear holocaust. She positively glowed in the mist, greeting Sylvia with the nonchalance of a sister coming over to borrow some sugar. Sylvia sensed that with the end of the concert, something of their friendship died too, as for twins whose shared being ceases at birth. And it was with a sense of mourning and regret that she welcomed Rebecca back, told her they were about to leave, and turned and listened with her to the last chords of Jimi's solo. Within several years, both the guitarist and the friend would be dead.

For Sylvia the weekend had been a lonely few days that reached their peak early on during the performances by some musicians she knew personally. It was the central irony of her time here, though, that she felt closer to a couple of guys playing on the stage hundreds of yards away than she did to the best friend with whom she had come to spend the three days. Sylvia picked up a muddied jacket and then tossed it back down to the ground; she looked at the garbage all around her and saw in it a reflection of the remains of her friendship. To others, the flotsam of the weekend, piled high and smelly, was the discarded chrysalis of the metamorphoses that took place here. Instead, Sylvia saw junk. Isolated from one another by the era's sexual ambiguities, the two girls would never again be as close as they had been.

It was a tired, haggard parade of Woodstock veterans that wound its way out of the brown bowl that Monday morning and back toward the cars still clogging the exit routes. Sylvia and Rebecca followed silently, talking only when they needed to exchange opinions about where they had left the Volkswagen. Sylvia wanted just to get home, get cleaned up and get into bed. When they finally found the car, they realized it wouldn't be that easy.

> We went back to the car and the battery was gone. And we just took another battery. We got in, put the key in the ignition, and couldn't start it. We lifted up the hood. "Just go and get another one." I remember being stunned that that was our mentality, but it was. And it was okay. I was stunned that this was happening, but it didn't bother me. Took the battery, and put it in, and drove away. Just amazing to me, that's how we were. I knew that if you were in a restaurant in Manhattan and somebody stole your battery, you didn't go take the next guy's battery. But here it was an acceptable action.

Common pragmatism probably had a lot to do with Sylvia's decision to steal the battery: she needed one, so she took one. But the deliberate and knowing breach of Woodstock ethics may well have been an unconscious attempt to separate herself from that world of hippie values, the same set of values that was coming between Rebecca and herself. They hadn't worked for Sylvia during the long and lonely weekend of peace and love, and she was not about to apply them now that she was back in the real world. Sex was good, ripping people off was bad: the hippie rubric was clear on certain things. But at this point Sylvia didn't care. She wanted to put distance between herself and Woodstock and wasn't about to allow Woodstock niceties to keep her from doing it.

It should not be surprising, really, that the disintegration of the Woodstock ecosystem, reflected in Sylvia's petty theft, was rapid and thorough. By Monday morning, society's vices, so tentatively held at bay throughout the weekend, crushed in on the delicate preserve. The field emptied quickly, as if all the festivalgoers suddenly remembered they had the rest of their lives to get on with. And in the midst of the exodus, greed. Penny Stallings, amazed that the whole thing was over so quickly, couldn't believe what she was seeing.

> As everybody was going, the ground fairly smoked. Almost like seeing Kirlian photos. It seemed to me like it got cold immediately after the festival.
>
> There continued to be things I disapproved of. I was still in my self-righteous mood. The Hog Farm took a lot of farm equipment. You can say that was giving the equipment to the good people, to the common people. But an awful lot of them were record execs who couldn't make it in the real world. These were some very hip people. Not spiritual people, not people of the earth. But LA dropouts. To see them take everything they could—I was very put off by the division of spoils.
>
> I had an argument with one of the bosses, who was saying the Hog Farm people could take the chain saws. I said, "If everybody takes all the equipment, then it won't be here for next year." I wanted it to happen forever. I wanted it to be my summer for the rest of my life.

Rufus Friedman had a similar reaction:

> I remember coming out from behind the stage and seeing the devastation. When we first got there, it was a beautiful alfalfa field, it was lush. This guy Shorty and I had driven the first semi up that hill three weeks earlier, full of trees. It was the first cut in the virginity of the area. The main thing I remember at the end was the smell and the devastation.
>
> I left my gear, my kit bag and my racing helmets, and when I went back to pick it up it had been stolen. I ran into the guy who stole it, three or four weeks later, at the Café Wa at a Grateful Dead concert. He was in my clothes. He had my Sergeant Pepper outfit on. I grabbed him by the throat, or by the lapels. He said,

"I'm tripping. I'm tripping." Then I said, "You're not worth beating up."

Naturally there was ugliness in the disillusionments that accompanied Monday's sunrise. Friendships were deteriorating, venality was encroaching on the love oasis. Still, the aura of the three days preceding persisted even as the thousands hurried from its imperfect sanctuary. Most of the departing thousands got out before the fall of Woodstock was complete, carrying with them the spiritual remains of the briefly flourishing culture. Their cars were lined up one behind the other in an irritatingly obdurate traffic jam, a gnawing reminder of the difference between the carefree weekend and real life. Most would find other reminders of the compromises, frustrations, disappointments and challenges real life promised, all the way home. Most were better prepared to handle them now than before.

Susie Kaufman hated to leave the one place where she had felt whole again. With an emotionally heightened intensity she hung on every note of Jimi Hendrix's final anthem as its twisted patriotism nudged her back into that world where she had felt so vulnerable and insecure.

Do I remember Hendrix! By the time he went on, everyone had left. I couldn't understand it. They were going to miss the most incredible part of the experience. I seem to remember waiting for the light to come up before he played. And as he started, the sun crested behind him. I wouldn't take my eyes off him. I mean, if someone believed in Jesus and he suddenly walked in, that's how Hendrix was for me.

I didn't want to leave on Monday. I didn't want to end the magic. It was over and I was sorry. The field suddenly looked a lot smaller than it had for the last two and a half or three days. All it was, was mud and garbage. I walked away slower and slower because I didn't want to go. But there was nothing left there, it was over.

It was awful to go back to the real world. Driving down the thruway, you still saw other cars and you passed your peace signs. We felt great, it had been fulfilling. Like a sexual adventure. When I hit Morristown with its colonial atmosphere, it looked very straight. We were covered with dirt and mud, and I wanted to tell people we had just come from Woodstock. "We're back now, you've been watching us in the news, and now we're back." In the house I said to my parents, "I'm so sorry, I'm not ready to talk about this, I'm going to go into my room." I told them I had a religious experience.

I wouldn't take off those muddy jeans for a couple of days. I slept on the floor for the next couple of nights, because I had a fancy canopy bed. I couldn't believe I was back in the world. I was very reclusive. I watched the news, and I remember there had been a lot of slants against it, such negative, bitchy things. Then suddenly it started to turn in our favor because there had been so many positive goings-on and so few negative happenings.

Scott Lane left in typical style: with a girl on his arm. He had met her sometime during the night, after leaving DiRosa in the woods by the showers. But his big buddy had promised him a ride home, and Monday morning they rendezvoused at the predetermined spot. Fred not the least bit surprised to see Scott had found yet another woman. The plan was for everyone to go to Scott's parents' apartment, where he knew they would indulge his sudden visit with two grungy friends. They always indulged Scott. Crashing at his parents' place in New Jersey, Scott sensed a change. He remembered how childlike he had felt when Mr. DiRosa looked down at him from his horse; he was unsettled about being here in his parents' house making love. Years of self-doubt and irresolution were to pass by before Scott would learn to channel his ability to charm people into a career.

Now accepted as one of the film team's own, Elen Orson drove home in one of the company cars. Sore from lugging film canisters all weekend long, she settled into the front seat, proud of what she had accomplished. She was just in high school, and she had helped film the documentary the kids back home wouldn't even see for a year. She had proven herself and as a result would be given adult responsibilities at the studio as soon as they returned. She looked back at the towers, now starkly overshadowing the wreckage below, and remembered the nightmare of their swaying in the wind, the horror of nearly dropping the film from the top platform. If Woodstock had been a fantasy, it had been one from which she had made undeniably authentic personal gains. She would scrape the mud off her boots once she was back home, and wrap it in cellophane. At the time she knew only that she would want to keep it to put in the garden of her first home; eventually she carried that clump of Woodstock dirt to Hollywood. But first there was the production company back in New York.

> There was work right away. We had to sync up the film. I had the great opportunity to relive the moment. The first thing I had to do was "eyeball sync." That means you didn't have a slate or a clapper, no point of reference. You just pick a roll of film—it could have been anywhere in the hour-and-a-half period—and you have to find the soundtrack for it. Our job was to find where in the track the picture went. The first one they gave me to do was Ravi Shankar! No vocals. It was real difficult. He never got into the movie.
>
> I remember Crosby, Stills and Nash's footage. They came to see their film. I had worked on some of it. It was six in the evening, and I wanted to get all my work done. The editor came into my room and said, "Put your work down. We're going to have a screening for them now." There was a couch in the back of the room. I was on the floor and they were back there in their leather jackets and long hair. And they were lighting joints and passing them. I remember getting a toke from David Crosby. I was in heaven. They'll never believe this. How am I going to tell this to the kids in school?

In the line of traffic, behind Elen's car, behind Scott, behind the slowly moving line of vehicles heading home, Jimmy Jordan and Evan sat, playing no music, feeling the silence between them. Like Sylvia, Jimmy sensed the festival had brought to a close a particular relationship, somehow arrested by the very freedom celebrated within the privileged precincts. The openness and caring exhibited over the three days pointed up how barren the relationship was. A last-minute truce had been called between them, which was to endure at least for the length of the ride home. But Jimmy knew this ride would be their last trip together.

> I remember Evan making up with me the last day, and we took a beautiful ride in the mountains there before we came home. It was so beautiful and it had stopped raining, and we didn't have to get back.
>
> I can remember coming back and people saying, "What was it like?" We had no idea that the eyes of the world were upon us. How am I ever going to tell anyone what this was like? And then to come back and realize we were the focus of history! It had been on TV and on the radio.

Bill Pelligrini didn't have a car, didn't really have any place to go. He wandered around the woods as the craftsmen broke down their stalls and packed up their wares. Gypsies, they were no doubt off to the next fair, to the next wooded bazaar. He had heard there would be work on the cleanup crew and was planning to stay on for the two weeks' employment that had been promised. But beyond that detail, his next step was already taking shape. Bill watched as a leather worker carefully placed his box of tools in the back of his van and drove off. Bill headed off to grab his plastic garbage bag.

> After Woodstock I stayed two weeks and helped clean up. I thought it was my duty. I was a very responsible guy. "Trucks over there, bags over there. We made this mess, people, we can clean it up." It was a point of pride. I was a Boy Scout and a good camper. And a good camper cleans up. It's just what you do. You're in the woods, and you see a can one hundred miles from nowhere and you bury it or you pick it up and truck it out of there.
>
> I drifted to Boston and saw a little shop on Mumford off Kenmore Square. And I went into this leather place and I said, "Hey, if you teach me to make leather goods, I'll work here for nothing." And they said, "Okay, sure."

Helicopter service had been halted by Monday morning, so entertainers found themselves stuck in the same big tie-up as did those they had entertained. Sitting there in the queue of cars, going nowhere, Country Joe McDonald and John Sebastian both had the first real opportunity to consider what this appearance might mean in terms of their careers.

John knew without a doubt that being here had been the right thing to do. Cut off from his group, he had again enjoyed the camaraderie and acceptance of the rock elite he once headed. More than that, he felt a connection with the counterculture, which his celebrity had made difficult. Like so many others, he realized for the first time that the things he talked about with his friends, the simple, peaceful life he wanted to find, were the goals thousands of young Americans were talking about. This had been a convention of 500,000 people who had always thought they were freaks, alone.

Still, there was an unavoidable uneasiness about Friday night's performance. Within the all-accepting arena of Woodstock he was certain his like-minded audience had gotten off on his slightly goofy show. But this had been no private party, no mere musical gig for a small group of friends. It was a piece of history. It was barely over and already he sensed its impact.

After being up all night, I remember getting in the car and rolling down the window to hear "The Star-Spangled Banner." I drove away in the car. I don't think I doubted there was going to be a fairly large number of people who were going to stay there for a couple more weeks. I think there were. But it felt as if this community had had its party now and that perhaps it was going to return to those smaller klatches of people.

The performance I gave there, which was so stoned-out and hippified, presented an image that was slightly askew. Not too far from who I am, but sufficiently askew to be an image that did haunt me to a certain extent. Difficult to overcome. It was an impression that was hard to progress from. I think people carried that image of me, tie-dyed and psychedelicized, long past the point it made any sense. This was not my main modus operandi, and now here is this huge impression left: a movie, an album, press reaction for years. There was a prejudice against that mentality. It was a slow, unidentifiable process. It dated me at a time when I was way too creative to be dated. I remember thinking, If it's damage it's already been done.

Country Joe also sat in the traffic, pensive. How would the aftermath of this massive event affect him personally? There was no way to judge, since there had never been a rock show this large. In a single gig one could communicate an image to so many people that it would be impossible ever to alter that image again. Given the proper preparation and skill, a rock performer could exploit that opportunity to lock into the public's consciousness in the most favorable light possible. Joe had appeared with neither the proper preparation nor the skill to control his image. He had simply run out there Friday night to keep the party rolling as it was just gaining speed. He suspected he would not be the first good samaritan to find himself penalized for the good acts he committed.

It launched me as a solo performer and stamped me with an identity. The identity fit well for the most part, but it's a little uncomfortable as far as a show biz identity is concerned. And I must say, I didn't like being that person for a long time. And I fought it. Now I can live with it. It's just that it's so visible and so sharp and clear and typecast in a way. The first Country Joe and the Fish album had only one song that was a protest song. The second had only one song that was a protest song. Those early years, which have a reputation for being full of protest music, were in actuality full of conservative music.

I became separate and outside. A symbol of Vietnam, of the Woodstock generation, of obscenity, of protest music, in spite of the fact that all of the protest was justified. As far as I was concerned, after 1970, I couldn't play in any municipal auditorium in the country; the federal government and the military were actually on my case. My line was tapped. The IRS was auditing my books every other month. And I worked outside the country for the most part. And the industry held me as a troublemaker and a totally noncommercial entity. You pay a penalty. Why it happened I have no idea.

The makeshift "Sha Na Na" sign on the side of the van had ripped when Jocko Marcellino finally had the U-Haul loaded up and ready to drive back to Columbia. He didn't even care that his group was the only one that had to pack up its own equipment. He was still high from performing, and every time kids drove by and cheered the sign, he got another rush. Just before the members of the band left, a contract releasing their performance for use in the film was shoved under their noses. They hardly read the terms, and quickly signed the contract with the hope they might possibly be included in some version of the movie. They had barely made it into the final hours of the three-day festival. Unless the film was going to be just as long, how would Sha Na Na ever be included? Someone handed them a check, and Jocko joked that with all the excitement of performing he had forgotten all about pay. He knew that the long-term benefit of appearing would be far greater than whatever they earned that night.

> At Woodstock, we made three hundred dollars. That was for the whole group. And the check bounced. They put us up, but we paid for the transportation. We got paid one dollar to be in the film. We signed the release for a dollar. Some big groups didn't, though. They were at Woodstock, but from the movie you wouldn't know it. We paid to be at Woodstock, but it was worth it. That put us in the international scene. Everyone except Dylan, the Beatles and the Stones was there. And even in the movie, we figured we'd get edited, but they put in "At the Hop." Our first gold single was "At the Hop."
>
> Afterward, it was like culture shock. We had a record contract and an agent at William Morris. We had to go on the road, down to Miami. We were playing at the Marco Polo Hotel. It was nice, but it was night and day. First a gig for a half a million hippies then this Vegas room in Miami Beach. Wild.

Tom Constanten, who with the Dead had beaten a fast retreat out of Bethel on Sunday morning, watched the news reports Monday from the hotel room in New York where the group was staying before their performance that night at the Fillmore. Aerial shots showed cars backed up for miles and panned the devastated cowfield, still emptying out. It looked like a major battle had taken place there, rather than a weekend of music and love. He was looking forward to the gig tonight: he needed a performance at a reliable hall with proper acoustics and adequate technical assistance to buoy up his confidence after the discordant jamming they had done Saturday night. Still, no matter how successful the gig tonight, Tom sensed his future with the group was as empty as that now gutted field. He looked at the wreckage of the amphitheater and saw in it the end of an era, both for himself and for his generation.

> Things had come to an end by the Woodstock Festival: it was the monument to the movement, rather than its startup. The movement started to get shrink-wrapped, the image was being distorted.
>
> Early in 1970 I left the band. My last gig was in New Orleans the night the band was busted. Those are totally unconnected. Pigpen and I were the only ones not busted. Incredible but true, we were totally clean when the police came to our room. It was a very cordial parting of the ways. Everyone recognized the situation. It was a turning of the page.

Ron Stone, who had also left early, disappointed in the frivolity of the festival when he had expected more political action, was watching the same news reports that Monday morning. He saw the cars crammed on the roads. Already his opinion about the event was changing: perhaps in its very escapism the weekend had made a political statement. Now back in Washington, he realized how positive the vibes at Bethel had been compared to the growing hysteria of the Nixon administration. He was still glad he got out before the deluge of Sunday and the crush of traffic the next day, but as uncomfortable as things must have gotten up there the capital was getting even creepier. Suddenly the cavalier disregard for society's rules and mores that flourished at the festival looked as if it had sent a very important message indeed.

> In January of 1969 Nixon had been sworn in and our whole world began to collapse. The Democrats and liberals were no longer in

control, and I had never seen that kind of change. I couldn't stand the man and couldn't stand the policies. I didn't like the men he was bringing to Washington.

While everything was falling apart in Washington, Woodstock gave me the sense that the culture was coming together in other ways. It offered great promise. There was always the sense of doom on the horizon, but this seemed like a counterbalance to it, even though it wasn't political.

To the people of Sullivan County, the fiasco in Yasgur's field was distinctly political, although not in the sense that Ron suggests. Having weathered the weekend without panicking, extending their kindness where needed, the locals united in a joint cry of "Never again." It was a response echoed around the country, as the very magnitude of the Woodstock Festival prompted nationwide concern over its recurrence. In Bethel, barely was the concert over than a campaign was initiated to oust the town board that had allowed the Ventures hooligans into Bethel. Skirting around the traffic-jammed main highway along the back roads he knew so well, George Neuhaus drove up to Max Yasgur's farm and savored the rot and ruination. In the heaps of refuse, in the stink that rose from the land, he could see the outlines of the platform that would sweep him back into office that November. The official issue was the reinstatement of zoning, which would provide the supervisor with the legal apparatus necessary to control the assembly. But that issue aside, everyone in town wanted to make sure a Woodstock never happened here again.

I wasn't thinking of this as an election issue at the time, I was thinking, Where are we going, and what are we going to do? Are we going to have a rerun of this a few years from now? A couple of weeks after the festival, a lot of people in the community came to me and prevailed upon me to run again.

The following year another group came in here and wanted to have a rerun festival. And I was in office. They made no arrangements, except with Max Yasgur, to use a piece of property down by the lake. And they were talking like it was going to be a few thousand. Well, it was about five thousand. But I was on the scene. I had the sheriff, we had the state police, and I immediately roped off all roads leading in, kept it quiet. It never got in the paper. We kept it under wraps.

Late one night, eleven or twelve, I was up at the four corners with the road closed off. No more cars could come in. Max came to me and said, "You gotta keep them from running through my cornfield."

And I said, "Max, you gave them permission. It's your problem. You got to go down and tell them to leave."

He made a few bucks off the first one. And he became their idol. He probably thought a few hundred of them was coming back, just to be on the small part of land he had on that lake. They had a flatbed of a truck and a band. But we have laws and we were enforcing them. We had adopted a local law to control any assembly. Not outlaw them, just control. We told Max he had to go down and tell them all to be out by daybreak. We kept the road closed off and let only local people with business up there go through.

Anne and Burt Feldman went out to their driveway and collapsed the table on which they had left food and water for the hippies. They took the light down from the tree and noted again, with satisfaction, that no garbage had been strewn about their property. They had heard all the angry talk from their neighbors and knew that it would most certainly express itself even more forcibly around election time. For the couple, though, the ending of the festival meant the excitement was over and the humid quiet of the Catskills summer would return. They felt abandoned in the rustic remoteness of Bethel. No security detail for Burt to work on, no cars for Anne to tow. The festival's liberating influence on their lives died that Monday, but as a local political issue, they knew, the concert and its impact wouldn't soon go away. Long after the festival was over they would be called on to defend the legend it generated right where it began, in Bethel. Nearly two decades after the last hippie had departed, the Feldmans would find themselves the standardbearers of a local movement to preserve the Yasgur site. Immediately after the concert they took a perverse pleasure in the effect whose lingering impact no amount of legislation could undo.

> BURT: There were portojohns only for a few thousand people. And the stench lingered for months. And it did ruin the crops. You can do this in China or other places, but you can't use human shit to fertilize a cornfield if people are going to eat the corn here. Crops were trampled; they had to be, no way they couldn't be.
>
> ANNE: All that summer and fall and into the next spring, if you drove in that area, the smell of human excrement was so extremely strong. It took about three years for it to dissipate. Every time it was warm, it just came up. I felt it was a shame, but you had these people here, what were they going to do? I sympathize with the people who lost their crops, but it's an act of God as much as anything. They were like locusts on the land.
>
> BURT: During the summer you can go there and almost always see people there. It has become a mecca point. Like the Alamo.

It wasn't the stench but rather the image of the drugged-out kids that remained with Dr. D'Amico. At the hospital one morning, he talked with some of his physician friends about the intoxication and overdose cases he had cared for and was surprised that the other doctors weren't shocked by the extent to which drug use had penetrated middle-class youth. Everyone seemed to be aware of the fact that substance abuse was common, although the degree to which it was evidenced at the festival was a little surprising. He found out that a number of cases even worse than those he was seeing had been flown into the hospital, and that one kid had died. He made his rounds thinking about his own children, and whether or not the drug problem in Sullivan County would end when all the festivalgoers finally left Bethel.

> If you told me then that I was going to become a specialist in the field of addiction, I would have told you no way in hell. I was saddened by it. In a way just felt sorry, not even repelled. I felt the young people were destroying themselves. Woodstock became a part of my career, when you look back at it.

For the young people who had been involved with the festival long before it officially began, for whom the three days represented but the culmination of months of excitement, growth and fun, Monday challenged and taunted them even more than it did any of the thousands now crawling away. What do you do as a follow-up when you've just staged the biggest cultural event of the decade, when you've touched the personal histories of so many of your peers, when you know that the "real life" that now awaits you will never be as real as the make-believe one that's receding in front of you? If you're young and have truly captured the spirit of the magic you've helped create, you pack up and move on to the next great adventure.

Henry Diltz, who had felt so at one with the mythology of the event during site preparation was, therefore, not surprisingly the most taken aback by the desolation of the farm Monday morning. Ruefully and dutifully snapping pictures of the mess, he used his camera to distance himself from the hellhole his paradise had become.

> What was left was junk, muddied junk. I remember thinking it looked like a battlefield. Bags of food, clothes, all soaking wet and trampled in the mud. I was conscious of this being the Civil War area. Whenever I get around New York or Pennsylvania, I think of the Civil War. I look around to see if I can find a musket lying in a bush somewhere. You think it could have been a day just like this when a battle took place here. With all this stuff lying around like dead bodies. You've seen those old pictures on glass plates, of battlefields, bloated horse bodies, cannonballs, dead soldiers lying in the field. That's what it looked like.

For Rufus Friedman, the close of the festival signaled the end of a three-month-long survival-camp fantasy. It had been his long-delayed chance to play tough, hang with the big guys, swear, sweat, cuss and carry on. But play can produce its lessons and logic too. Like most of the Woodstock Ventures personnel who had taken the stint upstate on a lark, he didn't have another job to go to. Still, he wasn't interested in the cleanup details offered to the grunts. This had been too special an experience to end knee-deep in debris. Maybe there hadn't been anything glamorous in the forest clearing and ditch digging, the pasture clearing and order taking that made up those three months of getting ready for the festival. But the sense of building something, using his muscle to make something happen, converted even the most routine construction task into an accomplishment. Then, once the concert began, he had gotten to wear a black jacket, he had escorted Janis Joplin. No, no way could he now do garbage. His tenure as a crew member had boosted his self-esteem. The image he formulated over the months of a gritty but proud laborer stuck in his head as he looked over the muck and mire that now remained behind, covering the hills into which he had cut the first path. Like a soldier of fortune when his job is done, Rufus decided he would head out as soon as the traffic cleared up. And like a mercenary, once out of the heat of the action, he turned from grand notions of valor to more practical concerns. A cowboy once, he was to be a cowboy evermore.

Midway up the management ladder, Lee Blumer saw in the steam and stench rising off the field that Monday morning the visions of a recording-industry career she had thought dashed just three months before. How right that it would be out of the rubble that opportunity rose. Little she had witnessed behind the scenes at Woodstock had reversed the pessimism her earlier rock career had instilled. The pursuit of the almighty buck had nearly catapulted this weekend into disaster, and each hour of the long, long concert brought more and more proof of management's cynicism and hypocrisy toward the ethic the event exploited. But Lee herself had been surprised at the way the people's spirit had moved her. Regardless of the chicanery behind getting the music to them, the kids in the field were truly grooving with the performers. The kids at the jails had found their only moments of escape through it. The kids at the concert had found their most intense moments of togetherness through it. And skeptic though she might have been, she couldn't deny the glow she felt from the camaraderie and sheer enjoyment she had shared during the intense months of preparation. Rock meant something to this generation, including many members of the crew, that no amount of entrepreneurial wheeling and dealing could undermine. As the focus of the entire counter-culture—and of the mass-culture bigwigs looking to reap profit from it—Woodstock attracted recording-industry executives, promoters, agents, many of whom took note of the Ventures personnel. Participation in this mega-happening served as entrée of unequaled clout, and without having a résumé Lee was in demand even before the concert ended. As she lay down to sleep that Monday afternoon, tendered offers buzzing vaguely in the back of her head, she couldn't think about the future in specific terms. All she knew was that something very different had happened to her understanding of the music and the people, and her role in bringing the two together. Having come to Woodstock as a recording-business burn-out, she would leave a woman whose belief in rock had been renewed. And whose future in it had been sealed.

> I can say this for almost anyone I was directly involved with: we didn't have a clue what was going to happen on August 18. All we cared about was August 15, 16 and 17. What we were going to do afterward never occurred to me. While I was up on Woodstock, I was offered record company jobs. I couldn't take them. Woodstock was such a shock to my system but it wasn't a career. When you've invited five hundred thousand people to your living room, what do you do for an encore? I went off to St. Thomas.
>
> Of all the experiences I've had in my forty years now, that was my favorite one. It's like a big accident, nobody had a clue it could be done. It had never been done before. By the time it was over, it wasn't a job anymore, it was the most personal thing I had done in my life. In some mythological way, it was something I always wished I could do: have all those people experience the same thing at the same time. I wasn't career driven, and I can't say many of the people I knew there were. They were being driven, but by many other things.

Penny Stallings was ready for a good long sleep that Monday afternoon as well. Rooms at the crew hotel were emptying out already, and she was able to move out of the cramped quarters she had shared with Lee and into one for her and Barry. Like the last few British colonialists who decide to stay on after some bit of empire has been returned to native rule, Penny had decided to remain with Woodstock Ventures through the lengthy disman- tling procedures ahead. In fact, not only was she going to help unravel the miles of administrative red tape left gnarled by the last three days, she was actually going to begin planning for Wood- stock II. In the end, the festival had gone so successfully there was already talk of testing the fates again with another. The first step was to disengage the organization from its local responsibilities— suits from farmers, businessmen, local property owners—and then reestablish the Woodstock Ventures office in Manhattan and start anew. Unlike Lee, Penny believed that Woodstock would lead directly to a fulfilling and profitable career in rock showmanship. After this, the world.

> We were in the catbird seat, it was a golden event for us. I thought it was going to be my profession. I didn't think, I did all this, but, Look where I get to be. But somehow what I had done allowed me to be right there in the eye of the hurricane. I came out a woman who did things. I couldn't think of it as feminist, because feminism wasn't really happening at the time. I was just tough, way tougher than I am now. I would try to be tough and in many respects I just didn't have the experience to back it up. It was a matter of style. I wasn't ready for it. I was probably insufferable for a while there.
>
> We were all quite carried away with ourselves, and I was, as much as or more than anyone else. And I thought I would be doing that kind of thing forever.

Little would turn out exactly as the young woman planned as she drifted off into an exhausted slumber that cool Catskill eve- ning. In the silent mounds of her pillow, her ears still hummed with the thunder of the crowd and the electric roar from the amps. In the darkness of her room the swarming collage of color from the field streaked clouds of contrasting hues against her eyelids' black. These were, she thought, the outlines of the rest of her life. To Penny, to the thousands who attended, to the millions who held their breath and watched it from afar, Woodstock must have looked like the future. But it was merely a one-way passage to the future, which rightfully disappeared once the chosen had passed through. Woodstock was after all a generation's shared birth canal, a pivotal corridor leaving a mark on each of the people who squeezed together to squeeze through. The Woodstock Festival of 1969 earned a place in history not so much for what went on during those three days as for the way it affected what came after.

Part III

THE
SUMMER
OF OUR
LIVES

COME NOVEMBER, December, January—when the warm rains of August had passed and the Catskill snows covered Yasgur's land—it became easy to make fun of Woodstock. An event so massive created a canvas so large that it naturally stretched anything genuine into a caricature. Naked skinny-dippers, dew-drenched hippies, peace-and-love-babbling performers: that already looked vaguely silly by the time the photos started hitting the newspapers and the taped footage started showing up on the nightly news. If anything of real or lasting value occurred on Max Yasgur's farm, the reflection of the weekend in the media mirror was twisted into almost instant parody. The kids left Bethel with a feeling of having shared a unique and powerful experience, only to discover that the whole nation was soon laughing at them.

At first, however, cultural analyses of the phenomenon in the field amounted to a love embrace as even the most staid of publications offered valentines to the peaceable kingdom that had just vanished into the Catskill mists. *The New York Times,* which had in its first editorial on the festival deplored its excesses, finally proclaimed the weekend essentially "a phenomenon of innocence."

Time magazine, in perhaps the best commentary on the significance of Woodstock, emphasized the message to America—and history—that the festival carried. Interpreting it as the sixties' most dramatic demonstration of the power and distinctive character of the era's youth, the essay treated with gravity and seriousness the sex-drugs-and-rock-and-roll ethic governing the weekend, and pointed to it as an embryonic value system that could forever change the national character. But despite the portents the essayist discerned, the column in the August 29 issue did in the end acknowledge an unforgettable, albeit chaotic, celebration. "The real significance of Woodstock can hardly be overestimated. Despite the piles of litter and garbage, the hopelessly inadequate sanitation, the lack of food and the night of rain that turned Yasgur's farm into a sea of mud, the young people found it all 'beautiful.' One long-haired teenager summed up the significance of Woodstock quite simply. 'People,' he said, 'are finally getting together.' The undeniable fact that 'people'—meaning in this case the youth of America—got together has consequences that go well beyond the festival itself."

Of course, the flurry of letters to the editor that newspapers and magazines received in reaction to their benign, accepting coverage of Woodstock showed that vast numbers of Americans were revolted by the goings-on at White Lake. A Fairfield, Connecticut, woman wrote to *The New York Times* that the event represented an exercise in mind control through drugs. An Oklahoma woman wrote to *Time:* "Your whitewash of this youth culture will precipitate the flood that will inundate us all. They plan to take over the helm—and apparently you've welcomed them aboard." Nevertheless, the magazine's editorial staff felt strongly enough about the festival to place it on the list—a bizarre roster—of top ten pop cultural events of the decade, along with the 1961 opening of Manhattan's first disco and Lord Snowdon's wearing a turtleneck with a tuxedo.

But it may well have been the mainstream press's reconciliation with the festival that tainted the Woodstock legacy, pushing it toward the cultural cliché it was to become. For three days Woodstock served as youth's sacred ground, its Promised Land. But once the mainstream press embraced it, the counterculture energy that had given the concert its vitality began to be sapped. How could an event that shared a top-ten list with turtlenecks and discos endure as an icon for rebellious youth? The shift of opinion started probably not so much in reaction to what happened during those three days in August as in reaction to the media image that emerged afterward. At first among radicals, then among the left and to the very heart of the generation, it became passé to praise Woodstock.

As early as December 1969, the Bay Area's *Ramparts* magazine was denouncing the festival as a sham. Woodstock, an article asserted, "provoked reams of self-congratulation in the underground press. Everyone seemed to think that the new age had indeed arrived, although when Abbie Hoffman grabbed the microphone and told the Woodstock crowd that their numbers meant nothing unless they could free John Sinclair, Pete Townshend clubbed Hoffman over the head with an electric guitar. . . . This is It! was the message broadcast from Woodstock. Paradise Now, the Aquarian Age. Look no further, and don't bring me down."

By the time the movie documentary from the concert came out, disdain for the Woodstock cult was the sine qua non for cool among media hipsters. You just didn't buy into that epiphany-in-the-mud crap if you were really with it. Andrew Sarris used his *Village Voice* review of the movie, which opened in New York in March 1970, to state his case by dispensing with the film and then moving on to an acerbic putdown of the concert itself. Acknowledging that he "wouldn't be caught dead or even stoned at an orgy of madness like the original Woodstock Festival," he took a jibe at those among his colleagues who had indulged in the "relentlessly retarded rhetoric of self-congratulation" that had heretofore filled the press. Then, to separate himself from the duped Woodstock advocates, he sent out this rallying cry for revisionists. "When you come right down to it what did Woodstock prove? . . . The notion

that everyone at Woodstock was deliriously happy is purely promotional demagoguery. What did fat boys and girls with pimples
do in the decades before the folk and rock scene? They sat home
and suffered silently while their parents ignored them. Now the
least of them can punish their parents for not appreciating their
uniqueness. . . . Another children's crusade has ended in drench-
ing disillusion."

Beyond media backlash after media overkill, external events
conspired to mock Woodstock too. The hostility and violence of
the Altamont Festival in late 1969 dispelled the notion, nurtured at
Woodstock, that America's youth were incapable of re-creating the
mean-spiritedness of society at large, and the belief that harmony
and cooperation through music was the birthright of the Woodstock Nation. The student deaths at Kent State in the spring of 1970
destroyed in an afternoon the aura of invulnerability and manifest
destiny that had hung over the concert weekend that previous
August. The gentle, protected, warm-spirited ambience of Woodstock seemed at best more and more remote, at worst downright
naive. Pop culture began its march through the Me Decade,
toward yuppiedom.

No artifact better marked Woodstock's fall from grace than the
success of *Lemmings*, a musical revue created by a team of writers
from *National Lampoon*. The show, which opened in January 1973,
devoted its entire second half to a parody of the festival, upping the
number of attendees to a million just for good measure and depict-
ing their suicide as the climax to the weekend. John Belushi introduced the Joe Cocker spaz routine he would bring to national TV a
few years later on "Saturday Night Live"; Joan Baez's Woodstock
plea for a pardon for her jailed husband, David, was lampooned;
even though neither Bob Dylan nor Mick Jagger was actually at the
festival, they were thrown in, possibly because by this time—not
even four years later—so many of the actual performers from the
festival were either dead or so unpopular as to be unsuitable for
ridicule. Typifying the cynical humor that would dominate the next
decade, *Lemmings* could succeed only if audiences were willing to
look back to the sincerity of the sixties, to recall the touchy-feely
intimacy of Woodstock—and laugh. It ran for months.

In time, Snoopy would develop a birdbrained friend named Woodstock. In sitcoms, kooky characters who were stuck in the past were dismissed as thinking they were still at Woodstock. A tenth-anniversary concert took place in a mall on Long Island; a fifteenth-anniversary reunion was held in the Borscht Belt hold-over resort of Grossinger's. Performers, eager to move on with their careers, refused to talk about their appearances at the 1969 festival. It dated them. To the larger world, the Woodstock Music and Art Fair became a curiosity of the past, thick with the dusty platitudes of a bygone movement, merely cute in its antiqueness, like flag-pole-sitting or jitterbug marathons.

But there are dungarees in closets today that were worn to Woodstock. There are packets of mud, now dried into caked squares of New York clay, that were carried home from Yasgur's farm and that still await a garden. There are tickets, unripped and cherished, that came home twenty years ago with kids who one Tuesday morning in August stashed them away and have main-tained a vigil over them ever since. There are performers, orga-nizers, local townsfolk and concertgoers whose experiences then and now will forever prevent the festival from truly becoming a cliché.

To pop culture at large, perhaps, the impact of the biggest youth happening ever has been diffused over time. The weekend seems to have been just that, a weekend. But there are lives that were touched, perhaps molded, by the events of August 15, 16 and 17. And it is in those lives that the true history of Woodstock is written.

THE FELDMANS

THE BOATHOUSE from which old Ben Leon watched the skinny-dipping hippies has been bought and converted into a dazzling lakefront summer home by a millionaire. The dilapidated barn where Hog Farm commune members crashed has been completely refurbished by a preservation-conscious interior designer who has turned a dump into a rural masterpiece. The number of permanent residents on the unpaved road where Burt and Anne Feldman live has quadrupled since 1969. What remains unchanged, however, these two decades later, is the Feldmans' support and enthusiasm for the festival, a stance that singles them out in this community where memories of the weekend can still raise hackles—and fists.

At first, Burt and Anne joined in with the local residents in campaigning for zoning laws that would prevent another such unruly event from happening in their county. Though they personally had enjoyed the excitement, the devastation of the countryside and the belongings of many of their friends couldn't be ignored. Local papers were full of editorial indignation. Burt himself accompanied a contingent of fellow Bethel men to Albany to petition the government to pass statewide laws forbidding huge gatherings like Woodstock.

But despite their espousal of an immediate municipal counterpunch to the festival, the Feldmans still recognized the significance of the event on a larger scale. For a week that August, Bethel was the center of the youth-culture universe. Sleepy Bethel, financially strapped Bethel, nearly forgotten Bethel had become a media flashpoint. If their fellow townspeople's shortsighted view of the concert concentrated on the negative impact it had produced locally, the longsighted view should focus on how to turn the calamity to the town's advantage. The fetid odor still arose from the fields with each rain, yet Anne and Burt began to mention to people that there might be some way of capitalizing on the site, some way to plug into the energy created here that explosive weekend. Few neighbors reacted very positively.

> BURT: I'm trying to convince those stupid bastards they have a potential gold mine. I don't care if you approve of the event or not. I said a classic example is a small village in Pennsylvania. Several thousand men came there and they were shooting at each other for several days and when they left there were barns burned and people dead and animals slaughtered. And no one is in favor of people dying or barns burning but last year two and a half million people went there to Gettysburg to see it. And they say, That's different; this was for crazy hippy bastards.

An aficionado of local history, Burt had the perspective of how time would immortalize the festival, while the rest of his neighbors just wanted to forget. Both he and Anne began their unpopular battle at least to establish some sort of historical marker on the site, and even that was met with hue and cry.

Along the way, the Feldmans began noticing that the world at large was recognizing the significance of the festival even if the hometown didn't. On anniversaries through the decades, radio stations and TV camera crews came to town, and were often directed to the Feldmans, who were emerging as the local authorities on the events of that weekend. At one point, Burt required a minor operation, and when he mentioned to his surgeon where he was from, the young doctor went crazy: he had been one of those hippies in the field years earlier. Slowly the cars that stopped at the site were changing from painted Volkswagens to late-model Volvos, and the faithful paying their respects at the field went from hippie to yuppie.

Inspired by the turnout for the fifteenth-anniversary reunion held at Grossinger's, the Feldmans decided to stop merely talking about the need for a historical marker and to do something about it. Between 1984 and 1986 the Woodstock sign became the center of controversy in Bethel, upstaging the debate over the sewage plant and the bungalow colony permit. Anne and Burt went to every town hall meeting to bring up the marker and eventually their persistence wore down the board members' resistance to at least considering it. When they finally agreed in theory that it could go up, they couldn't decide where: on the road, down in the hollow where the stage was, out near the main highway as a direction guide. Then no one could agree on the wording: they didn't want to sound too celebratory of an event many still considered a violation; they didn't want to sound too negative, or why bother putting it up?

In the end, after fighting for the installation of an official historical landmark sign, the Feldmans were upstaged. The owners of the acreage, who had bought it from the Yasgur estate, had no such qualms about commemorating the site and, on their own, placed a plaque on the most prominent corner of the field, where it still stands today. Emblazoned with a re-creation of the Ventures dove-on-the-guitar logo, the stone sculpture reads: "Peace and Music. This is the original site of the Woodstock Music and Art Fair Held on Aug. 15, 16, 17, 1969." It is simple, unobtrusive, but hard to miss. About a hundred yards away, the cows, now the field's only population, ignore it and those who seek it out. As for the marker the town finally decided to erect, it was so spindly and poorly secured that it was gone little less than a year after it went up in 1986. A two-inch-story filled a hole deep inside *The New York Times* a week after it was installed.

Burt and Anne still have hopes that the town will wake up to its own history. Now sixty-six, they are odd oral historians of this giddy, youth-oriented incident in their town's past, unlikely repositories of the legend. But in remembering it, cherishing it and perpetuating its legacy, they have found the weekend continues to do what it did for them twenty years ago: even as they face their golden years, devotion to the nation's greatest youth event ever keeps the Feldmans young.

> BURT: I realized that it was an event of seminal importance to American social history. It was the coming of age of a new era, what's the phrase, the Age of Aquarius, whatever the silly thing was, it doesn't matter. What you had here was a half a million young people under the most abysmal conditions who were being treated terribly, being abused, and yet there was peace.
>
> ANNE: It's not like we would want it here again, but it happened and we think we should be proud of that.

DR. PAUL D'AMICO

A SMALL-TOWN doctor, a devout Catholic and father: Dr. Paul D'Amico no doubt seemed a most unlikely rebel to the hundreds of kids he treated back in 1969 when, suddenly, the back roads of Sullivan County became the main street of the American drug-crazed counterculture. He fairly typified the straight-arrow world of home and hearth. He personified traditional values and conventional success. He was, passing up and down the rows of cots where acid-laced teens twisted, the very epitome of the establishment. Or was he? Beneath the standard white jacket of his profession and behind the thick glasses that made him seem even more intellectual, there were the mind and soul of a man whose maverick philosophy and antiestablishment theories would eventually grab headlines, work wonder cures, jeopardize his career. Woodstock uprooted Dr. D'Amico's book-and-journal-inspired mindset, planting the seed of independent thinking in its place. Within two

decades he'd be paying the price for demonstrating the very rebelliousness that went unrecognized by the self-fashioned rebels he
treated at the festival.

At Woodstock D'Amico's contact with drugs was so new that he
barely recognized the clinical distinction between the recreational
drug use he saw in such profusion there and true addiction. To his
eye it was all nearly the same thing. Soon after, though, the doctor's practice began to take on more and more patients with full-
fledged substance dependencies. Though his formal training had
included little direct preparation for managing this often refractory
disease, he found he couldn't ethically turn the needy away—
though other medical professionals in his area obviously felt little
of the same responsibility. As he remembers it, he started to build
a reputation as the county's leading addiction doctor because
nobody else around wanted to compete for the title. Despite his
lack of schooling in this area, he was learning an enormous amount
simply by doing, and much of the experience he was gaining
contradicted academic guidelines concerning rehabilitation. Into
the 1970s he grew more and more dissatisfied with the sanctioned
approach to addictions, specifically with New York State policies
concerning methadone. That substitute drug merely continued
addiction under an approved form, he believed. Instead, he
wanted to cut out all opiate substances and treat the addicted with
beta blockers, drugs he believed subverted the need for the body's
dependency on heroin all together.

But before initiating a program for this treatment approach on
his own, D'Amico was sidetracked by a charismatic rehabilitation
director who invited him to join the staff of a new center for low-
income alcoholics and drug addicts he was building locally.
D'Amico was flattered that his good work in his small practice had
brought him to the notice of someone willing to pay him a great
deal more than he was making, to continue treating addictions.
The association was to end in disaster, and it gave D'Amico his first
taste of the legal hassles that await mavericks attempting to inno-
vate within the restrictive structures of the medical-governmental
establishment. D'Amico's employer was investigated for allegedly
attempting to place patients in menial jobs as part of their rehab,

reserving a portion of their wages for their upkeep. D'Amico asserts it was a legitimate strategy to get the patients off welfare, to mainstream them into the community while maintaining the supervision without which they would return to full drunkenness or addiction. Government agencies saw it differently, shut down the operation, and sent D'Amico off with an extremely bitter taste in his mouth.

If anything, the closing of the rehab program only convinced D'Amico further that the governmentally approved protocols for handling the addicted—be they alcohol- or drug-dependent— were hopelessly out of date and mired in bureaucratic mumbo-jumbo. That conviction persuaded the board at a newly constructed hospital in the area to put D'Amico on staff and eventually allow him to set up an entire ward for treating heroin addicts without methadone. Initially the results were encouraging—rehab in general had such a poor success rate that any index of accomplishment looked enormously positive. And the doctor who never even specialized in psychiatry or pharmacology had emerged as something of a statewide hero in drug treatment. He remained on the fringe, partially because that's where the medical community always places its pioneers, but also because his personality removed him from more respectable circles. His inclination toward a drug-conspiracy theory was growing and his messianic sense of mission simply made him seem kooky. Through vanity presses he began publishing a series of self-help books that documented his belief that it was decadent society that was unwilling to curtail the addiction it secretly propagated as an enslavement of its people. Somebody was benefitting from the substance abuse he was trying to address, and that somebody became the object of some rather ill-focused ranting on his part. His accusatory posture inclined him to incriminations about nonmedical mischief as well: he believed the Vatican was populated by sham papists, that the real pope had fled to Spain and the current pontiff had been placed there by secret agents of evil. Nevertheless, personality quirks aside, he seemed to be helping people, and for a while that seemed like enough.

He's still not sure what first drew the attention of state medical

authorities to his operation in the mid-1980s. By then he had
added lecturing to his hospital practice and had even begun selling cassette recordings of his theories. But he thinks it was his
stance against methadone that probably first kindled the flames at
the stake where he was tied in 1987. First he learned of a criminal
investigation against him, an attempt to link the heroin-overdose
deaths of several of his outpatients to his failure to maintain them
on the prescribed methadone treatment. At the same time several
state agencies complained officially that his practice of treating
drug- and alcohol-addicted patients within the same program violated current standards for abuse management. A psychiatrist
from New York City was sent to conduct a formal assessment of
D'Amico's program, and filed a negative review of what he found.
Finally, his own hospital's review board got skittish and questioned D'Amico's procedures. The allegations of poor judgment
mounted and the dossier of incriminating evidence grew fatter,
until in July he was dismissed from the staff and had his license
suspended for an undetermined period. The doctor who had
learned firsthand at 1969's rebel festival how widespread drug
abuse had become was being punished for taking rebel steps to try
to curtail its devastation.

> They would die on the street, and if I hadn't taken them off
> methadone, the state claimed, they would be alive. I found out
> that I was going to be indicted on murder charges. When I was
> suspended from the hospital I realized the noose was tightening
> around the neck. The secretary at the health department told
> mine that they were doing an underground investigation of how
> many I had taken off methadone who later died. I really thought
> I was going to go to jail. They were going to accumulate ten,
> fifteen cases and then indict me. The committee at the hospital,
> the quality-assurance committee, came against me. That was
> enough. That would be enough to dismantle my program, so
> there was no need to bring the criminal charges.

D'Amico says it has cost him upward of $25,000 to defend
himself, and he is still not sure he will ever be able to practice
according to his own principles again. He plans to make a living

through administration or teaching if he fails to win back his right to practice in New York. Dr. D'Amico's case remains one of the more ironic twists in the labyrinth of personal histories that link Woodstock and today. In the orgiastic psychedelia of Woodstock, in that giant surge of childish disobedience, he saw nearly demonic degradation. Yet all of those kids, no matter how overwhelmed they were, got off their cots eventually and set off for home, their weekend of druggy insurrection against the straight world's code of ethics forgiven, unpunished. Dr. D'Amico, on the other hand, would leave that celebration of rebelliousness and slowly start on his own divergent journey. As the years raced by, that journey accelerated and grew ever more and more risky. Finally he found himself twisting hopelessly, not on a cot in a makeshift hospital, but in a courtroom and in the newspapers. It's unlikely that in the middle of his nightmare there will appear some well-meaning caretaker who will be able to step in, calm him down, get him through it all safely. And when the nightmare ends, it's unlikely Dr. Paul D'Amico will be able to get up and just go home unscarred.

GEORGE NEUHAUS

MAYBE THERE are no villains in the Woodstock story. Perhaps that is the story's uniqueness. George Neuhaus might have epitomized the sort of reactionary politician who seemed, back in 1969, the antithesis of the Woodstock spirit; he might have stood scowling on the sidelines during the weekend-long flowering of the hedonistic nation; he might have detested the entire lifestyle the Aquarian Exposition celebrated.

But then so did most of the parents who sat home watching the television reports about the festival, worrying that their sons and daughters were participating in this heathen hoedown. So did most of the older generation wondering what the events in Bethel signified about the future of the country. George Neuhaus, former Bethel town supervisor, family man, father, just happened to be present at the creation of the Woodstock Nation, but aside from the coincidences of location he was little different from parents in other parts of the country. Because the event took place in his hometown, it would forever change his life. But for all intents and purposes, George Neuhaus was no more a villain than every mom and dad who resolved that weekend to take action against the gathering storm of immorality they saw at Woodstock.

For other parents that vow became a quiet, hard resolve that perhaps erupted into domestic squabbles now and then over the next couple of years, whenever Johnny and Janie announced they were about to embark on some endeavor Mom and Pop judged too far out. But for George the resolve became a campaign slogan, one that earned him an instant following among the disgruntled residents of Bethel, who one August morning woke up to find their little town adopted as the New Eden by a mass of weirdos.

"Who Spit in Bethel's Pot?" queried a headline in the *Catskill Shopper* on October 1, 1969, just a single salvo in the unrelenting fusillade of recriminations that rocked through Sullivan County politics that fall. Outrage was focused on then town supervisor Jerry Amatucci, whose campaign for reelection sputtered hopelessly on as Neuhaus announced his bid for the post and blithely sat by and watched as memory and local gossip did the rest. In the elections that November, according to the *Sullivan County Democrat*, "all present supervisors [returned] to office, with exception of Daniel 'Jerry' Amatucci, town of Bethel, who lost to George Neuhaus." It was a vote Neuhaus read as a mandate to accept the mantle of Catskill Savonarola, protecting the entire country from hippie invasions, mass concerts and drugs.

Barely two months after he took office, Neuhaus successfully drafted and got passed a town resolution, the first in the county, controlling public assembly. "No person," it read, "shall use, allow, let or permit to be used property for the assembly of persons in excess of 10,000 unless a written permit authorizing such use shall have been obtained from the town board." In other words: no more Woodstocks. Throughout the next summer, the residents looked fondly on that bit of legislation as all around them other communities were threatened by the endless number of Woodstock IIs promoters tried to organize in the wake of the Great Coming Together of 1969. Neuhaus himself helped squash the Bach to Rock series slated for nearby Mountaindale, which eventually was derailed thanks to a restraining order from the state attorney general. "I'm proud of my son, who is willing to go out and serve his country, instead of sitting in the hills of Mountaindale smoking pot," Neuhaus told the local paper in triumph, putting in a plug for his boy then enrolled in the service.

Meanwhile that same August, in Powder Ridge, Connecticut, an al fresco fiasco of giant proportions took place when promoters— with 18,000 tickets sold—were told at the last minute to fold up their operations. Thirty thousand kids had already showed up and were refusing to leave. Injunctions against performances didn't prevent folksinger Melanie from taking the stage, thereby convincing the kids that eventually more entertainment would follow, which in turn convinced them they should just sit and wait. At one point, the frantic promoters attempted to rent Yankee Stadium as an alternative, but were rebuffed, leaving them with nearly 30,000 hippies waiting for a show. The debacle proved just how miraculous the Woodstock weekend had really been; even nude swimming and pot smoking at Powder Ridge couldn't entertain the kids forever, and the vibes grew more sour with each hour that passed without the promised music. Residents of Bethel sighed with relief: because of George Neuhaus, Powder Ridge had the problem this summer, not they.

The goodwill engendered by his anti-Woodstock reputation persisted for two more two-year terms, but eventually the vicissitudes of local politics caught up with Neuhaus. In 1975 he was out, only to be returned to office in the election of 1979. He was out again in 1981, then back in 1983, staying until he was again rejected in 1987. Without a platform as powerful as the anti-Woodstock cause, his electability has varied greatly from year to year.

The only man to have built a political career out of the festival, and specifically out of criticizing it, George Neuhaus actually is far less of an anti-Woodstocker than he might imagine. The weekend was a fluke, a three-day wonder the very essence of which is its irreplicability. Because he worked so diligently and efficiently to assure its never happening again, Neuhaus has helped preserve the once-in-a-lifetime nature of Woodstock. Others like the Feldmans may be more obvious proponents of the mythology, more dutiful tenders of the flame. Others may in their lifestyle better represent the durability of the values crystallized that weekend. But even though he came to the position from the rear, Neuhaus shares with every hippie in the field the acute realization that Woodstock belonged to a particular time and place, never again to be repeated. Implementing elaborate legal devices and employing the rhetoric of God and country, he nixed any repeat of the festival, any crass, commercial and possibly dangerous attempts to restage the magic. And far from making him the villain, that valiant diligence in ensuring "never again" has allowed 500,000 memories to remain intact, unchallenged, untainted, alive.

ELEN ORSON

Elen Orson drives a Mercedes. Bought used, she is quick to point out. And she drives it not for status but because it is, she says, simply a very good car. The car is parked in the garage of her home, high in the Hollywood Hills, where two dogs, a swimming pool and a husband attest to some of the changes in her life over the last twenty years. Her attitudes about that life, though, and something about the way she confidently and thoughtfully expresses them connect her strongly to the independent-minded New Jersey kid who left her grounded boyfriend behind and took off for Woodstock.

After the festival, Elen worked in regional theater, collected unemployment, and eventually wandered to Los Angeles, the movie capital, where she thought she might concentrate on the editing trade she had been dabbling in since Woodstock. But LA proved tougher than she had expected. Here was a city jammed with technicians who had more sophisticated skills than she did at the time. There was none of the collegiality and congeniality she had benefitted from back in the New York studio. And very little of the nonsexist thinking that flourished there. Here editing, especially sound editing, was male dominated. And more important, all the men had union cards. Unable to find studio work, the young woman edited independent shorts and public service documentaries; it was work that guaranteed long hours and low pay.

But while editing this material she first realized how influential she could be in controlling the final thrust and message of the piece: her precision work could serve as a vehicle for her political ideas. For example, when a large fuel company hired her to cut a documentary about an African country it was interested in developing, she made sure footage of the native Bedouin population received substantial play. The effect was subtle, but she at least felt she was doing something that left her imprint on the final product. Ever since, she has continued to marry her work and her political beliefs as she has moved into ever-more lucrative jobs. She finally broke into the union, and now has a job at a sound studio that services the motion picture and television industries. The girl who dangled precariously over the crowds with canisters full of performance gold is now a woman who sits comfortably on the porch of a Hollywood home she makes movies to pay for.

By the strict value system of the Woodstock era, such comfort would be considered hopelessly bourgeois. By the less unrealistic standards by which we judge ourselves today, Elen has just made out fine. Her upscale drift through meaningful work is an eighties ideal. And in the little ways she imposes her ideology on her surroundings through that work, she is perpetuating something of what she learned at Woodstock. She has refused to work on several slasher movies that have come into the shop, because she believes they glorify violence and embody antiwoman stereotypes. She removed her name from a film she thought was sexist. Such flourishes are hardly monumental. Yet it is the way she brings a liberal's world view to her workaday decisions that perhaps best reveals her Woodstock roots. At seventeen she refused to accept certain things about the way American society ran; at thirty-seven she still does.

Several years ago she fell in love with and wed a man who served in combat in Vietnam. Such an individual—he was a southerner, and he enlisted!—would have been the last type of guy she would have envisioned marrying a decade earlier. She still considers herself a feminist and a pacifist, two characterizations which back in 1969 prompted her boyfriend's father to deny his son permission to go to Woodstock with her. And yet now she identifies her living with a former soldier, one who was wounded in action, as the greatest learning experience of her life. She can barely believe her own ears when she hears herself saying it, but she can now understand that there were two sides to the Vietnam controversy. A veteran of the protest movement, Elen married a vet from the war and is proud of it.

The first to admit that significant changes have occurred since Woodstock, Elen also cultivates her nostalgic memories of that weekend. She sees in it both a global significance—it proved something to the world—and a personal one. Her work today traces its résumé right back to the three days she spent in Yasgur's field, and often that work brings her into contact with the special fraternity of filmmakers who collaborated on the movie.

But the weekend is cherished for more than the professional bonuses it has delivered. Although she slaved away through most of the concert, the time spent there holds a sacred place in her memory: she still owns the dungarees and belt she wore there, not as current pieces of her wardrobe but as exhibits in the personal museum of her life. She has preserved as a special emblem of honor the now battered red pass that designated her as a member of the camera crew. In the movie she helped make, she appears for two seconds in a shot taken just as the Sunday thunderheads rolled over the mountains. Wind is whipping through her hair, and there's a look of panic just beginning to register on her face. She is delighted that she has been captured weathering a storm the winds from which still blow through her days. As with many of the thousands there, Elen rejects the cliché notions about the concert as a sixties joke. In her life it has proven to be so very much more.

Woodstock spread like ripples through the society. We're the only ones who knew what really happened there, the ones who were there. Others heard about it but they had no concept from which to judge. Maybe with the film they had some idea. There's no way to describe the feeling, the warmth, the mass happiness—everyone was just gaga that they were there. And the mass ripples of that have gone back through society, so when you have the harmonic convergence or the US festival—big things, big gatherings—when those happen they always compare them to Woodstock. It's the base upon which all other things have been judged, the paragon. It's become part of my fiber.

There's this cartoon we do called *Jemm*, about a rocker girl. And there's this bad group with a guy named Technorat, who is always trying to thwart the girls. A couple of weeks ago he sent Jemm and the Holograms back through time and I said no, no: it was the Woodstock Festival, and I was laughing my head off.

I don't think anyone who lived through that time actually wants to go back. It was a time of conflict. The whole reason it happened was conflict. We made some ground and Woodstock was a celebration. But I don't want to live in that time. I've had to make more things happen in my life. I still have my jeans from Woodstock, and my leather belt. But I don't want to wear that now.

COUNTRY JOE MCDONALD

"THE WAR," says Joe McDonald emphatically, "is over." But in many ways the war continues to haunt the singer who twenty years ago sang the conflict's most famous protest song, a song he now argues has been misunderstood all along as antimilitary. And that misunderstanding has boomeranged through the decades that separate him from the era of his greatest popularity, an era that culminated at the Woodstock Festival. Locked into an image that fateful weekend, Country Joe McDonald walked off the stage in Bethel and into a future that would hold greater and greater obscurity. The next twenty years of his life would be spent fighting an uphill battle against the tide of public opinion that slowly and inexorably began shifting away from him soon after the concert appearance. The only individual to perform twice at the biggest media event of the sixties, Country Joe is also one of Woodstock's most astonishing casualties.

Almost immediately after the concert, the long-rumored breakup of Country Joe and the Fish finally occurred. The members' affiliation had been rocky for months and several trial separations culminated in disintegration by 1970. Still high from the Woodstock appearance and other well-received performances during 1969, Joe embraced the breakup as an opportunity. His first solo album, *Thinking of Woody Guthrie,* was released in January 1970 to reviews that favorably compared him to the folksinging great. And by November of the same year, he released another solo effort, recorded in Nashville, with a country-western flavor, *Tonight I'm Singing Just for You.* An agreement to appear with the Fish in the spoof film *Zachariah* reunited him briefly with his former colleagues during production—they played a group of bumbling banditos. But the rupture was complete and there would be no performing musically together again.

At just about the same time, though, Joe began to encounter difficulty with bookings; he suspected that his antiwar statements and songs were inviting hostility from the conservative boards that supervised large arenas. Then the IRS began a series of harassing audit demands, and Joe also thought he detected the presence of tapping noises during phone calls. Indignant and paranoid, Joe decided he'd be better off out of the country for a while; he headed to Europe, where his music was enjoying more popularity than stateside. At first he approached the continental tour as a good way to master his solo act away from the scrutiny of American fans. He was to discover, however, just how fickle those fans could be. Out of sight, and out of mind, Joe played Europe as the American record buyer forgot all about him.

Exposure to anti-American sentiments while in Europe inflamed Joe's antiwar ideology, and he became even more radical. Upon his return he joined up with Jane Fonda and Donald Sutherland in the Free the Army program, a series of entertainment tours designed to bring the leftist-pacifist political message to the soldiers themselves. But Joe's own military past soon asserted itself, and discomfort over what he feared was the stars' patronizing attitude toward the service personnel grew. It was clear to him that Fonda had no idea what the men who served were all about, and her basic premise—that by accepting conscription, the draftees were perpetuating the conflict—had no basis in the reality of the day. He parted company with FTA, convinced he knew the military mindset better than the troupe's leaders, convinced that even his "Fixin'-to-Die Rag" was understood better by fighting men than civilians.

> You know, it didn't really make fun of the military at all. Almost all vets will explain that it doesn't make fun. It never implied that we would not do a good job fighting. I asked, What are we fighting for, not whether or not we could fight. We will fight, but what is it all about? The question hasn't been answered yet.

Throughout the early seventies Joe continued to deliver solo albums that ran a spectrum of musical styles: among them, *Hold On, It's Coming*, recorded in London with Spencer Davis; a concept album based on a book of World War I poems, on which he played all the instruments; and another live album in 1972. Joe was experimenting and growing as an artist, but unfortunately the Woodstock label lingered on. By 1975, the war over, Joe had moved on to address other social issues on his *Paradise with an Ocean View* album, which included songs about saving the whales and third-world inequities. But people didn't seem to be listening to the music. Instead they were listening to their memories. And in their memories Country Joe became associated with Vietnam and all the war's unhappiness. He is certain that in the great cultural sublimation of that war that took place in the late seventies and early eighties, he, too, was pushed into the very deepest recesses of the generation's collective consciousness.

Professional frustrations took their toll on his personal life. In 1975 Joe got married for the third time. By 1982 he was getting married again. He never stopped writing and producing records— he set up his own company, Fantasy Records in Berkeley, for just that reason. But they often failed to get air play and his concert schedule tapered off to the point that royalties from his sixties music comprised more than half his annual income. But if the public seemed determined to forget him along with the war, Joe

himself couldn't loosen his fascination with Vietnam. Around
1985 he began work on what he calls his *Guernica*, his magnum
opus, with which he hoped to come to terms once and for all with
what the war had meant to him and his country. Called *The Vietnam
Experience*, the album contained the song "Welcome Home," which
has become something of an unofficial anthem of several veterans'
organizations. In conjunction with the album, Joe codirected a
rock documentary, uniting the songs from the LP with footage
from the sixties. Joe describes it as "a tribute to those who fought
and those who resisted. It includes the antiwar experience of those
within the military as well. It was a form of outreach and a thera-
peutic healing device, to help us Americans, the vets, their families, to get some closure on this experience." But the work failed to
generate much media attention when it was released in 1987. While
the public seems to be comfortable with dramatic depictions of the
war—the Oscar-winning movie *Platoon*, for example—McDonald
says, musical treatment of issues stemming from the Vietnam
experience seems still to be a no-no with the masses and more
intensely within the record industry itself.

There is resignation in his voice when Country Joe assesses the
current state of his career. He bemoans the fact that his performance schedule is so spotty, but then on the other hand he figures
he's amassed five million miles on the road over the past twenty
years and that's enough for him. He still spends two hours a day
practicing guitar and voice, but goes into the Fantasy offices less
and less. He became a father again in 1988 and directs much of his
energy to raising his four children. His work with veterans—he's
involved in the drive to build a Vietnam memorial in California—is
his most high-profile activity, and one that still provokes the most
questions. Country Joe, isn't he the protest singer? What is he
doing with the vets?

> Journalists always ask that question. "Isn't it inconsistent? You
> sang the 'Fixin'-to-Die Rag,' and now you're working with the
> vets." Well, they forget I am a vet too. Vets have no problem with
> the song, they understand what it's about.

My kids are mystified, that's for sure. About a lot of things, about me. They know about the song and about Woodstock, sort of, but I perform so rarely now they don't really associate me with that. My daughter hasn't ever seen me perform; she's seven. Hasn't seen me. Well, you know, the chances of them seeing me perform these days are pretty slim.

RON STONE

Ron Stone loved the American political process, loved Washington, loved being part of the history-making decisions there during the sixties. And in 1970, not a year after attending the Woodstock Festival, he left all that he loved behind. A lottery was run, he was assigned number 26, his college deferment elapsed, and his draft notice was sent. Ron bought a ticket to Canada and stayed there for seven years.

The young man, who had served four years as a congressional page, was not proud of dodging. It seemed not merely cowardly but also antithetical to his patriotism. He was enamored of politics, specifically American politics in all its forms. This was, after all, a guy for whom even a playful concert weekend in New York held potential political implications. All through those years on the Hill and then afterward, as a student in the nation's capital, Ron had harbored hopes of building himself a career in government. He had worked alongside the most famous legislators of the decade, had been educated in the arcane ways of Congress, and had become familiar with that most heady of governmental seductions—power. More significant, he had watched as his idols in Congress argued against the war and ceaselessly tried to curtail its expansion. Now Ron's own future as an American, and as an American statesman, was being placed in jeopardy by the failure of elected officials to stop the war. After years of listening to doves haranguing the hawks, Ron was now dodging.

The steady flow of resisters northward was at its peak when Ron arrived in Montreal that summer. Work permits were difficult to come by, so Ron set up a bogus corporation, hired himself, and through that employment finagled the Canadian equivalent of a green card. The work he was able to find with that visa wasn't very satisfying: he washed dishes, he did gardening. He had never thought of himself as particularly entrepreneurial—his experience had all been directed toward preparing himself for a political career. But with necessity as his inspiration, he quickly refined his business acumen and bought into a thriving rolling-papers operation, importing goods from Spain. In 1972 a college buddy inherited a small amount of money and asked Ron to help him start a natural gas business in Vancouver. And for the next five years, in a city Ron still says is the most civilized in the world, the two young Americans struggled to become titans of Canadian industry.

During this long period of estrangement from his birthland, Ron grew fond of his new home but never really considered himself an expatriate. He would devour magazines and papers from the States, following closely the reelection of Nixon in 1972 and the Watergate debacle that ensued. It riled him that he had to watch from afar as so intriguing a scandal unfurled in Washington. Even as the Republican hegemony unraveled, Ron never held much hope for the amnesty he heard other resisters talking about. As far as he was concerned, he would never be able to return home permanently. His grandmother died, his sister got married. He was unable to go back to Chicago for either. He did make one trip back early on, and his paranoia was so intense he never dared try it again.

I made one surreptitious trip back. I was in a friend's apartment
and, like, fifteen police cars surrounded the building. I really
freaked. I was running from roof to roof. It was enough to scare
the wits out of me. They were just responding to a fire alarm.
And then, when I was flying back, through Seattle, there's an
announcement for me to come to gate six, and at the same time
an announcement for airport security to come to gate six. And
when I finally get there, there are all these guys in suits, FBI guys
I'm sure. They were just calling my name for stand-by. And
before we take off, these guys come on the plane. And after they
leave and we start to take off, we have to stop and go back and
they come on again. I'm sweating and almost throwing up.
Finally we do take off and the guy next to me says, "Son, I can tell
you've never flown before, but you'll be all right." Of course, I
had flown a thousand times before. It just wasn't worth the
anxiety to go back.

In 1977, after many months of sputtering finances, the fuel
business neared collapse. Just as things looked their bleakest,
Jimmy Carter declared the amnesty for draft dodgers, as others
had predicted he would. And Ron, accepting stock as a buyout,
left the Vancouver company, packed his bags and headed home.
After being legally prevented from visiting America for the better
part of the decade, it's not surprising that Ron's next few years were
spent nearly nomadically, first in New York, then in Fort Lauder-
dale, then in Chicago, before he finally moved to Los Angeles in
1979. There, establishing permanent residence, he was again able
to concentrate on his abiding passion, politics. He became involved
in the long, hard and eventually successful drive to incorporate
West Hollywood as an independent city. Ron saw the new city as
the perfect place to launch the political career he had put on hold in
the seventies. Sentiment against the war had been nearly universal
there and his history as a draft dodger would actually earn him
respect. Besides, the public interest in West Hollywood's incor-
poration would transform the city's officials into media celebrities,
far more flashy than run-of-the-mill bureaucrats. But Ron was
never to realize those ambitions. In 1984 he ran during the first city

elections and suffered a heavy defeat. Shortly afterward, he found out that he had AIDS.

After that diagnosis, Ron has beaten the odds in fighting off the ravages of the killing disease. Still, he has lost forty pounds and fatigues so easily that he has been forced to curtail all his political activities. He secured a license as a corporate arbitrator and now free-lances as a negotiator in partnership squabbles. Oddly, the man who always thought he would be a politician has avoided joining any of the organizations currently fighting for more government spending for AIDS research and care. In extremis, the politico who never was elected has decided to sit this one out.

> I've had a hell of a life really. I have no regrets. Even though I have so much free time and a little bit of money, there's really nothing I want to do. There was a point when I thought things were building to a major climax in my life. And now I just realize that was life. You may never write your masterpiece, but every little experience you were a part of counts. You were there.

JOCKO MARCELLINO

T HERE IS perhaps no better proof of the unpredictability of the era Woodstock epitomized than the fact that of all the groups and supergroups who performed there, of all the famous singers and idolized rockers who dazzled that crowd, few would go on to enjoy the popularity, commercial reward and enormous exposure that awaited, of all groups, Sha Na Na. Without question, here is the most astounding and unexpected success story of the entire show.

Sitting in his English Lit class the September after the concert, Jocko Marcellino still could not believe his scruffy little act had shared the stage with the likes of Hendrix, Slick, Guthrie, Crosby, Stills and Nash. The turn of events was made no less remarkable by the fact that now, barely four weeks later, he found himself back on the same Columbia campus, doodling in his notebook as he had in May. "And now, greased up and ready to kick ass, Sha Na Na." He could still hear the announcer, and the roar from the crowd—even diminished as it was by the time they got to perform—was still loud enough in his memory to bury the drone of the professor in the front of the room. He didn't know it then, but he was to experience that crowd appreciation for the next twenty years.

Although the group had secured several gigs immediately after the concert, none of the members considered their prospects for making the act a full-time job promising enough to quit school. As the other students around them protested, resisted, rallied and partied, the Sha Na Na Columbians crammed and dashed, studied and rehearsed. Soon, though, demand for Sha Na Na exploded, and it was to become absolutely unrelenting once the Woodstock movie came out and introduced them to an entire nation of rockers.

> We brought our books with us to appearances. I remember once leaving a notebook I was studying for an exam from on an airplane. But I always got it done. I wrote a paper on what it was like to appear at Woodstock. I did another paper for a psych course relating rock-and-roll music to what was going on in the counterculture. That one I actually was asked back the next year to give as a lecture. For one class—it was after the movie came out—I compared *Gimme Shelter* and *Woodstock*. My premise was, you could take all the footage of the films and re-edit them and make one film look just like the other. You could easily have cut *Woodstock* to look like a nightmare.

For Jocko, though, the editing job done on the movie was just fine: surprising them all, it included their version of "At the Hop." And that produced the group's first gold single. Buddah Records increased the promotion campaign behind the group's albums, and Sha Na Na collected three gold LPs, signifying sales of 500,000 units. Inevitably Sha Na Na's success invited imitation, and when it came it came with a vengeance: the musical *Grease* opened on Broadway in February 1972, barely two and a half years from that night in August when the group sang "At the Hop" to a throng anxious to hear Jimi Hendrix. Hendrix had died over a year before. Jocko says the producers of the show, recognizing their debt to the group as the inspiration of the musical, asked the members to be in the production, but they decided they didn't want to participate. It would restrict their touring, and the eight-shows-a-week schedule was incompatible with the classes they were still determined to attend. The show ran for more than 2,000 performances.

Actually, Jocko would have loved nothing better than to appear on Broadway: his yen for real acting was increasing and the Sha Na Na shenanigans weren't quite enough to satisfy his desire for serious theatrics. And so, with graduation from Columbia on the horizon—and with the freedom to tour full-time—Jocko decided to register at NYU for a master's in dramatics. Two more years of juggling school and greasing-up followed, but he thrived on the stage, playing meaty parts like the cowboy in *Bus Stop*. Dreams of a full-time acting career remained just that, however. Unlike most frustrated New York actors, his hopes were dashed not by lack of luck but by good fortune. When both the Beach Boys and Chicago turned down a producer's offer to star in a weekly TV comedy show, Sha Na Na's managers urged the group to accept. And since several members of the original group had already dropped out, Jocko didn't want to dilute the ensemble further. He headed to California, and on to one of the most successful syndicated variety shows of the decade: called simply *Sha Na Na*, it ran three years and made Jocko, to say the least, a very comfortable rock-and-roller. And more than comfortable, it made him competent. A kooky, fast-paced half-hour, the show nevertheless required an immense amount of music, and in producing it week after week, Jocko became a vastly improved performer. And the greaser who as a Columbia frosh had, naturally, felt inferior to the greats on the Woodstock stage started to take himself seriously as a musician.

We made ninety-seven half-hours. We would do two hundred fifty songs a season. Eight tracks a day. It was like a machine. But that was the thing about the TV show, we got to back everybody, from Conway Twitty to James Brown. James Brown came in and laid down some tracks and said, "Who's drumming?" And I said, "Me." I was nervous, I thought I had done something wrong. I was a rhythm-and-blues nut and he was my god. He said,

"Brother," and gave me five. One of the high points of my career. We really got good at it during our television show. We were learning a lot. It was campy and shticky, no doubt about it. We knew we were doing sort of zany things, and then a couple of years later this show really got hip. It was an attitude.

Nearly a decade had passed since the group's canny amalgam of irreverent nostalgia and stagey charisma kicked off youth's fascination with early rock. Through the seventies that new interest would blossom into a growing number of golden-oldie radio stations, an increasing appetite for rock revival concerts, and a new respect by mainstream pop stars for the hits of the fifties and early sixties. Perhaps the most noticeable embodiment of that nostalgia craze was the movie version of *Grease*, which became the biggest box-office smash of 1978 and the most successful film musical of all time (twice the domestic revenue of *The Sound of Music*). This time around Sha Na Na knew better than to turn down the offer to participate, and the group's soundtrack from the film was nominated for a Grammy. In the rollicking "Hand Jive" dance number of the movie, Sha Na Na plays the band Johnny Casino and the Gamblers as John Travolta and Olivia Newton-John hoof.

It wouldn't be Hollywood if there weren't a downside to Jocko's success, and he has paid for Sha Na Na's triumph. These days the group—he's one of the two original members still in the act—plays the big rooms in Las Vegas, tours the Orient (where it is fabulously popular), and may soon make another TV series. But Jocko's heart is still in acting, and his association with the greasers has stereotyped him; convincing Hollywood casting directors that his Sha Na Na persona is just an act has been difficult. He's appeared in a number of character parts in TV series and landed a role in the talking-horse comedy *Hot to Trot*. But the meatier, flashier parts have eluded him.

Eight years ago Jocko got married; he now has one four-year-old son and a sixteen-year-old stepson. The acting frustrations are minor glitches in a life the performer rightfully recognizes as rich in rewards. Rock and roll, and Woodstock have been very, very good to him.

It's not really ironic that I'm here now and so many others from Woodstock aren't. It's what you do with your life. That was an incredible time, a time when there was a lot of experimentation, a lot of experimentation with drugs. You tried it—"Hey, this is great"—and then the people who didn't stop got toasted, and they were gone. I came from that period, but now I have a son, and he is my main chore in life. I don't drink or do drugs. I'm a jock, I play basketball and jog. That's hip.

I have a stepson who is sixteen. He and a couple of his buddies came over recently, and one said to me, "You were at Woodstock?" And I said yeah. And he said, "I was born that weekend." And I thought, Boy, am I old.

SYLVIA GREENE

WITH STARTLING frequency into the seventies, the stars who shone at Woodstock died. Obituaries and headlines about Janis, about Jimi darkened newspapers, underscoring the festival's recession further and further into history. The deaths separated now and then, lengthening the shadow that distanced the event from the present. Though no one ever really expected there to be another Woodstock, the finality of each death magnified the fact that the magic of that weekend was irrecoverable. With each celebrity who fell, the Woodstock Nation as a whole took note of the passage of time and the widening fissure between its momentary explosion on the cultural landscape and the present. Other less celebrated concertgoers died during the decade after the festival, too, kids from the field whose passing commanded no national attention— but members of the Nation whose deaths nevertheless compounded the irretrievability of those precious three days. Rebecca died in 1975, a stroke victim whose unborn child expired along with her. When she heard of her friend's death, Sylvia Greene ran to her room and surrounded herself with the items she most strongly associated with Rebecca, including some of the clothes she had worn to Woodstock. As she wept, she knew she would never again think of the concert without thinking about Rebecca. And then, suddenly, she realized she never had.

The years after the concert had been troublesome for the friendship between the two young women. It was more than just a case of drifting apart: the intensity of their relationship in high school created an odd form of attraction-repulsion. The rivalry they had shared lingered throughout their college years in the complicated emotional connection between them. By then Sylvia was dating full-time and acting as sexually liberated as Rebecca. Then Rebecca mentioned that she had been experimenting with bisexuality, and Sylvia—though fascinated—couldn't help thinking that in some perverse way Rebecca was just trying to one-up her again, claiming to be making forays into yet unexplored sexual terrain.

This rivalry did not really weaken the bond between the two. Years might go by when they would not see each other, but no matter how long the interval between contact, Rebecca would remain present to Sylvia, if only in her dreams. Indeed, Sylvia's own travels in the seventies made it hard for her to have any other sort of contact with her high school friend. Like so many of those who were drawn together at Woodstock, Sylvia blew through the early part of the next decade like a feather in the wind, seeking contentment through a sometimes chaotic, frequently far-flung series of relocations, uprootings, quests. Dropping out of NYU, she flitted to a San Francisco commune and shared a four-bedroom house with fourteen other seekers. A stint in the drama program at California Institute of the Arts in Valencia still didn't amount to enough classwork for a degree, so when Sylvia journeyed back to Boston around 1974 she enrolled in her fourth university sequence, this time at the University of Massachusetts. There, finally, she earned a bachelor's degree, but graduation found her no less unstable. Motivated by a crush, she moved to Maine, where for the next year she taught school in an experimental program among the state's most deprived neighborhoods. The romance that brought her northward sputtered and died, so after one year of $50 paychecks, Sylvia moved back to Boston, to waitressing and bookkeeping while she decided what to do with the rest of her life. Occasionally she would hear from Rebecca, but the sporadic conversations were cryptic, and often Sylvia's friend seemed deliberately to keep significant news from her.

> When she got married, that's when I was the most angry with her. I wasn't invited to the wedding. I was livid. There was no excuse for that. I was so angry and hurt. I should have been at her wedding, that's what I kept thinking. She got married in November. The next February I got a phone call at two in the morning and it was Rebecca. And she was calling to say that she loved me more than anyone in the world. It had been months. I realize now she was dying on some level. I truly believe that in some way she was communicating with me and letting me know what was going to happen.
>
> A couple of months later I had an invitation to a wedding in Pennsylvania. And again Rebecca called me out of the blue. We talked for a long time, forty-five minutes. I didn't bring up the fact about the wedding. I said, "Rebecca, you are happy." I was so happy for her, as you are when you know someone has arrived home. It transcended the anger. I made plans to visit her on the way home from the wedding in Pennsylvania.

The visit would never take place. Just days before leaving for the trip, Sylvia got a call from Rebecca's mother relaying the outcome of a tragic accident that had occurred in upstate New York, where her daughter and her new husband had taken up residence. It had been sudden, instant. She was gone.

On a profound level the death of the friend from her youth brought an end to Sylvia's wanderings. The unfocused longing for community the two girls shared with the rest of the Woodstock pilgrims shifted for Sylvia when Rebecca's death jolted her off the random trail she had taken since the festival. Something of the adolescent innocence she celebrated at Woodstock withered that afternoon. The great rivalry of her youth—the sexual competition unique to the era, the intense personal involvement the times encouraged—was over. Sylvia was free to set about making the adult decisions that would form the blueprint for the rest of her life.

She went to a kibbutz in Israel, and then moved to California again, where her mother had relocated. The next few years were characterized by a growing commitment to her Jewish heritage and to her career as an educator. She finally met the man she would marry, a former music producer who is now a chiropractor. She lived with Allen for several years before wedding, first in a traditional Jewish rite, backed up several days later with a Taoist ceremony. In 1984 Sylvia wrote a reading-aid book. She is now the mother of two daughters.

Woodstock, and the hippie mores it represented, all seem far away to Sylvia, who says she's not ashamed to be called a yuppie now, since the designation fits. But there are still elements of sixties thought, and whether she's talking about the spiritualism she's found in her return to Judaism, or about her bond to her children, it's easy to identify her as someone whose roots extend back to the field in Bethel.

Nonetheless, a significant link between then and now has been severed by the death of the girlhood friend who accompanied her to the festival. And while the closure of the relationship with Rebecca reaffirms the rarity of their Woodstock weekend, it indicates that for some those three days are most treasured for their precious finality, as the rich ending of something dear and memorable. For Sylvia—as for many others—Woodstock was a farewell.

BILL PELLIGRINI

OF ALL things Woodstock has been called, no one has ever described it as a vocational-guidance workshop. And yet that is exactly what it turned out to be for Bill Pelligrini. Bill fell upon a career as he stumbled around through the Aquarian mud those three days. A lost boy wandering into manhood, the onetime derelict watched as throughout the woods surrounding Yasgur's farm long-haired artisans crafted rough materials into fancy ornaments, pottery, jewelry—goods for sale. It seemed right, it seemed viable; making something honest and selling it. The next twenty years of Bill's life—a saga of Dickensian gains and losses, booms and busts—would be directed by this chance encounter with the honest economy of hippies who sat hammering and weaving and welding and smiling in the backs of the psychedelic vans they drove to Bethel that hot weekend in August 1969.

Within weeks Bill was in Boston picking up the tools and the skills of the craft at a leather goods store. There is a Horatio Algeresque poignancy to the early stages of his subsequent rise. He returned to New Jersey from Boston, where for several years he and a buddy supported their aspirations to a rock-and-roll career by making the hippie-era vests, belts and handbags that became immensely popular after Woodstock. He was invited to set up shop in a boutique that serviced suburban kids' appetite for "counterculture" goods, and quickly realized that for every belt he sold, the store sold ten silver bracelets, for every vest he sold the store sold fifty silver necklaces. He observed the boutique's jeweler, asked questions, saved his money, and bought a set of silversmith tools. Maintaining his hide-crafting skills, he expanded his abilities to include the more profitable precious-metals market. By 1974, just five years after he panhandled his last handout on the Bowery, Bill Pelligrini was running his own fine-crafts shop in Monticello, New York, just ten miles from the very site of the Aquarian Exposition.

For several years the shop prospered, but eventually the dismal economy of the area dragged Bill's business under. Not unlike many of his Woodstock peers, he was finding the seventies a tough time to live out the life-fulfilling promises of the sixties. He returned once again to New Jersey, uncertain about his future as a craftsman.

> I took a year off to try my hand in vacuum cleaners. My father was working for Electrolux, and he asked me to come down and help him and fix some cleaners one afternoon. While I was there, he said, "Get on the phone and try to collect some of these back bills." And while I was on the phone, the district manager came in, heard me, and offered me a job. I was in Wheeling for six months, and then Pittsburgh for six more, and then I moved to Erie. It was good enough money, but no satisfaction.
>
> The company did weird things. They took this old guy who was in management for years and years and demoted him to the field. I saw this old man carrying boxes through the snow in Erie, and if he didn't do it they were going to cancel his pension. One day I saw a little old lady come into the store, she must have been eighty-five. And she had the hose in the wrong end, that's all.

Otherwise this cleaner was perfect. And I heard another sales-
man tell her this and that, that the whole thing was broken and
she needed a new one. Something snapped. I was fed up. I quit
right then and there.

Once again, Bill found himself broke, at loose ends and on the
bottom. He knew one thing for sure, though: he did not want to
work for anyone else. And since the only thing he really knew how
to do on his own was the handcrafting, he decided that was his
route to independence. He was right, for a while.

Friends back in New Jersey were setting up a silver-importing
business, but as of 1977 they were operating exclusively as distrib-
utors and wholesalers. When Bill showed up, he convinced them to
let him set up shop with them; they could increase their profits
markedly if they manufactured jewelry in addition to merely operating as middlemen. Within a year, the company had expanded to
twenty-two employees and sales increased to $2.5 million. A
decade after he had been kicked out of high school, Bill Pelligrini
was a small-time magnate. But almost inevitably, he very soon
began to experience the emptiness of the prosperity he was enjoying. As the business expanded he found himself doing less and
less of the hands-on craftswork he loved, and spending all his time
with management functions. He was becoming a Babbitt, and he
didn't like it.

As it turned out, he was not destined to spend much more time
with the company. The partners were thriving and looking toward
the Christmas season of 1979 to do record business. The theft of a
silver shipment, however, deprived them of the raw materials they
depended on to meet their orders. They were overextended and
unable to deliver, and the Christmas that was supposed to be their
heyday turned into a financial disaster. By the end of the year, they
were in bankruptcy.

Resourceful and resilient, Bill picked himself up from the rubble
of his former empire, brushed himself off, and recognized the
situation as yet another invitation to start over again. A relationship
with a woman living in California had been heating up, and during his high-rolling days he was flying out to see her often. With

the prospects looking dim for the continuation of that expensive arrangement, Bill decided to move out to Los Angeles and get married. That turned out to be a big mistake: unable to find work for eight months, Bill began to suspect his wife's interest in him had stemmed from his former prosperity. He became the object of her criticism and hostility. Bill moved out to California on the ominously appropriate date of April 1, 1981; by October he was separated from his wife. And no sooner were they apart than he located a job managing a jewelry factory and started moving upward again.

During the mid-eighties Bill again drifted away from hands-on craftswork and into management positions in the industry. And each time he did, the same duality of success and emptiness that was gnawing at his entire generation of achievers settled into his life again. The spirit of the sixties that Woodstock distilled into a momentary utopia had left its mark. Bill's situation merely dramatized it: the Woodstock ideal of self-reliance and self-actualization through honest labor kept banging into the American equation of upward mobility through bureaucracy. But it wasn't until he was mugged in 1987 that Bill once again opted to chuck the routine and break the cycle. Late for work because of his injuries, he was fired for irresponsibility; the inequity made him decide to leave Los Angeles altogether.

Today, Bill, along with his new wife, has a job as a condo manager: free room in exchange for maintenance chores around the northern California ski chalet compound. It is, he is the first to admit, a go-nowhere, dead-end job—and that's just why he loves it. For now it affords him the luxury of time with minimal responsibilities other than those he owes to his relationship and himself. It's a hiatus from the whirlwind he's been riding, as have so many others since 1969—a break many of his contemporaries are considering in one way or another. During this interval in the mountains he's reading the Oriental philosophies he likes so much, fixing a sink now and then, and thinking about his future. Not surprisingly, he sees it leading back East, back to where his journey began twenty years ago, back to his roots as a proud and still-growing child of Woodstock.

Today's kids really scare me. These kids: going to business schools with their blinders on, choosing their careers when they're four or five years old. I find out there are colleges that are dropping humanities. I feel bad for these people; their lives are based on acquisition. I have acquired things and I have lost them. And I am better off. They will say I am just a loser, they will laugh at me. I've been reading a lot of Taoism, where you learn that the more you store up, the more you have to guard, the more things have a way of turning back to dust. No way you can keep material things from decaying.

The experience of going to Woodstock was one of reassurance and euphoria. The first time in my life people were not being acquisitive or conniving. It showed how things could be, even though it was just a bubble. It existed like a Camelot for a short time, before reality came in. But the feeling of it, to experience it, gave me confidence that alternatives, even if they failed, could be tried.

JOHN SEBASTIAN

THE REAL Woodstock, the picturesque little town that lent its name to the concert, is today still very much as it was twenty years ago. A small artists' community thrives there; vacationers drive down its quiet main drag, sighing at the rustic charms of the village. Many make the same mistake as the hundreds who two decades ago flocked here, thinking the town was actually the site of the festival that bore its name. There is a certain irony to the fact that John Sebastian has chosen to make his home here, in the town that has been trying for all these years to correct an incorrect association with the festival. No, the Woodstock concert did not take place here, the town dwellers are constantly telling visitors. And no, John Sebastian would like everybody to know, the performer he was back then is not the same performer he is now. But these days he worries about it less and less. He lives, prospers, grows in Woodstock—and in a way his residence there signifies the broader comfort and peace John is now making with his Wood-stock past.

At first his unscheduled appearance at the festival gave his post–Lovin' Spoonful solo career the push it needed. Though to this day he complains that the drugs he took destroyed the quality of his performance that evening, he came across quite profes-sionally in the Woodstock movie, which further propelled his fame. In addition to being included on the soundtrack LP, he released an album of his own in 1970, *John B. Sebastian*, which included the hit single "She's a Lady." He continued to tour around the country, and even began to develop an international following. At the famous music festival on the Isle of Wight in 1970, a crowd of 200,000 gave him a standing ovation and kept him on the stage for two hours.

Soon after that, though, John detected a change in the air, in music and certainly in his popularity. The warm reception he could always count on began to die down; the number of bookings started to fall off. His subsequent albums failed to sell. In fact the only hit he had during the entire second half of the decade was the theme song for the TV sitcom "Welcome Back, Kotter," and that sold mainly because heartthrob John Travolta was in the show. Sebastian, saddled with his seemingly unalterable image as the tie-dyed groovy guy, became increasingly passé.

> Around the time of disco and then punk, I was really getting killed by the critics. I think they may have thought they had to distance themselves from the sort of sincerity I bring to a perfor-mance, that laid-back style. I've been through times when it's been hard to be me. I've done a lot of work before hostile audi-ences. I have stepped onto the stage and during the first couple of tunes seen the guys in the first couple of rows visibly being made uncomfortable by the poor reception I was getting.

Like so few of the chart-jumping rock stars of the sixties, Sebas-tian rightly felt the inequity of rejection since he was truly talented. In concert he wisely delivered the old hits associated with his heyday, but time and time again he found it painful when his

newer compositions would leave the audience listless. Others of
his generation and echelon—James Taylor or Stephen Stills—were
allowed to grow through the seventies, but John reaped no such
benefit. So obscure did he become that a reviewer in *The New York
Times* seemed genuinely surprised to have enjoyed a performance
by the former Spoonful vocalist at a New York City club in 1974.

Finally, in the mid-eighties, John began to come to a very cagey,
very realistic and ultimately rewarding realization: he didn't want
to be locked into the image created at the Woodstock Festival, and
yet he didn't feel it necessary to reject it completely either. He
didn't want to suffer the ignominy of reinventing himself as an
eighties-friendly rock personality; on the other hand he didn't
want to pander to the equally self-degrading spectacle of merely
re-creating the hippie past. Instead he seized on a few projects that
allowed him to tread a middle ground: address the past in distinctly hip and contemporary ways.

The first project he signed on for seemed the perfect amalgam of
old and new. MTV and the video clip had revolutionized the way
people related to music. Nearly every major contemporary release
now had a music video produced to accompany it, to explain it, to
hype it, to get people to listen to the tunes. It didn't take long for
someone to realize that the roots of rock deserved the video makeover too, and thus "Déjà Vu" was born. Planned as a weekly
syndicated show, "Déjà Vu" featured a half-hour's worth of newly
produced video clips using vintage rock-and-roll cuts. And who
better to host the program than John Sebastian: after all, he himself had contributed mightily to the upheaval of the sixties,
when traditional folk and provincial instruments and tunes were
souped up with the most up-to-date electronic technology and
rock-influenced riffs.

But while record companies were fully aware of the impact a
popular video could have on the sales of new releases—and were
ready to pay the hundreds of thousands required to generate that
impact—they remained unconvinced of the value videos would
have on their catalogues of older material. Funding for the clips
dried up quickly, and the show failed. Still, the media exposure,
and more important the personal reconnection with the past that

"Déjà Vu" afforded, inspired John to mine his own history further. At present he is working on a movie script that is heavily autobiographical; it relates the story of a sixties quartet that rockets to fame, and depicts a world of fame with very little fortune, he says, a time when rock's most successful figures couldn't dream of the catered, indulgent lifestyle that's now par for the course. But it is also unabashedly nostalgic: an exercise allowing him to relive the glory days leading up to Woodstock, and an attempt to resolve the distance he has traveled since then.

> I was surprised at how the media didn't understand the sixties when it happened, and I am astounded at how little they have learned in twenty-five years. It's been fun to show some of this to my son, who is sixteen. He is the inspiration for all this. It's nice to fill him in on the reality of it and explain it was not all one tie-dyed fantasy.
>
> Songs are funny things. They can become dated and make you feel like a nerd singing them. Without ever calculating or planning it, I've been lucky that many have stayed fresh. Many of these songs have aged remarkably well. I feel kind of lucky that way.

SUSIE KAUFMAN

Jarrett Lennon Kaufman was born February 1, 1982. In modern style, the delivery, which took place in his mother's home, was videotaped, an auspicious on-camera debut: he has since gone on to be a successful child actor in both commercials and movies. A slight growth-hormone imbalance will keep him smaller than normal for most of his youth, which in fact only guarantees that the cuteness he's capitalizing on will remain marketable for a long time. He is adorable, intelligent and unmannered. He is, says his mother, the most wonderful thing that has ever happened to her. Yes, of course, even more wonderful than Woodstock, but he might never have happened if she hadn't decided at her shrink's advice to go to Bethel that weekend twenty years ago.

During the early seventies, maintaining the self-acceptance Susie first felt at Woodstock took some bizarre forms. She admits now that she overcompensated for the rape and its negation of her sexuality by becoming involved with too many men. Lovemaking reaffirmed her identity as a desirable woman, and the woman who was a virgin until she was raped became a bedmate to more men than she likes to think about. In addition, as part of her revolt against the past, she abruptly left New Jersey, finding work on touring staffs for several rock bands. She was little more than an elevated gofer, and the craziness of the road provided her with no security whatsoever. But like the promiscuity, the chaos energized her, providing her psyche with the overstimulation it needed as an antidote to depression. Woodstock's high shook her the way her shock therapy never could, and without really thinking about it she went about re-creating the festival's go-go-go frenzy in her own life.

The path that led from Woodstock through the years of sex and rock and roll forked for Susie as she neared her thirtieth birthday. She found she wanted to reconnect with another mainstream, one that extended out of what she had experienced at the festival. It was there that she had felt the stirrings of her nurturing instinct for the first time since her rape, as she cradled the bleeding foot of the boy cut by glass. In some of her sexual encounters since then, and even in the way she watched over the performers with whom she toured, much of the same mothering response expressed itself. Finally she decided to put this response to more direct use.

> I was getting the maternal urge. More and more I was watching women breast-feeding. About five years before the pregnancy I began to really plan it. I decided to settle in California, so I wouldn't be chastised about having a baby on my own at my home. I figured I had to have a job so I could work out of my home and take care of him. So I became a typist; it was the only thing I could do that would keep me home, no bosses. I tried it and it worked. I said all right, I'm getting closer to making Jarrett.

And Jarrett was to be made with specifications worthy of a high-performance race car. Because she knew he would be an only child, she wanted the baby to be born an Aquarian. She herself was a Libra and, through consultation with astrologists, understood Aquarius to be the most compatible sign. In addition, Susie wanted the child to be a boy: she wanted to avoid the potential for the sort of mother-daughter conflicts she had gone through during her own childhood. And she wanted the child on her own; she had no intentions of marrying simply to accomplish what she knew she needed only one night to achieve.

On February 1, in the bed in which her child was conceived, Susie began her labor.

Her son is named Jarrett after Keith Jarrett, a jazz musician Susie adores, and Lennon after John Lennon. In raising the boy, she is following many of the rubrics of behavior she learned as a child of the sixties. For example, she has opted not to send him to school yet, conducting his education at home herself. Public schooling, she believes, inculcates hostility and encourages children to associate standing up for themselves with aggression. No doubt she recalls the relentless taunting in grammar school and hopes to protect her undersize son from the same. She's also intelligently skeptical about medical authority and has decided not to allow her son to receive the experimental growth medications recommended by some physicians. In fact, with admirable ingenuity, she has decided to turn his potential disadvantage into an asset. A mother who named her son after the Beatle she fell in love with as a girl watching "The Ed Sullivan Show," Susie has, naturally enough, gotten the boy into show biz. He's licked his fingers on Kentucky Fried Chicken commercials, he's sung the praises of Yoplait yogurt on national TV. Coming full circle, during a trip to New York several years ago for the filming of a mini-series, Susie and Jarrett made a pilgrimage to the Dakota, the Manhattan apartment house outside of which John Lennon was shot.

The late sixties exist as a mottled blur of pain and confusion for Susie, through which only several clear incidents of joy can be recollected. The first time she saw the Beatles on TV is one. Woodstock was another. Did it change her life? Who knows. What is clear is that a period of unhappiness and damage ended for her

those three days, and a new era began. And no matter how imma-
terial and transitory the Aquarian Exposition may have seemed,
something happened there that put a young damaged woman on a
road to recovery. Part of Susie Kaufman was reborn there; twenty
years later it's living on in her son.

JIMMY JORDAN

THERE WERE roughly 500,000 people at the Woodstock Festival in 1969. There were roughly 500,000 people gathered on the mall that October afternoon in 1987 when Jimmy Jordan realized this was the largest multitude he had been part of since the concert. That was then, this is now. That was three days spent with another man, isolated in their gayness in a crowd of straights. This was a mass exercise in gay pride, during which he drew strength rather than discomfort from the immensity of the gathering. And yet it was because he had been to Woodstock and passed through its aura that he truly appreciated this massive gay march on the capital— and the changes in his life that brought him there.

Jimmy quickly moved beyond the disappointment of the affair with Evan and the muddy memories of the festival. At Woodstock he felt himself an outcast among a throng of outcasts. But as he moved into the seventies, the feelings of alienation the concert weekend had brought to a head began to subside. The accelerating power of the gay pride movement in New York caught him up. At first hesitantly and then with full conviction Jimmy joined in: participating in consciousness-raising groups, writing for gay lib publications. The lifestyle celebration that Woodstock had been for straight baby boomers was echoed in the do-your-own-thing banquet Jimmy and the rest of gay America were enjoying several years later.

If Jimmy was able to walk away from Woodstock and into a new decade of gay openness, he was unable to escape the concert's seismic effect on the music scene. Rock, which had been king throughout the seventies, became godlike in its hold on the performance front. The music may have lost the raucous edge that made it so vital to the kids of the previous decade. But fueled by the magnitude of gatherings like Woodstock, rock in the seventies became big, big business. So big in fact that it nearly obliterated all the other forms of music that had thrived during the sixties in clubs and cabarets around Manhattan. Jimmy started the decade singing jazz at talent shows, winning contests and weekend gigs at the then thriving network of basement joints. But little by little the number of outlets for his kind of vocalizing grew smaller and smaller. Rock was it, and a jazz singer just wasn't going to make it.

At one point Jimmy had harbored hopes, buoyed by much positive feedback, that someday he would be able to make a living from singing. He had hoped that eventually the spot gigs and intermittent applause would come together into a career, so he could get off the work treadmill he was running, from one bad job to another. But as the cabaret scene died, so did his dreams of singing full-time. Sing rock, he was urged by agents who refused to represent him unless he plugged into the more commercial sound. Find a bar band. But he couldn't do it. He knew he could bring down the roof with standards like "My Funny Valentine," and "Here's That Rainy Day" and knew, as good as his pipes were, he'd only sound foolish trying to rock. Jimmy had gone to Woodstock and watched Roger Daltrey and Jimi Hendrix, had seen Sly Stone and the Grateful Dead. The notion of giving up jazz standards for that sort of music seemed as foreign to him as the entire festival. The concert receded into history, but the reverberations shook through the seventies. By decade's end, the music had completely passed Jimmy by.

For that matter, so had the gay movement. The free-for-all had begun to produce its burn-outs, and Jimmy was one of them. Satisfying years of pent-up sexual frustrations and compensating for years of identity-bashing was great—at first. But for the sensitive the ecstasy of liberation soon grew tepid and the expectations that it would lead to something more substantial met too often with frustration.

> I remember I went through a two-year period when I didn't sleep with a man. I was gay. But I didn't want to feel used sexually on any level, and that's what we were doing on a lot of levels. By the same token that men had always used women, men were using other men. I really wanted to relate to someone as a human being and relate to another man as such. But into the eighties, I retreated again.

The twenty-year anniversary of Woodstock finds Jimmy a far more optimistic individual than did the tenth. Deprived of his musical outlet and defeated by the emptiness he perceived in the gay community, he lurched through the early part of this decade in an extended depression. Relationships faltered and his work disappointed him. But by late 1986 something inside him snapped, and his period of passivity ended. He isn't sure what the catalyst for the change was, but it may in part have been his decision to pursue his singing career again actively that initiated the metamorphosis. Jazz clubs reopened, and Jimmy again began the round of one-night performances that had given birth to his ambitions in the early seventies. Soon enough he began to receive the positive feedback he remembered from so long ago. He is now considering the option many Americans have in the past: touring Europe, where jazz flourishes, to establish his reputation.

Jimmy has also entered a new period of gay activism, one that he says is more informed and mature than his earlier involvement. A member of several AIDS awareness groups, he views commitment to change as a lifelong process, a realization that perhaps he and his generation lacked during the activism of the sixties.

> If I had to sum up in a line or two what I learned at Woodstock, a lesson, it's that the things that have any real value in life take a lifetime of work. That was a thing in the sixties: a lot of people thought that by having a few marches and stirring up a little action, things were going to change. Thinking about it, if there is anything to be learned, you don't go on one march and think the world will change. It's a lifetime effort: if you are going to work for meaningful changes it's a lifetime thing. But at that time, you thought everything was changing and you were living a utopia that was permanent. Part of gay liberation was part of that utopian feeling that things were changing and you were a part of it. You realize as time goes on a lot of that was surface.

Twenty years ago Jimmy Jordan went to Woodstock hoping to solidify his relationship with a young man. The weekend turned out to be a demonstration of just how challenging it was to be gay in a heterosexual world. To various degrees Jimmy has been confronting that reality for the two decades since. But like the kids who trouped to Woodstock in rowdy display of their right to be different, Jimmy is today drawing strength from his sense of being joined with others in free expression of his chosen lifestyle.

TOM CONSTANTEN

"*T* AROT IS an interesting failure. A good idea haphazardly thought out and badly realized. The energy of the music only underscores the impotence of the action." That's how a critic reacted in *The Village Voice* to Tom Constanten's musical *Tarot*, the project that in 1970 offered him an excuse to leave the Grateful Dead. "Close your eyes . . . and just go with the music, and you may have a decent time. The show itself is tedious, pompous, inefficient and amateurish," said another critic, in *The New York Times*. The off-Broadway production lasted four weeks. Tom had written the score and was playing organ in its five-man ensemble. Meanwhile, 3,000 miles away, the Dead—minus Tom—sold out another performance, and another, and another.

There is in Tom's post-Woodstock story the look and feel of misfortune, miscalculation, mistakes made and later paid for. The dismal history of his first project after leaving the Dead introduced a series of unpromising career decisions and moves, none of which in the most remote fashion ever equaled the fame and influence he experienced as a member of the legendary band. The Grateful Dead's following has remained devout for two decades, earning each of the group members his own pedestal in the rock pantheon. The further Tom traveled along the path that diverged from the Dead, the clearer it became that his was a road into relative obscurity.

But it was a road to contentment as well. The past two decades in Tom's life are something of a tribute to the spirit of Woodstock: he has followed his own dictates, adhered to the doctrine of his own world view. He has pursued self-fulfillment and eschewed celebrity. If that course has not produced fame or riches, Tom Constanten, former keyboardist for the Grateful Dead, is the last to complain.

For a short interval after his departure from the group, it looked as though his solo career would be as blessed as the Dead's. Around the time of the musical, he formed a new group called Touchstone and landed a contract with a record company. The executive who sealed the deal was interested in both the group and the soundtrack from the show. Things started to fall apart quickly, though: the critical panning doomed the show, and with it the soundtrack's potential. Then the record company fired the VP who had negotiated the deal; Touchstone sank into bureaucratic limbo and eventually disbanded.

Feeling a little frazzled by the demise of his group and the show, Tom accepted a temporary teaching position at the State University of New York at Buffalo.

> I was teaching twentieth-century music and methodology. And I know it was because I had been with the Grateful Dead that many of the students signed up for the course. But they were truly interested once they got there. I didn't make connections between the Dead's music and classical music to popularize the classical music, or to make it more accessible. I made those connections because they are there. The shoe fits. Certainly Jerry's improvisations have many points in common with the twentieth-century avant-garde.

If the irony of that eluded Tom, the reality behind it didn't: most of the composing he would do for the rest of the decade would take him further and further from rock and back to his roots as a classical pianist. His most prestigious piece, *Déjà Waltz*, was written as his contribution to an acclaimed series of commissioned modern waltzes, whose other contributors include John Cage, Philip Glass and Roger Sessions. Other experimental work would follow, much of it published though little recorded.

With time, Tom developed his own live act, an odd collection of pieces he calls his *American Survey*. It includes ragtime, symphonic pieces and solo arrangements of Grateful Dead tunes like "Hesitation Blues" and "Dark Star." Since Pigpen died, Tom allows himself to be billed as "the only surviving former pianist of the Grateful Dead." The billing, he knows, helps identify him and helps sell tickets.

> On a typical tour I play college campuses and bars. To be fair, I have played in pretty sleazy places. I have played at places where the bikers come up and park their bikes at the stage. But I asked myself "What am I doing here?" more when I was with the Grateful Dead. Playing at a place like that either you come through the trial by fire or you burn up. But it's on your own. There's another benefit of not being so high-profile: your bombs aren't remembered by so many. Luckily I haven't embarrassed myself. I have maybe had a half-dozen note-perfect performances.
>
> Sometimes I slip-stream the Dead. That's what I call it. It's a term from auto racing: they break the wind for you and you save fuel. I'll play in the same town a week to two weeks after they've been there. I sold out in Syracuse, two nights. It was worth a four-digit figure for me. Of course, the Dead had played in the Carrier Dome and sold out. But they made what I got possible.

Tom liked the Buffalo teaching position and since then has accepted short-term assignments at Harvard and at the San Francisco Art Institute. But he lives in Oakland, and his full-time commitment is to a nonprofit community music center in San Francisco's Mission District. Three days a week he is a piano teacher. On weekends he is the resident pianist for KQED-FM's "West Coast Weekend," a musical variety show he compares to "Prairie Home Companion," only urbane. When John Adams, whose *Nixon in China* was the rage in 1987, failed to show up as scheduled one week, Tom led the show's regulars through an impromptu skit called "Khrushchev in Disneyland." The radio show may go national, according to Tom.

Since there was no acrimony in his leaving the group, Tom continues to see his former colleagues whenever their touring brings them to the Bay Area. Content with the low-profile life he has made for himself, Tom bears no grudge against his celebrity buddies. With his oldest friend, Phil Lesh, he is still able to share the appreciation of fine classical performances that brought them together in the first place. And with the group he shares another tie: because he contributed to several of their albums, he still receives a small royalty check every now and then. It's just pin money, an irregular reminder of his time with one of the biggest groups in rock history.

On Valentine's Day 1986, Tom married a woman from the registrar's office in the community music center. They share an apartment in the rear of a house in a nondescript neighborhood in Oakland, the major attributes of which are low rent and a variety of ethnic restaurants. Tom moved here in 1976, and although he would like to spend more time in Europe—his following is growing there—he has no plans to move. In a lot of ways, Tom lives the life many of the kids who watched him on the Woodstock stage envisioned they would be living twenty years later. It's not the glamorous life they imagined a rock star would lead, of course. It's the life they imagined for themselves, hoped for themselves, in fact: simple, honest, down-to-earth. Happy.

I see myself as an answer to trivia questions. They say of Stravinsky that the tragedy of his life is that he wrote his masterpiece, *The Rite of Spring*, when he was thirty years old. I don't think of my life that way. My experience with the Dead gave me a hoop, something I can continue to aim for in terms of public exposure. The enticements of that life are always agreeable.

You'd have to be a fool to say you don't miss them. Fast-lane living. On the other hand, that's not the only place those entice- ments are to be found. But it is hard to say I miss them. What's to miss: I close my eyes and I remember them. I can go on a plane and play music in another city again. I've done it, and it's ten times as gratifying when they're sold out for just me. Even if it's a smaller place.

SCOTT LANE

INVULNERABLE, IMPERVIOUS, lucky: Scott Lane personified these traits, characteristics that have always marked youth's sense of self and that pervaded the group consciousness at Woodstock. The nineteen-year-old felt protected, perhaps even privileged, having sailed through the sixties and into the festival on a stream of good fortune and narrow escapes that reinforced his confidence in his quick wit, good looks and charmed existence. He had danced blithely on the brink of personal disaster on a number of occasions, and skirted back nimbly at the last second each time. In this he was not unlike the festival itself, a gaudy orgy prevented from realizing its own self-destructive potential only by a mob's conviction that nothing bad could happen. Scott went to Woodstock in search of good times, thinking, What's in this for me? And as the furies miraculously stayed at bay that weekend, he made love and dropped acid, and had one decade-climaxing bang-up good time.

The festival ended that Monday in August, and with it the sanctuary the 1960s had provided young men like Scott. The 1970s, it would turn out, was payback time.

It didn't take Scott long after Woodstock to get a taste of what life in the no-nonsense future was going to be like. That Halloween, drunk, he "borrowed" a roommate's car to drive a girl home, without informing the owner. On the way back home, he rammed the station wagon into a telephone pole. His instincts told him to get out of there fast, and to deny knowing anything about the whereabouts of the car. When the police came to follow up on the robbery report his worried friend had phoned in, they noticed Scott was bleeding from the forehead and there was windshield glass in his hair. He spent the weekend in jail. An out-of-court settlement cooled the owner's eagerness to prosecute; still, the incident was a clear indication that the carefree high jinks of adolescence needed to be put behind him.

By 1972 Lane had decided to get serious about the acting career he had been flirting with, and he moved to New York. He was an attractive, youthful-looking newcomer and found commercial work relatively easily. He made a cologne ad with Sandy Duncan; he got a walk-on role in the George C. Scott movie *The Hospital*. Things seemed to be shaping up well; but the wild ways of the sixties were catching up with him.

> I had lived such a fast and furious acid-fueled experience. It affected my career. I could never settle down. I was having serious déjà vu all the time. And terrible dreams. Violins were playing off key. Weird sexual things with people I knew, or gay people all over me. Recurring nightmares. I had to wake myself out of it. And then I would have feelings that someone was standing over me.
>
> Then in 1972 I auditioned for a movie called *Sexual Freedom in Brooklyn*. And I went out for the lead in it. And I pretty much got the lead on the way I looked, but I had no confidence in acting. I didn't have the technique, but just needed a little more help. I was trying to get the acid out of my system. So when it came around to it, the name was changed to *The Lords of Flatbush* and

the original cast was me, Richard Gere and Sylvester Stallone. Richard Gere and I got fired.

With his hair still cropped into the fifties do required for *Lords,* Scott turned his back on New York and headed to Los Angeles. The next few years are classic struggling-actor material: a string of guest appearances on shows like "Barnaby Jones" convinced him he could make a go of this acting life. But with each successive bit part, the big breakthrough role seemed to become more and more elusive. He joined a workshop/performance troupe, and before long the other struggling actors in the ensemble—Teri Garr, Richard Dreyfuss—were making the career moves that would turn them into celebrities by mid-decade.

Things weren't clicking for Scott as quickly as he had hoped, and even a trip to London for acting study didn't improve his opportunities. He got married upon his return in 1975, and he and his wife had a son in December 1976. The marriage lasted another three years, a period during which Scott's résumé of parts he almost landed became quite impressive.

> I started having lots of headaches, and I had to take lots of aspirin. Then I was taking lots of codeine, I had hurt my knee. Work wasn't happening, marriage was going bad. I was stuck in the sixties. I kept thinking that I would dive under these waves and just come out on top of it.
>
> Then, in 1979, I staged my great escape. I was only getting lousy TV stuff. And coming in second all the time. Everybody else was starting to make it. So all of a sudden, I'm twenty-eight, twenty-nine, and all these movies are for, like, twenty-three, twenty-four. And I'm not getting it. I split.
>
> I know lots of people you'd never know did acid, but they have this same restlessness, can't get on with serious lives. I had such an abnormal restlessness.

The "great escape" ushered Scott into the eighties with a kick in the pants. He was looking at thirty and beyond, and was still not much more sure of his future than when he had left Woodstock over a decade before. He experimented with stand-up comedy, and did what everyone in LA who doesn't have steady work does: write screenplays. He got occasional parts in peripheral movie projects.

And then, one day in 1987, he made a phone call to a broker he had met at a party. The financier invited Scott in and discussed telemarketing with him, explaining how those who had mastered their interpersonal communication skills can clean up by selling over the phone. If you can charm people, you can make money. Scott is now a broker.

> This is an interesting period. I'm still writing a screenplay, and working on stand-up material. But I can afford that now. I brought in seven hundred thousand dollars' worth of business this year. I never thought the name security would be that close to my name, but now I am a member of the National Association of Security Dealers. People on the other end of the phone get this sense that I really care: it's personality. I don't really have the mind for it; I sell on energy and enthusiasm. At the office they call me "Uzi." I've made over a hundred thousand dollars in commissions.

Scott hopes to be able to develop a clientele of venture capitalists whose trust in him transcends the portfolio he represents. Eventually he wants to invite the same clients to invest in his own film company, a production-distribution outfit that would make his own movies and acquire those made by others. He is hoping, in short, to become something of a mogul. Perhaps he will. And if he does strike it rich in Hollywood, his lucking out again may simply prove that among those thousands of self-gratification junkies who headed half-stoned into the realities of adulthood in the seventies and beyond, well, maybe there were those special few who were truly blessed. Maybe there were some kids who were just destined for the sweet life. It's as potent a mythology to have emerged that weekend as any.

> I still have an outrageous, slightly funky yet horny attitude about what life has to offer. I haven't lost that one iota. You put the

quarter in the machine and you pull. Unfortunately, you don't get any free plays. I've always been hyperkinetic, only I feel like I'm calming down now. I feel more in control. I think I'm a lot more trustworthy than I was.

One time during the sixties I was tripping and I thought I had found the meaning of life. I wrote it down so I would be sure to remember. And the next day I looked at it again and it said, "I'm hungry."

RUFUS FRIEDMAN

THE CANALS in Venice, California, are deceptively still and murky. The moats that crisscross this tiny little stretch of beachfront between Santa Monica and the more yuppified stretches of Marina del Rey to the south appear clotted with reeds. No yachts are docked along these shallow manmade estuaries, only single-motor skiffs can negotiate them. But in the crazy-quilt pattern of land values that is Los Angeles real estate, these seemingly downscale canals and the sites that face them are among the city's hottest properties. It is on a vacant plot he bought here several years ago that Rufus Friedman—the lowliest and proudest grunt of Woodstock Ventures—is building his dream house. It's costing roughly half a million dollars.

Rufus will tell you, when he picks up the phone for a conversation, that he has to make it short. His clothes are in the laundromat across the street from his office, also in Venice, and he doesn't want someone to steal them. The problem of the homeless in the area is pronounced, and while he holds sympathy for the lot of the vagrant poor in his neighborhood, he still doesn't want them to walk off with his underwear. He's been lucky here since neither his home nor his workplace has been broken into, but he knows of many other residents who haven't been so fortunate. An area in transition, Venice may be the perfect spot for Rufus Friedman, successful businessman and former Woodstock beast of burden. He wants his community to prosper, but he can't really imagine Venice without its bums, without its murky canals. The way it is now—part rough around the edges, part high-tone—suits him just fine. In fact, it's the ideal locale now that the Bastard Son has grown up. No matter how far he's come since he dug ditches on Yasgur's farm, he cherishes the honor of having been one of those indefatigable, downtrodden, no-glory grubs whose sweat fueled the Woodstock phantasmagoria. Like White Lake that summer, Venice allows Rufus to cultivate his image as maverick survivalist, to continue to wear the badge of distinction he earned in 1969.

For a long time after Woodstock, it was his newly developed self-confidence that kept him from succeeding. For nearly a decade Rufus would repeat the same work pattern: his handyman skills and make-it-work pragmatism would get him in the door; his intuitive ability to figure things out would prepare him for greater responsibility; eventually he would become so savvy about the business (and maybe a bit too obnoxious about his savvy) that he'd alienate the bosses and get sacked. The very instincts that permitted him to bloom at the festival were his undoing in the years following.

After Woodstock, Rufus returned to Manhattan and found work in the SoHo art district—mostly contracting on conversions of raw industrial space into residential lofts. It was while living there that he met a woman named Strawberry at a gallery opening. She rebuffed his advances at first, but his bravado prevailed and he managed to finesse his way into her life. In 1971 they married, but like many of the projects he initiated as an exercise in chest thumping, the union was doomed from the start. They moved to San Francisco so that Rufus could work on a communal housing project that friends were putting together; soon after, Strawberry returned to New York without him.

The rest of his San Francisco period followed a familiar routine. He went to work for a company pioneering the application of holographic technology, in a capacity not much higher than the grunt status he occupied at Woodstock. His pay: $5 a day, and a pair of cowboy boots someone had left behind. Soon his construction-handyman responsibilities opened up to include more sophisticated craftwork and eventually he was participating in the commercial holographic work at the cutting edge of the company's future. Regardless of his contributions, however, he never was able to penetrate the inner core of the company's power elite, never able to shake the fact that he came into the business as a laborer. Content to be a grunt when it was grunt work he was doing, Rufus balked at subservient status once he had mastered the boss's trade.

> I began producing and directing film for holograms. It was used in everything from commercials to wedding portraits. We did a cigarette commercial that was on display in Grand Central. We had write-ups in *Rolling Stone* and [executive editor] Jan Wenner came to visit me. We made a lot of money for a while. But I was getting a lot more famous than the others. I was getting a lot more work. And it started a lot of partnership squabbles. I gave my world-famous termination speech. "I don't mind being fucked. But I do mind being fucked and not making any money or having any fun." My sense of esprit de corps comes from Woodstock—a lot of that ease of understanding, just going with it. But it has to be nobody getting ripped off, everybody has to be getting something out of it.

At Woodstock, Rufus had been the perfect Aquarian employee: responsible when those above him were reckless, clever while his superiors were merely conniving. If occasionally he laughed out loud at his employers, his mockery didn't devalue his strong and willing back, his energetic devotion to accomplishing the day's required tasks. But for all the aptitude he demonstrated for fixing and building at the concert, and for all the knowledge he showed afterward in picking up and mastering craft after craft in on-the-job training, Rufus failed to learn the one thing the Woodstock Ventures brass and all his subsequent bosses knew all along: to make it, you've got to work for yourself. Fifteen years after the festival, Rufus finally did the next best thing: he went to work for his father.

Having left home while still in his teens, Rufus was able to accept his dad's offer without the concomitant sense of dependence which might have otherwise accompanied the arrangement. Henry Friedman, who had established himself as a successful commercial producer in New York, wanted to expand to the West Coast, and promised his son a hands-off deal that would set up Rufus as the head of the new branch office. Rufus also got a new car out of the bargain.

Rufus has responded very well indeed to the new status as boss—so much so that his father intends to turn over the entire operation to him soon. The pace he maintains in the executive position is killing: accounts in Australia, London and San Francisco keep him in the air as often as two days a week. But simply because he is now in charge doesn't mean that Rufus has become any less charged up than he was as a lowly laborer. He still relishes the rewards of hard work well done, only now, instead of mowing down alfalfa fields, he places models in them and films them. And he makes good money doing it.

Perhaps the one characteristic that links Rufus to so many of his Woodstock brethren on either side of the stage is his belief that, despite his success, he's still the same rebel he was in 1969. Perhaps in a way he is. He's happy to be the one man on the shuttle to San Francisco not wearing a tie. He has a son with a woman with whom he's been living for several years but to whom he isn't married. And he still lives in Venice, still keeps his offices there. These are small lifestyle choices, but they add up to a personality that still owes part of its development to what happened twenty years ago at White Lake, New York. He went there a scrawny little teenage lackey looking for a big new playground. He left having discovered his almost innate lumberjack capacity for self-reliance, perspicacity and sheer diligence. Rufus laughed when he looked up out of his ditch one hot August afternoon to see Michael Lang fall from his horse. He's still laughing. But he is also convinced that he's a better boss today because of the grunt he was at Woodstock.

HENRY DILTZ

DAVID CROSBY, Stephen Stills and Graham Nash on a frumpy couch on a plain wooden porch. The Eagles collected coolly around a desert campfire. James Taylor smiling, benignly embodying the title cut from *Sweet Baby James.* Annie Lennox in leather harness belting out "Missionary Man." Buster Poindexter working a club crowd into a frenzy with "Hot Hot Hot." These images from album covers and music videos form a train of pop icons back to 1969, and each is a photograph Henry Diltz took since then that now serves as a visual link to the festival. Henry's favorite from his gig as official concert photographer is of Jimi Hendrix closing the weekend with his electric "Star-Spangled Banner." But with that single shot and thousands of others still undeveloped in his bags, Henry left Bethel with his camera pointing toward a future that would hold twenty more years of capturing images, defining for all of us the history of rock. With each year, the reputation as an ace photographer that first brought him to Woodstock progressed and grew. Behind his expertise was something else, though. No aloof recorder of superstars and mega-events, Henry Diltz used his lens to bring himself closer and closer to the one thing he loved even more than photography: music. Eventually, in an unexpected way, he would return to his first passion.

Henry had known many of the Woodstock performers from his own performing days with the Modern Folk Quartet and from his years as part of the Lovin' Spoonful's retinue. After the concert he hooked up with Stephen Stills, for whom he had shot the cover photo of the best-selling CS&N album. For the next year he traveled in grand style with the suddenly famous singer-composer, who was, thanks to his appearance at Woodstock, enjoying the height of his fame. Henry went to Colorado to shoot the artwork for Stills's first solo album, and then on to London, where Stills relocated for an extended rehearsal period for his second. Although Henry had been working with rock stars throughout the 1960s, he had never before experienced the luxury of this lifestyle, a sumptuousness typical of the upscale self-image and income level that would become more and more common among musicians into the 1970s. Installing themselves in the country manor formerly owned by Peter Sellers and later by Ringo Starr, the Stills entourage became a magnet for the most prestigious recording artists of the day. Diltz remembers Eric Clapton and Bill Wyman, the Rolling Stones' bass player, dropping by. One day Peter Sellers came to see his old home, and Diltz took a picture of Stills and Sellers with John, the gardener who worked on the estate under very disparate owners. Stills included a song about the day in that second album.

Much of Diltz's work was with the Eagles, who soared to popularity in the mid-seventies, selling millions of the albums for which Henry had taken the photos.

> For the first Eagles album, we went out to the desert late at night. We left from the Troubadour club at two. We got out there around four. We walked up the side of the mountain, built a fire, and watched the sun come up, making some peyote tea. We drank

that watching the sun come up, and spent the day out there taking a lot of pictures and talking to a lot of cactuses.

The second album was *Desperado*. We went out to an old abandoned movie set of a western town and played cowboys. The band played the bank robbers, and the producers and roadies were the posse. I was up on a ladder photographing the whole thing. Lots of rifles and pistols and blanks. Everybody got so into it, they were shooting so much and made so much smoke, eventually the fire squad showed up thinking that the hillside was on fire.

Around this time, Henry noticed a lot of changes in the lifestyle of the rock elite, which made the lush life he lived with Stills seem modest in comparison. Coming from the sixties, when touring meant trucks and buses and maybe hops in two-prop puddle-jumpers, Diltz was astonished at the accommodations rock personalities now enjoyed. With the Eagles it was Learjets, but when he photographed with the Barbarians—a temporary offshoot of the Rolling Stones led by Keith Richards and Ron Wood—the entire company, roadies, equipment and groupies included, all traveled aboard a giant jetliner rented specifically for the length of the tour. The legendary excesses, the airborne parties, the all-night drug binges that one associates with seventies touring: Henry insists they were real—and he has the pictures to prove it.

As the eighties approached, and Henry's reputation brought him to the attention of a new generation of musicians, he began to notice not merely material changes but deeper differences as well between the artists he had known when he first began and those he knew now. Approaching fifty himself, he became acutely aware of how unlike the 1960s the music scene had become.

It's a different crowd of people. The people I photographed in the seventies came out of a folk movement, and they had a little more warmth. They were more like hippies. It came out of that Woodstock thing, all those artists. Nowadays, I'm not sure where they're all at. There are a lot of bands, well, their music is like them, kind of brash. I go to a heavy-metal concert—what is the melody? There isn't one line that I remember, I can't remember a thing. I don't come away humming a single tune. Not one line, just a lot of noise.

It's not likely that the crudity of metal alone was what prompted Henry to begin reconsidering his own musical career. But around the same time that the head-banging music became popular, he joined again with his former buddies from the Modern Folk Quartet, all three of whom were living in Hawaii. For the first time in decades they vocalized together, and for the first time in decades Henry felt the sweet high of performing. For years he had been successfully exploiting his instinctive understanding of the musician's temperament to become one of the most successful rock photographers around. By putting his own performing career on hold, he had been able to ride the coattails of other singers on opulent tours of the world. His lens and his musical sense had brought him to the stage at Woodstock, where he stood feet away as Hendrix gave a performance that would eventually touch millions. But now he found that singing in a small club with his three old buddies was just as intoxicating.

Fearful of dating himself—since he still works extensively as a rock album and video photographer—Henry speaks somewhat shyly of the sort of material the Quartet now offers. Their two recent albums, produced by a tiny independent label, contain four-part harmonized arrangements of Hawaiian songs, and hits from the forties. Actually, as performers as disparate as Linda Ronstadt, Paul Simon and U2 have proven, rock no longer sets itself apart from either provincial music or the standards. Henry's ongoing appreciation of both is quite contemporary and hip. If Henry doesn't fully realize that, others do. A friend of Michael Nesmith, he performed "Moonlight Serenade" on the former Monkee's short-lived "Television Parts" video series on NBC. Diltz's personal favorite from the Quartet's repertoire is "Stella by Starlight." Although he plays on cruise ships, not concert stages, the renewal of his singing career at the same time he continues his photography allows him to pursue two loves that brought him to Woodstock twenty years ago.

I still have all those same feelings about love and peace and brotherhood. It was love, peace and brotherhood—through music. At that time those feelings were very real, and to see it in such masses, that's satisfying. And I love taking pictures. I don't love the busy-work part in the lab. I love looking through the lens and capturing the picture, framing up what moves me and capturing it.

I loved "Stella by Starlight" long before Woodstock. I probably was humming "Stella" as I took those photos of those lovely naked Pig Farm ladies bathing with their babies in the lake in the woods that afternoon.

PENNY STALLINGS

PENNY FELL hard at Woodstock, and as for any young person, getting over that first romance was tough. And when what you fall in love with is something as elusive as the crazy, kinetic zing Penny felt every day she was working at the festival, the rebound can last months, or decades. Woodstock turned Penny into a thrill junkie: August 18, 1969, found her hopelessly hooked to "the action," that ever-mutating, ever-mobile creative center where genius, hipness and celebrity collide and explode. Where, she wondered, would she get her next fix?

Her first option—the planning and mounting of the follow-up concert—never materialized. In fact, in almost inverse proportion to the sizzle that built as the first festival came together, the follow-up fizzled into a nonevent by the time of Woodstock's first anniversary. Penny doesn't even remember being taken off the Woodstock Ventures payroll; it all just sort of disappeared.

She and Barry had already decided that mega-events were probably a thing of the past and that the new "action" had shifted to more controllable musical shows. Same rock-and-roll energy; less risk at the gate. Their introduction to concert promotion started modestly enough: they booked an arena in Dallas, flew Sly and the Family Stone in, and took a percent of the gate. Sporadic bookings led to a more profitable gig, one that allowed Penny to put into operation all the assertiveness training she had received at Woodstock. The summer education turned out to have been an incomplete course; Penny had yet to master the difference between strength of character and obnoxiousness. She promoted the touring company of *Jesus Christ Superstar* and soon found out that creating the action rather than just witnessing it could be an arduous task.

> It was, Hey, kids, let's put on a show. It was like Woodstock all over. But it was a mean world too. I went into town first, I printed the tickets, made the hotel arrangements. And I was the person who dealt with the unions. And I got ripped off: they'd double the price an hour or day before the show. There were a tremendous amount of payoffs, and I just said no. I tried to be as tough as I could, thinking because of Woodstock that I was way beyond where I really was. It was like getting triple-promoted at school. And then all of a sudden you're in that new class. And you really don't know, you haven't done the stuff in between. I was wearing a suede miniskirt, a peasant top and no underwear, and trying to deal with the union people.

Real-world realities made the fun of White Lake seem like the summer camp it had in fact been. Now Penny had to deal personally with the nitty-gritty of the entertainment business, whereas before she had only watched it from afar. She tried to throw around weight that she didn't have, with working men still unaccustomed to dealing with a woman manager of any stripe, much less a pushy one. Even Barry didn't completely understand her new persona. He wouldn't let her in the room when he and the show's agent counted receipts at night. She remembers being relegated to the corridor outside the ticket booth—and crying.

When the *Jesus Christ Superstar* tour ended, Barry and Penny took a year off with the money they had made, and regrouped and decided what to do next. They soon joined with comedy writers Michael O'Donoghue and Anne Beatts, whom Barry had known from his Electric Circus days. Together they went to see *Lemmings*, the off-Broadway hit, on which O'Donoghue had collaborated, that spoofed Woodstock, hippies and the divine excess of the sixties. And together they talked about a new, experimental late-night show NBC had approached them about. It was going to be different, hip, topical. "Saturday Night Live" was going to be, Penny quickly became convinced, where the action was.

How much had changed in her life, in the generation's life, since 1969: not even a decade after Woodstock, the smart-ass, middle-class, collegiate humor "Saturday Night Live" dished out had become the accepted comedy style of the moment. Sincerity, honesty, loyalty, cooperation—SNL aimed weekly barbs at just these hippie virtues. In a way, in fact, the entire show during its first wildly successful years operated as a distancing technique between the self-exposure of the late sixties and the new, trendy aloofness. But as Penny saw it, the TV show wasn't really all that different from what had happened at Woodstock. It embodied the same youthful rebelliousness, the same fun-loving irreverence, the same antiauthoritarian cheek and chic. And now that mass gatherings like Woodstock were a thing of the past, television served as the generation's meeting ground. Half a million received the message on Yasgur's farm that weekend in 1969; even on a bad night, twenty times that number shared communally in the youthfest that was SNL. She wanted to be a part of it.

As it turned out, Penny never got the chance to join the new show. Back in Dallas, her mother developed a terminal illness, and Penny returned there just as the final planning stage for "Saturday Night Live" was being entered. Barry became the agent for O'Donoghue, Beatts and several other young writers on the show, while Penny missed out on the ground floor. By the time she got back, the show was on the air, developing the cult following that would make it the sensation of late-seventies television. Because of her relationship to Barry, she became part of the inner circle of SNL, but she was never really a creative part of the process the way she had been at Woodstock.

So she developed her own creative outlets. Borrowing from the attitudes the show popularized, she collaborated on *Titters 101: An Introduction to Women's Literature,* and wrote both *Flesh and Fantasy,* a comedy compendium of Hollywood trash gossip, and *Rock 'n' Roll Confidential,* an all-the-dirt-you-wanted-to-know-about-pop-stars-but-were-afraid-to-find-out cocktail-table volume. All three books exhibit the same keen eye for parody and a sharp sense of the absurd in everyday pop culture that she deployed at Woodstock to entertain the other working women there. No pop icon was too lofty to be shot down; no belief too deeply held to rip up. In *Confidential,* for example, she took great delight in pointing out that at junior college Bruce Springsteen was so unpopular that the other students circulated a petition to have him thrown out. Much of the book is devoted to pictures of today's biggest rock figures as scrawny high school kids.

The books drew Penny to the attention of the producers of "The MacNeil-Lehrer Report," who were anxious to improve their viewership demographics by appealing to the thirty- to forty-year-old audience, which in the mid-1980s became a prime news consumer group. Penny came on board as a weekly "columnist," delivering a segment in which she would comically detail a contemporary concern or observation from the baby-boomer perspective. For three minutes a week, in slickly presented sound bites and flashing images, she documented the changes she'd gone through—the changes we'd all gone through—since Woodstock; she personified the dominant memory style of the Woodstock generation, that trendy impudence for the passions of our youth coupled with a heart-tugging nostalgia for the way we were. She had one foot still planted on the stage in the cowfield in 1969, and the other planted firmly in front of the camera in the present.

Penny's success in writing and her crossing over into TV satisfied her need to achieve, to become something. The recognition of her accomplishments allowed her to settle into the sort of self-possessed tranquil strength she had admired in Jean Ward so many years earlier. But this time she wasn't riding tractors or nimbly wielding buzz saws, nor was she stridently bossing others around. She had mellowed into a clear-headed and determined woman whose power expressed itself through competence, control and clout.

Still, at 42, she senses the same conflict so many women her age do: the wrestling match between commitment to family and the yet unknown opportunities that commitment may preclude. Woodstock took a green little sorority deb and showed her the excitement this life could hold; ever since August 1969 she's had a taste for the action. She just doesn't know whether or not she can give it up.

> I used to think we would go from one project to the next, one more spectacular than the previous one. If I could just continue that kind of school schedule, where September through May you work on something and then you graduate and go on to the next. That was how I spent the last twenty years. Can I ever live in that same way? I have to have children now if I am going to have them. And as much as I would like to be a sixties person, have the kid and just put him in a papoose, that is no longer the way to take care of a kid. Do I want the next adventure, and do I hold out for it? That little bit of unknown magic is still there, I can always still get the call.

LEE MACKLER BLUMER

It has taken nearly all of the twenty years since she stood on that stage at Woodstock and realized what she had just pulled off for Lee Blumer to come full circle, again to be standing at the center of a major youth event, again to be placed face to face with rock and roll's magnificent vitality, again to feel closely, essentially plugged into the power that vibrates globally when pop music connects with a social consciousness. Again, in short, to believe. During the three months of preparation for Woodstock, virtually every one of Lee's doubts about the integrity of the rock business in the sixties had been confirmed and compounded. Then, for the three days of the concert itself, something of the magic that had first drawn her to the industry reinsinuated itself. The weekend had worked, the party had been pulled off, the music she loved had filled the air. And she had been a part of making it happen. Two decades would pass before she would experience anew that same invigorating rush.

It was, in fact, the crash afterward that impeded her at first from moving on to the next career high. What do you do as a follow-up? It was a question that confounded nearly all the young men and women who had joined together to ride the Woodstock Ventures caravan to chaos. Initially seeking some rest, Lee wrapped up matters in White Lake and headed to the Virgin Islands for a short vacation, a mental-health holiday during which she would consider her future. Two years, one miscarriage, too many acid trips and a stint as a drama teacher later, she was still considering. The miscarriage frightened her; she attributed it to the drug use and promptly curtailed it. Depleted emotionally and still longing for the communal high of the festival, she became interested in Scientology, which was flourishing in the Islands among hippie dropouts there. Soon she became a full-time follower of the cultlike religion and decided to move to Los Angeles, where the largest community of sect members lived and where she would be able to live and work within the church.

> I was embarrassingly into it, I was going with it almost as far as I could go. I was able to minister and teach, and I did a lot of administrative things. It was full of a million people from backgrounds like mine. The growth of Scientology was directly proportional to what was happening in the late sixties, when there was such a thrust toward spiritual growth. Scientology managed to position itself as a way to access those spiritual needs.
>
> One day, though, I was standing on the step of a building they had bought. They were getting into real estate before anybody else. And this young black kid came up and said, "Hey, man, what is this place?" And this arrogant old man, this church elder, said, "Hey, this isn't for you." I said, "How dare you turn this kid away when he comes to us!" It crystallized many things for me that I had been secretly feeling about the church. It eventually became the seat of my dissatisfaction. For a long time it was like a subconscious departure, I was not aware how much I was pulling back. But I ceased to be involved.

By 1980 Lee had moved back to New York and dropped out of Scientology completely. She realigned herself with a group of the original Woodstock organizers who were promoting a flashy tenth-anniversary reunion concert, complete with film deal. But that effort petered out—mostly, she says, because of ineffectual management—and its failure surprised her not a jot: the original had worked, she had long ago realized, by accident. The concert weekend in 1969 had become WOODSTOCK only because of a miraculous series of coincidences that permitted the bungled chain of management decisions to go undetected. Woodstock was a once-in-a-lifetime thing; Lee knew that trying to keep its spirit alive by making it twice in a lifetime was futile.

Having reconnected with the Woodstock crowd after her years in California, Lee embarked on a long association with Ventures alum Bert Cohen, a rock entrepreneur whose contributions before the concert were generally acknowledged to have gone nowhere. Driven and egomaniacal by Lee's account, Cohen was one of the Woodstock graduates who had never really moved beyond the sloppy hippie business style that barely suited the sixties and certainly had no place in the eighties. For a while in the seventies he had run a successful publishing, advertising and promotion company—he helped turn the Grapefruit Diet into a national sensation for about an hour. But in 1981 he whispered a single word to Lee which, like some secret shibboleth, made her overlook all her trepidation concerning Cohen and hook her immediate future to his vision. He said: Movies. Let's make 'em.

The ensuing three years amounted to a disaster, during which Lee learned that the only enterprise that rivaled the music industry in chicanery, ineptitude and heartbreak was filmmaking. During all her years in Hollywood she had managed to avoid the lure of the silver screen, and now, back in New York, she fell head over heels. But for all the dead ends and bum steers she encountered, it was a helluva ride. First, Cohen convinced the Hungarian government that he was the man to make the Bela Lugosi bio pic the Hungarian national film board had been eager to see produced. Then, when that project fell through, he raised money for a low-budget thriller called *Shhhh*, on which Lee served as assistant producer, meaning casting agent (she recruited Karen Black from their Scientology days together), script doctor, hand holder and back scratcher. *Shhhh* actually entered production and for a while dreams of a career in movies danced before Lee's and Bert's eyes. She then realized that the dreams Bert was seeing were heavily influenced by cocaine. Bert's health then started to give out. Midway through filming, he had a massive heart attack and died. And Lee, who had deferred pay until the picture could be sold, looked down at her waistline and sighed. She was eight months pregnant.

After being told years earlier that she could never have children, Lee had been astounded herself to find that her affair with a Polish émigré had left her pregnant. It's impossible, the doctor said when she went back to him. And though she had no sense that the father was anyone she wanted to marry—he had told her bringing children into this world was a sin—she was determined to have this child. She found another doctor, a woman, who encouraged her to bring the pregnancy to term. Alex was born on February 18, 1985.

> I tend to think having Alex made me a lot more optimistic. I don't have any chance but to make things work, I don't give myself a lot of time thinking about things not working. I work a lot harder than I ever did in my life. I have found so many answers to so many questions in my life by having a child. I enjoy it tremendously. I've been everywhere else, it was the thing I needed to do to finish my song. It's not like I'm about to retire, but this gives me the impetus for the next thing I have to do, it focuses me in a way I wasn't focused before. I'd like to have my son live in a society that is a little safer, a little happier.

Lee fell into a free-lance position with RCA Records that eventually turned into a full-time staff job at $40,000 per year. The security she finally felt for both herself and Alex proved to be temporary; she was let go in a budget cutback in 1986. The dismissal may have been the best thing for her. Thrown upon her own resources, she started doing publicity out of her apartment and eventually landed a major account: domestic promotion of the 1988 Human Rights Now! tour, the fund-and-consciousness-raising series of rock concerts conducted to aid the work of Amnesty International. With support from the group U2 and superstars Bruce Springsteen, Sting and Peter Gabriel, Amnesty International emerged in the late 1980s as one of the most powerful means of reaffirming rock's political potential. Music again was prompting action, and not just on the dance floor. At Amnesty concerts, petitions were circulated, issues addressed, thoughts provoked. Having a good time could also mean making a statement.

The promise of Woodstock was coming true for Lee Blumer. With her own child as her connection to the next generation, she approaches the twentieth anniversary like a runner proudly passing the baton. The Aquarian Exposition had ended, and for many years she forgot what it was all about. But the undeniable lessons of that weekend survived, and now she is delighted and enthused by her part in spreading the message again. The woman who toured with the Monkees, paid off cops at the Fillmore East, and trembled as Woodstock teetered on the brink of disaster knows firsthand the sordidness that surrounds the pure heart of rock and roll. But now as then she also knows that pure heart still pounds away, and wants to believe—perhaps even more now than then—that its beat can change the world.

My secret idea is that the nineties will have a very sixties flavor; kids won't sit still and watch things go down in an inequitable manner. We've woken up a whole generation. I've been to a lot of Amnesty concerts and I see these little babies who look like all they are interested in is Bono's tushy, and they're talking about petitions and political prisoners. It's really heartening.

I get to say I was at Woodstock. And often I hear the kids say they envy me. "How wonderful!" I talk to sixteen-year-olds, and their vision of it is this vision of community, and wonder that all who could be there cared about the same thing. And all that is true. Aside from the mud and the rain and all that, that's what really happened.

ABOUT THE AUTHOR

JACK CURRY was born in New York City in 1952 and received a degree in journalism from Syracuse University. He worked as an editor for the New York *Daily News* and *Look* magazine before joining the staff of *USA Today,* where he is entertainment editor. He has contributed articles on popular culture to many publications, including *Cosmopolitan, TV Guide* and *American Film.* Jack Curry divides his time between Washington, D.C., and New York City.